AUTHORITY IN BYZANTINE
SOCIETY, 950

The imperial government over the central provinces of the Byzantine Empire was both sovereign and apathetic, dealing effectively with a narrow set of objectives, chiefly collecting revenue and maintaining imperial sovereignty. Outside these spheres, action needed to be solicited from imperial officials, leaving vast opportunities for local people to act independently without legal stricture or fear of imperial involvement. In the absence of imperial intervention provincial households competed with each other for control over community decisions. The emperors exercised just enough strength at the right times to prevent the leaders of important households in the core provinces from becoming rulers themselves. Membership in a successful household, wealth, capacity for effective violence and access to the imperial court were key factors that allowed one to act with authority. This book examines in detail the mechanisms provincial households used to acquire and dispute authority.

LEONORA NEVILLE is Assistant Professor of History at The Catholic University of America, Washington DC. She has written various articles on Byzantine bureaucracy. She has held the Bliss Prize Fellowship.

AUTHORITY IN BYZANTINE PROVINCIAL SOCIETY, 950–1100

LEONORA NEVILLE

The Catholic University of America

CAMBRIDGE UNIVERSITY PRESS

CAMBRIDGE UNIVERSITY PRESS
Cambridge, New York, Melbourne, Madrid, Cape Town, Singapore, São Paulo, Delhi

Cambridge University Press
The Edinburgh Building, Cambridge CB2 8RU, UK

Published in the United States of America by Cambridge University Press, New York

www.cambridge.org
Information on this title: www.cambridge.org/9780521838658

© Leonora Neville, 2004.

This publication is in copyright. Subject to statutory exception
and to the provisions of relevant collective licensing agreements,
no reproduction of any part may take place without the written
permission of Cambridge University Press.

First published 2004
This digitally printed version 2008

A catalogue record for this publication is available from the British Library

ISBN 978-0-521-83865-8 hardback
ISBN 978-0-521-10117-2 paperback

Contents

List of illustrations	*page* vi
Acknowledgments	vii
List of abbreviations	viii
Map: The central provinces of the Byzantine Empire	xi
Introduction	1
1 Imperial administration and Byzantine political culture	5
2 Activities of the imperial administration	39
3 Provincial households	66
4 Provincial households and the imperial administration	99
5 Regulation of provincial society	119
6 Contention and authority	136
Conclusions	165
Appendix: guide to sources	168
Bibliography	181
Index	205

Illustrations

Map: The central provinces of the Byzantine Empire   *page* xi

1. Seal of Pardos, *c.* 950–1050   21
   Diameter 26 mm., weight 12.14 g. Dumbarton Oaks
   Collection no. 55.106.4222. Dumbarton Oaks, Byzantine
   Collection, Washington, DC. Photo credit: Joe Mills.

2. Seal of John, *c.* 1000–1100   21
   Diameter 27 mm., weight 12.34 g. Dumbarton Oaks
   Collection no. 55.1.2869. Dumbarton Oaks, Byzantine
   Collection, Washington, DC. Photo credit: Joe Mills.

3. Ring of Michael Attaleiates   75
   Dumbarton Oaks, Byzantine Collection, Washington, DC.
   Photo credit: Joe Mills.

Acknowledgments

Many people have helped shape the thinking behind this book through their writing, teaching, and conversation. I am grateful to all and hope that I can repay a portion of that debt by providing this book in return. I mention here only a handful of individuals whose contributions have been particularly significant. Judith Herrin and Peter Brown encouraged my dissatisfaction with simple explanations and taught me to think boldly about history. Thomas Tentler read an early version of this work that had a sixty-page chapter on taxation. I am sure that readers will join me in offering him sincere thanks for advising me, among other things, that this was a bit much. At a later stage, Paul Stephenson also read a draft and offered equally valuable advice. The reports of the anonymous readers for Cambridge University Press challenged my thinking on several key issues and led to great improvements in the text. Eustratios Papaioannou generously shared his great expertise in Medieval Greek. Joel Kalvesmaki provided valuable editorial help. The remaining errors in this work are, of course, my own responsibility.

I completed most of the research for this project in the Dumbarton Oaks library, as a junior fellow in 1997–98 and as a local reader subsequently. Irene Vaslef (now retired), Alice-Mary Talbot, Sheila Klos, and Deborah Brown deserve praise for maintaining the excellence of the Byzantine library and nurturing a warm scholarly community. Students at The Catholic University of America have pushed me both to articulate clearly what it is that I have been doing and to get on with it. Of the many, John Beetham and Erika Franz deserve special thanks.

At one point in the composition of this work my husband Stephen inspired further progress by likening Byzantine provincial society to a platypus. While I am not prepared to defend the analogy, the book is dedicated to him for this insight as well as his unfailing encouragement.

Abbreviations

AD	*Archaiologikon Deltion*
BCH	*Bulletin de Correspondance Hellénique*
BMGS	*Byzantine and Modern Greek Studies*
BF	*Byzantinische Forschungen*
BSA	*Annual of the British School at Athens*
BZ	*Byzantinische Zeitschrift*
Cadaster of Thebes	Nicolas Svoronos. "Recherches sur le cadastre byzantin et la fiscalité aux xie et xiie siècles." *Bulletin de Correspondance Hellénique* 83 (1959): 1-166. Reprinted in *Etudes sur l'organisation intérieure, la société et l'économie de l'empire byzantin*. London, 1973. The text is on pp. 57–63.
Docheiariou	*Actes de Docheiariou*, edited by Nicolas Oikonomides. Archives de l'Athos 13. Paris, 1984.
DOP	*Dumbarton Oaks Papers*
Esphigmenou	*Actes d'Esphigmenou*, edited by Jacques Lefort. Archives de l'Athos 3. Paris, 1973.
Iviron I	*Actes d'Iviron*, edited by Jacques Lefort, Nicolas Oikonomides, and Denise Papachryssanthou, vol. I. Archives de l'Athos 14. Paris, 1985.
Iviron II	*Actes d'Iviron*, edited by Jacques Lefort, Nicolas Oikonomides, Denise Papachryssanthou, Vassiliki Kravari, and Hélène Métrévéli, vol. II. Archives de l'Athos 16. Paris, 1990.
JÖB	*Jahrbuch der Österreichischen Byzantinistik*
Kekaumenos	*Cecaumeni Consilia et Narrationes / Sovety i rasskazy Kekavmena*, edited by Gennadii Grigorevich Litavrin. Moscow, 1972. Reprinted with Greek translation by Dimitri Tsougkarakes, *Kekaumenos Strategikon*. Athens, 1993.

	Cecaumeni Strategicon, edited by Basil Wassiliewsky and Viktor Jernstedt. St. Petersburg, 1896. Citations to Kekaumenos include the paragraph numbers assigned by Litavrin, which are reprinted in Tsougkarakes, and the page numbers of Wassiliewsky and Jernstedt's edition.
Lavra	*Actes de Lavra*, edited by Paul Lemerle, André Guillou, Nicolas Svoronos, and Denise Papachryssanthou, vol. 1. Archives de l'Athos 5. Paris, 1970.
Life of Lazaros	*Life of Lazaros of Mt. Galesion*, translated by Richard P. H. Greenfield, *The Life of Lazaros of Mt. Galesion: An Eleventh-Century Pillar Saint*. Byzantine Saints' Lives in Translation 3. Washington, DC, 2000. Edited by the Société des Bollandistes, *Acta Sanctorum Novembris 3*. Brussels, 1910.
Life of Luke	*Life of Luke of Steiris*, Demetrios Sophianos, ed. *Hosios Loukas, ho vios tou*, 2nd edn. Athens, 1993. Text available in the Dumbarton Oaks Hagiography Database: http://www.doaks.org/saints2/TEXTS/64.html.
Life of Nikon	Denis Sullivan, ed. *The Life of Saint Nikon: Text, Translation, and Commentary*. Brookline, MA, 1987. Text available in the Dumbarton Oaks Hagiography Database: http://www.doaks.org/saints2/TEXTS/87.html.
Life of Paul	*Life of Paul of Latros*, edited by Hippolyte Delehaye, "Der Latmos" in *Milet: Ergebnisse der Ausgrabungen und Untersuchungen seit dem Jahre 1899* 3.1, edited by Theodor Wiegand (Berlin, 1913): 105–35. Text available in the Dumbarton Oaks Hagiography Database: http://www.doaks.org/saints2/TEXTS/81.html.
Marcian Treatise	Franz Dölger, *Beiträge zur Geschichte der byzantinischen Finanzverwaltung, besonders des 10. und 11. Jahrhunderts*. Byzantinisches Archiv 9. Leipzig, 1927.

Pantocrator	*Actes du Pantocrator*, edited by Vassiliki Kravari. Archives de l'Athos 17. Paris, 1991.
Saint-Pantéléèmôn	*Actes de Saint-Pantéléèmôn*, edited by Paul Lemerle, Gilbert Dagron, and Sima M. Cirkovic. Archives de l'Athos 12. Paris, 1982.
Typika	John Thomas and Angela Constantinides Hero. *Byzantine Monastic Foundation Documents: A Complete Translation of the Surviving Founders' Typika and Testaments.* 5 vols., Dumbarton Oaks studies 35. Washington, DC, 2000.
Vatopedi	*Actes de Vatopedi*, edited by Jacques Bompaire, Jacques Lefort, Vassiliki Kravari, and Christophe Giros, vol. 1. Archives de l'Athos 21. Paris, 2001.
REB	*Revue des Etudes Byzantines*
TM	*Travaux et Mémoires*
Xenophon	*Actes de Xenophon*, edited by Denise Papachryssanthou. Archives de l'Athos 15. Paris, 1986.

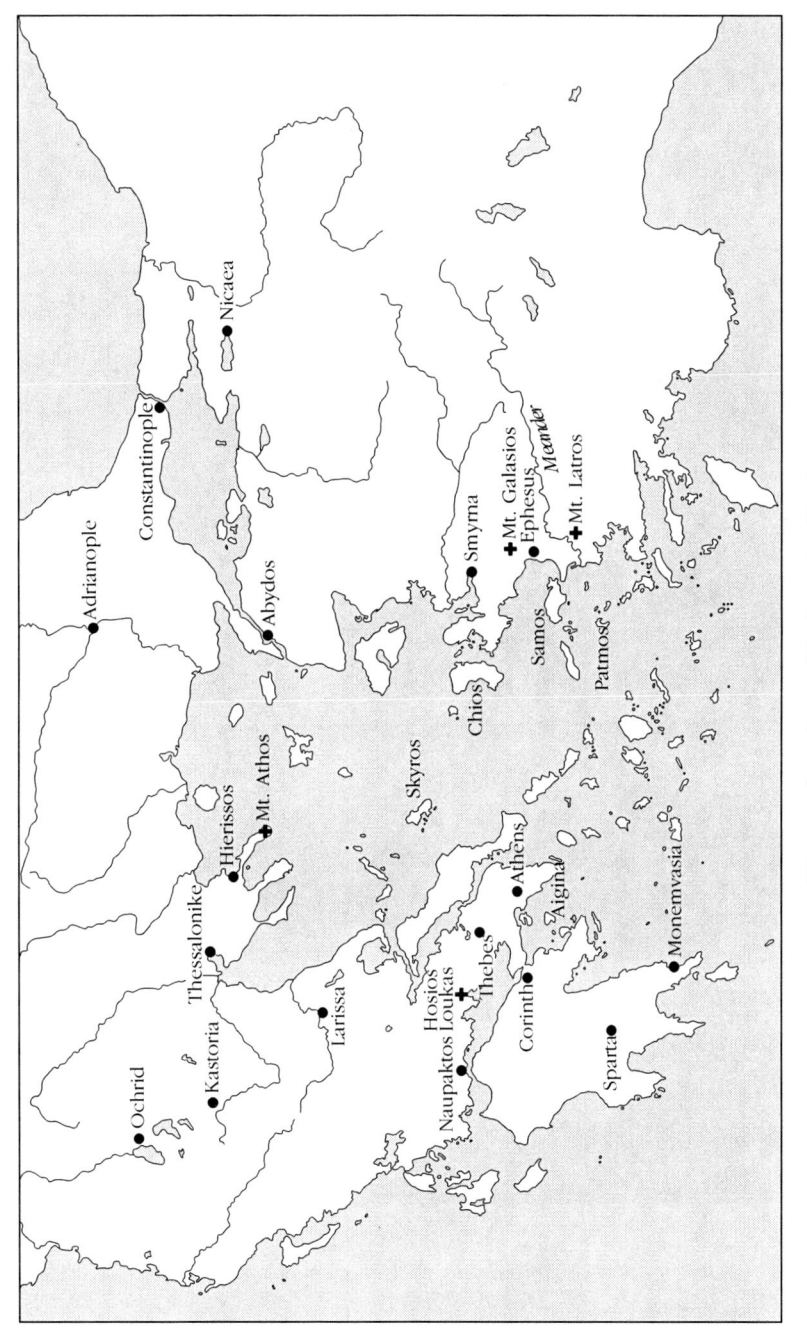

The central provinces of the Byzantine Empire

Introduction

The Eastern Roman Empire maintained a continuous imperial government for over a thousand years. Understanding how the formal stability of imperial rule may be reconciled with the adaptations that necessarily accompanied the transition from antiquity to early modernity forms the larger framework of inquiry behind this study. That the political continuity of the empire masks a mutable and occasionally dynamic society is no longer in doubt. The mid-twentieth-century conception of Byzantium placed it in strong continuity with Rome and in contrast with the West. Revisions in the models of Byzantine urbanism and economic development since the 1970s have increased estimations of both Byzantium's disjuncture with the classical past and its commonality with Europe. The Byzantine Empire is now seen as sharing with the West the same essential trajectory of economic growth from the ninth through thirteenth centuries. How much further changes in Byzantine society should be assimilated to the experiences of the western transition from ancient to medieval society remains open to question, as does the nature and extent of discontinuities with the Late Roman Empire. This study attempts to add nuance to our understanding of the changes in Byzantine society and government by examining the exercise of authority in the core provinces of the empire from the mid-tenth through the eleventh centuries.

Understanding authority in Byzantine provincial society requires addressing fundamental questions about the organization of society on the level of the family and local communities on the one hand, and the imposition of imperial government on those families and communities on the other. Such an inquiry thus nearly amounts to a study of provincial society in general. Yet here social structures have been examined with the specific goal of uncovering common means of manipulating and coercing behavior. Authority is broadly conceived as the ability to effect change in a given situation through any form of persuasion, manipulation, or coercion.

The primary conclusion drawn from this inquiry into the practicalities of authority in the core provinces is that the imperial administration touched lightly on provincial society yet maintained a monopoly on sovereignty, allowing much of social regulation to be undertaken by individual provincial households. The emperors and their agents acted in the provinces almost exclusively to further a limited set of objectives: maintenance of imperial sovereignty, suppression of revolt, and collection of revenue. The imperial government was generally effective in meeting its goals, but those goals did not encompass the close regulation of provincial society. Provincial people felt and tested the strength of imperial authority where their lives intersected with the desires of the imperial administration. This left many aspects of provincial life free from government intervention. Personal freedom in the provinces was constrained more by neighbors and rival households than by the imperial government. The ordering of society was left to individual households and communities who competed for control with little concern for the intervention of imperial officials.

While apathetic about regulating provincial society, the emperors effectively prevented provincial individuals or households from usurping systematic governmental authority. As the maintenance of imperial sovereignty was one of the chief aims of the emperors, locally powerful people in the core provinces seem to have been anxious not to look like rulers, at least so long as the imperial authorities were paying attention. The fear of false accusations of disaffection and the central administration's aggressive suppression of revolts seem largely to have maintained the imperial monopoly on outright government, without necessarily suppressing various forms of local authority and social regulation.

The provinces under consideration are those outside the vicinity of Constantinople but firmly within the sphere of imperial control, specifically the areas surrounding the Aegean: Thrace, Hellas, Peloponnesos, and western Asia Minor. These provinces formed the core of the empire, where we would expect imperial administration to be most direct and thorough. The Aegean provinces contrast with the outer provinces and frontier regions, where the nature of government seems to have been quite different. Recent work on the empire's frontier has posited that the aim of imperial control of the outer provinces was to maintain stability and prosperity in the inner provinces. In this model the frontier regions were lightly governed through positive incentives offered to local potentates rather than through the heavy-handed imposition of imperial administration.[1] This study

---

[1] Paul Stephenson, *Byzantium's Balkan Frontier: A Political Study of the Northern Balkans, 900–1204* (Cambridge, 2000), 317. The eastern frontier seems to follow a similar model: Catherine Holmes,

addresses the sources of authority of the inner provinces, whose prosperity and revenue were vital to the maintenance of imperial power.

Before engaging directly with provincial society, this book opens with an examination of the cultural expression of imperial politics and administration in Constantinople. It makes the case that Byzantium's traditional reputation as a state with an extensive and pervasive government arose because, until the late eleventh century, Byzantine political culture was expressed with characteristics that can look bureaucratic to modern observers. That political culture, however, was grounded in an ideology of empire that was substantially different from the ideologies of civil service that underpin modern government agencies. The evolution of Byzantine political culture in the late eleventh century into a form that appears less bureaucratic does not necessarily correlate to any significant changes in governing the provinces.

From this discussion of the shifting cultural expressions of imperial administration, the book turns to the actions of that administration in provincial society. The major activities of the imperial administration in the core provinces involved maintaining imperial sovereignty and collecting revenue. Maintenance of sovereignty was achieved through skillful diplomacy and military policy, control over fortifications and suppression of revolt. The efforts of the imperial administration to extract wealth affected provincial life more regularly and profoundly. The hand of government fell with considerable intensity in a few particular contexts. Aside from maintaining sovereignty and extracting wealth, the administration did little to govern provincial society.

After considering the strength and interests of the imperial administration, the argument turns to examine provincial society and the relationships that ordered that society. Chapter 3 describes the relationships within a household, *oikos*, the extension of household terminology into non-familial settings, the establishment of hierarchy among households, and the ways households formed associations. The model of provincial society developed in chapter 3 is then used in subsequent discussions of the interactions between prominent provincial households and imperial officials, and of the regulation of provincial society. Finally, to see how authority was exercised in the face of serious opposition, chapter 6 examines how provincial households prosecuted disputes with each other.

The temporal boundaries of the project are set loosely at 950 and 1100. Given the paucity of sources dealing with provincial society, I needed to

---

"Byzantium's Eastern Frontier in the Tenth and Eleventh Centuries," in *Medieval Frontiers: Concepts and Practices*, ed. David Abulafia and Nora Berend (Aldershot, 2002), 83–104.

cast a wide net for information. On the other hand the changing nature of Byzantine society and culture required temporal restraint. Change over time is more readily seen in the chapters that deal with the imperial administration, because the political culture of the capital is both better documented and understood, and the changes are clearer. In the chapters dealing more directly with provincial society, I have tried not to trace changes over time but to lay out an aggregate description.

The sources selected for this study either originate outside of Constantinople or deal substantively with provincial society. As most of the sources used here are little known to those who are not experts in medieval Byzantine history, they are described in the Appendix.[2] The bulk of the evidence derives from monastic archives, provincial hagiography, and instructive literature.

---

[2] With the exception of quotations from the following, all translations are my own: Richard P. H. Greenfield, ed., *The Life of Lazaros of Mt. Galesion: An Eleventh-Century Pillar Saint* (Washington, DC, 2000); Gyula Moravcsik and Romilly Jenkins, eds., *De administrando imperio: Constantine VII Porphyrogenitus*, new rev. edn (Washington, DC, 1967); Denis Sullivan, ed., *The Life of Saint Nikon: Text, Translation, and Commentary* (Brookline, MA, 1987); John Thomas and Angela Constantinides Hero, *Byzantine Monastic Foundation Documents: A Complete Translation of the Surviving Founders' Typika and Testaments*, 5 vols. (Washington, DC, 2000); F. A. Wright, trans., *Liudprand of Cremona: The Embassy to Constantinople and Other Writings* (London, 1993).

CHAPTER I

Imperial administration and Byzantine political culture

For many years the existence of a centralized literate bureaucracy was commonly considered one of the chief characteristics of medieval Byzantine civilization. This bureaucracy was thought to have allowed a particularly high level of state control over society.[1] This view of the Byzantine government is partially responsible for making "Byzantine" a derogatory term for inflexible and overly intricate organizations.[2] Yet a scholarly consensus has been growing for some time that the bureaucratic model does not fit Byzantine realities particularly well and that the provincial administration cannot have been as efficient and pervasive as had been thought.[3] It is here proposed that the reason anyone ever thought the Byzantine government was bureaucratic is that the political culture of the ninth and tenth centuries had characteristics that, through deceptive analogy with modern experience, can look bureaucratic to modern observers. The actual meanings and messages of Byzantine governmental ritual are foreign to us while bureaucratic regimes are familiar. Aspects of Byzantine political culture

---

[1] An extreme contemporary view: "Byzantine society, originally defined by the state, was constantly changed by it." Warren T. Treadgold, *A History of the Byzantine State and Society* (Stanford, CA, 1997), xvii. Other scholars have posited a high degree of government control over life: Alexander Kazhdan and Giles Constable, *People and Power in Byzantium: An Introduction to Modern Byzantine Studies* (Washington, DC, 1982), 19–36; Nicolas Oikonomides, "Title and income at the Byzantine court," in *Byzantine Court Culture from 829 to 1204*, ed. Henry Maguire (Washington, DC, 1997), 200. Bureaucracy continues to be singled out as one of the most notable characteristics of the Byzantine Empire: Rosamond McKitterick, ed., *The Early Middle Ages* (Oxford, 2001), 40.
[2] Admirers of Byzantium have tended not to dispute the existence of a large state apparatus, but rather expressed an appreciation of bureaucracy. See Paul Lemerle, "Présence de Byzance," *Journal des Savants* (1990): 259–60; Thomas F. Carney, *Bureaucracy in Traditional Society: Romano-Byzantine Bureaucracies Viewed from Within* (Lawrence, KS, 1971), 148.
[3] Hans-Georg Beck, "Theorie und Praxis im Aufbau der byzantinischen Zentralverwaltung," *Bayerische Akademie der Wissenschaften. Philosophisch-Historische Klasse Sitzungsberichte* 8 (1974): 3–33. Ralph-Johannes Lilie, "Die Zentralbürokratie und die Provinzen zwischen dem 10. und dem 12. Jahrhundert. Anspruch und Realität," *BF* 19 (1993): 65–75. Jean-Claude Cheynet, "Point de vue sur l'efficacité administrative entre les xe et xie siècles," *BF* 19 (1993): 7–16. Ihor Ševčenko, "Was there totalitarianism in Byzantium? Constantinople's control over its Asiatic hinterland in the early ninth century," in *Constantinople and Its Hinterland*, ed. Cyril A. Mango and Gilbert Dagron (Aldershot, 1995), 91–108.

having to do with the ritual exaltation of imperial majesty can give the appearance of an extensive administrative apparatus, with large numbers of functionaries and rigid assignments of duties and powers. When expressions of political culture are separated from administrative phenomena it is possible to get a clearer sense of both how the government appeared and what it was able to accomplish.

The discussion of Byzantine political culture and imperial government is complicated because neither stayed the same for very long. The period from the middle of the tenth to the end of the eleventh century is regarded as a key turning point in the administrative history of the Byzantine Empire, in which government through a pseudo-meritocracy of officials gave way to government through the personal relationships of aristocratic kin. I would like to distinguish between changes in government practice and challenges on the one hand and changes in political culture on the other. The period saw significant changes in government administration: monetary policy, fiscal practice, military organization, judicial administration, and poor relief. The circumstances in which the government needed to function changed: economic activity increased, provincial towns grew, neighbors were alternately quiescent and belligerent, and territory was gained and lost through conquest. Concurrent with these changes were also shifts in the insignia of political culture: in the markers of high social status, in ideas about what creates power, and in what constituted desirable personal virtues. Changes in political culture affected more the way the government looked than what it did. Changing ideas about the constitution of imperial authority and membership in the imperial hierarchy were significant for the culture and experience of the urban elite and of the great families involved with the government in Constantinople. They did not necessarily have a significant impact on the strength of the imperial administration in provincial communities.

The distinction between changes in administrative structures and changes in political culture should not be pushed too far because the phenomena are deeply intertwined. The distinction is helpful, however, both to understand why Byzantium has been perceived as a bureaucratic state and to identify changes that had real impact on the government's regulation of provincial society.

DEVELOPMENTS IN GOVERNMENT ADMINISTRATION

In keeping with the goal of distinguishing changes in political culture from changes in actual administration, I summarize here some of the

Imperial administration and political culture

institutional, economic, and political changes of the later tenth and eleventh centuries. Fine analyses have been made of the developments in the offices and hierarchy of the imperial administration.[4] The more modest task here is to sketch the changes in institutional structures, economics, and politics relevant to the development of Byzantine political culture and ideology in the eleventh century.

The Byzantine civil administration was formed in the seventh century as part of a large-scale consolidation of power in the capital. As provinces were conquered and cities of the Balkans and Anatolia declined in the seventh century, Constantinople experienced a profound increase of its share of imperial wealth and power.[5] The seventh-century transformation created a government based on a marked disparity of power between the capital and the hinterland.[6] The seventh-century consolidation established a slim government for an empire greatly reduced in size and complexity. Late Roman provinces were replaced by four large districts known as *themata*. Soldiers of a particular *theme* army were settled in that province and expected to meet most of their expenses out of the revenue from their property. By the middle of the ninth century the *themata* were administrative as well as military districts. The general of the *theme* army also acted "effectively as generalissimo in his province, with at the very least a supervisory authority over fiscal and judicial officials."[7]

The economic revival of the empire now seems to have been underway at the beginning of the ninth century and to have continued through the twelfth century.[8] As the empire recovered militarily and economically, the size and importance of the professional military units increased, as did the number of administrative districts. The generals were relieved of their duties in civil administration, as judges were appointed to each province.[9] The armies of the *themata* were augmented by an increasing number of professional mobile military divisions. The number of *themata* increased as

---

[4] H. Glykatzi-Ahrweiler, "Recherches sur l'administration de l'empire byzantin aux IXe–XIe siècles," *BCH* 84 (1960): 1–111. Nicolas Oikonomides, "L'évolution de l'organisation administrative de l'Empire byzantin au XIe siècle," *TM* 6 (1976): 125–52.
[5] Anthony Cutler and Alexander Kazhdan, "Continuity and discontinuity in Byzantine history," *Byzantion* 52 (1982): 468.
[6] John Haldon, *Byzantium: A History* (Stroud, 2000), 117. John Haldon, *Byzantium in the Seventh Century: The Transformation of a Culture* (Cambridge, 1990).
[7] John Haldon, *Warfare, State and Society in the Byzantine World* (London, 1999), 84.
[8] Angeliki Laiou, "The Byzantine economy: an overview," in *The Economic History of Byzantium from the Seventh through the Fifteenth Century*, ed. Angeliki Laiou (Washington, DC, 2002), 1146–56. Michael F. Hendy, "Byzantium, 1081–1204: the economy revisited, twenty years on," in *The Economy, Fiscal Administration and Coinage of Byzantium* (London, 1989), 9–18.
[9] Helen Saradi, "The Byzantine tribunals: problems in the application of justice and state policy (9th–12th c.)," *REB* 53 (1995): 173.

border districts, *kleisourai*, were upgraded to *themata* once they stabilized. Eventually the older armies of *themata* became irrelevant as the "field armies both along the frontiers of the empire and within the provinces were composed increasingly of either mercenary, professional troops or forces sent by subordinate and vassal princes and rulers of the various smaller states bordering the empire."[10] By the early eleventh century, rather than having soldiers of the *themata* support themselves from their land, taxes from their lands paid for professional soldiers.[11]

This increasing professionalism of the military contributed to the empire's great territorial revival of the tenth century.[12] Imperial generals enjoyed significant success in expanding the borders of the empire to the east and increasing control over the Aegean. In 961 Crete was reconquered by the future emperor Nikephoros Phokas (963–9) and local shipping became significantly safer as pirates were eliminated. Nikephoros and his family developed effective techniques for fighting Muslim raids and pushed the eastern border beyond the Taurus Mountains. The political disintegration of the Abbasid caliphate contributed to their success. The incorporation of northeastern territories in the Caucasus led the way for a recovery of northern Syria.[13] Several Georgian and Armenian princely families, persuaded to cast their lot with the empire, allowed their territories to be annexed. Bulgaria was incorporated into the empire as a consequence of John Tzimiskes' (969–76) effort to drive out the invasion of Sviatoslav of Kiev. The rebellions that broke out after Tzimiskes' death were eventually subdued by Basil II (976–1025).[14]

Some areas in the newly conquered territories in the east appear to have been converted into imperial estates that provided the administration with a direct source of income in the early eleventh century. New major posts were created in the fiscal administration to manage imperial estates and charitable houses. These offices reflect the increasing importance of direct

---

[10] Haldon, *Warfare, State and Society in the Byzantine World*, 85.
[11] *Ibid.*, 124. Nicolas Oikonomides, "The role of the Byzantine state in the economy," in *The Economic History of Byzantium from the Seventh through the Fifteenth Century*, ed. Angeliki Laiou (Washington, DC, 2002), 1022–3.
[12] On the political consequences of the increased strength of the army see Catherine Holmes, "Political elites in the reign of Basil II," in *Byzantium in the Year 1000*, ed. Paul Magdalino (Leiden, 2003), 38–56.
[13] Jonathan Shepard, "Constantine VII, Caucasian openings and the road to Aleppo," in *Eastern Approaches to Byzantium*, ed. Anthony Eastmond (Aldershot, 2001), 19–40. Catherine Holmes, "'How the east was won' in the reign of Basil II," in *Eastern Approaches to Byzantium*, ed. Anthony Eastmond (Aldershot, 2001), 41–56.
[14] Stephenson, *Balkan Frontier*, 47–79.

exploitation of property by the imperial administration.¹⁵ Further changes in fiscal administration in the eleventh century also point to more direct exploitation of resources by the government now acting as landowner rather than tax collector.¹⁶ Cultivation of estates gave the government the option of conducting non-monetized transactions. Imperial estates also produced cash revenue through the sale of produce and may have become a significant source of cash for the government. It is possible that at the beginning of the eleventh century the state drew more revenues from its estates than it did from taxes on land.¹⁷

From the eighth through the tenth century the economy of the government was highly monetized. Salaries were paid in gold and most taxes were collected in gold. One of the chief burdens of paying taxes was the requirement that taxes be paid in gold *nomismata* coins. Assessments ending in more than two-thirds of a *nomisma* were rounded up to the next full gold coin and change was given in silver and bronze.¹⁸ The imperial administration functioned as the chief force for moving currency through the economy: "The state was able to pay salaries and collect taxes in money without the use of that money becoming general (or rather, before it did so). The money with which to pay taxes thus became yet another scarce (and probably expensive) commodity."¹⁹ While the *nomisma* was juridically valued by weight of gold, its status as the only acceptable means of payment must have led its exchange value to exceed its nominal value.

The population of the empire increased steadily through the tenth century.²⁰ The territorial and demographic expansion of the empire throughout this period would necessitate an expansion in the money supply.²¹ The

---

[15] Oikonomides, "Role of the Byzantine state," 992, 1005–7. Oikonomides, "L'évolution de l'organisation administrative," 150. On the political role of imperial ownership of estates see James Howard-Johnston, "Crown lands and the defense of imperial authority in the tenth and eleventh centuries," *BF* 21 (1995): 86–97.
[16] Oikonomides, "L'évolution de l'organisation administrative," 137.
[17] Jacques Lefort, "The rural economy, seventh–twelfth centuries," in *The Economic History of Byzantium from the Seventh through the Fifteenth Century*, ed. Angeliki Laiou (Washington, DC, 2002), 288. The evidence for the rapid growth of direct imperial exploitation of estates is far from conclusive. See Catherine Holmes, "Basil II and the government of empire: 976–1025" (DPhil thesis, Oxford, 1999), 256–74.
[18] Cécile Morrisson, "Byzantine money: its production and circulation," in *The Economic History of Byzantium from the Seventh through the Fifteenth Century*, ed. Angeliki Laiou (Washington, DC, 2002), 944.
[19] Oikonomides, "Role of the Byzantine state," 978.
[20] Alan Harvey, *Economic Expansion in the Byzantine Empire, 900–1200* (Cambridge, 1989), 47–56. Laiou, "The Byzantine economy," 1147.
[21] Morrisson, "Byzantine money," 912. Oikonomides, "Title and income," 200. D. M. Metcalf, "Monetary recession in the middle Byzantine period: the numismatic evidence," *The Numismatic Chronicle* 161 (2001): 114–15. The Byzantine monetary system was multi-denominational and far more complex

efforts to integrate the Bulgarian economy with the rest of the empire in the eleventh century also created new demands for coinage. The expansion of the empire required coins not only to facilitate normal economic exchange, but to pay for the continued good-will of frontier elites.[22] The silver content of the gold *nomismata* increased very slightly between 914 and 1041, by an average of 0.04 percent per year.[23] Between 1041 and 1071 a more aggressive devaluation of the *nomisma* brought about a yearly increase in monetary supply "on the order of 1% (or an increase by one-third in monetary units over thirty years)."[24] The debasement of the coinage became rampant between 1071 and 1091, when the percentage of gold in the *nomisma* fell from 70 percent to 10.6 percent. Silver and bronze coins were also debased.

The devaluation of the coinage was one symptom of the increasing difficulty of the task of government in the eleventh century. The current paradigm of roughly increasing population and economic prosperity from the ninth through twelfth centuries has profound implications for our understanding of government.[25] In the eighth century Constantinople was the only city in the empire that could command the resources necessary to be a center of power. The government in Constantinople was able to maintain a highly centralized state because there was a vast power differential between the capital and the hinterland. When, with increased economic prosperity, towns grew, the relative power of Constantinople decreased and the government faced increasing challenges in accomplishing the same set of tasks.[26] As the eleventh century progressed, the growing prosperity of the empire created an impetus toward decentralization that made the task of governing the empire from Constantinople increasingly difficult.

In the second half of the eleventh century the empire faced great reversals in its military fortunes. Southern Italy and Sicily were lost permanently to the Normans. Imperial authority in eastern Anatolia collapsed quickly in the face of the Seljuk advance in the 1070s, and the establishment of the sultanate of Rum significantly reduced imperial territory. By the 1080s the Seljuks had established a capital at Nicaea. More successful efforts were made to repel the Norman invasion of the Balkans under Robert Guiscard. This invasion was practically concurrent with several rebellions in the Balkans.

---

than those in place in the medieval West until the thirteenth century. Thomas J. Sargent and François R. Velde, *The Big Problem of Small Change* (Princeton, NJ, 2002), 93.
[22] Stephenson, *Balkan frontier*, 135–6. [23] Morrisson, "Byzantine money," 922. [24] *Ibid.*, 924.
[25] For a statement of the current paradigm see Laiou, "The Byzantine economy," 1147–56.
[26] Hendy, "Economy revisited, twenty years on," 12–18.

Some of the empire's adversaries had become more dangerous since the seventh and eighth centuries as they developed more sophisticated state organizations that allowed them to put larger and more professional armies in the field. Developments in heavy cavalry, particularly among the empire's western opponents, minimized the tactical advantages of the Byzantine military. Emperors of the later tenth, eleventh, and especially the twelfth centuries "had to recognize that they were, for the most part, dealing with people or states who were no longer their organizational and logistical inferiors."[27] The empire also faced enemies with new goals. The advance of the Seljuk Turks differed from previous Muslim invasions by being a migration of people determined to settle in Anatolia. The generals of the empire had been familiar with the regular Arab Muslim practice of seasonal raiding, which did little to alter the boundaries between Byzantine and Muslim territory.

It has become fairly standard to consider the territorial expansion of the late tenth century as a dangerous overextension of the empire's resources.[28] The territorial expansion made the task of government more complex as buffer states became border provinces. The long-standing policy of defense in depth was replaced by efforts to control frontiers directly.[29] How significant this difference was depends on one's view of the nature of government control over frontier provinces. The case has been made that, at least along the Balkan frontier, "the imposition of a fully functioning administration across the whole Balkan peninsula was never imperial policy."[30] Rather, the empire was always concerned to manage the frontier region so as to protect the core provinces of the empire from attack. This was done through securing the loyalty of "a multiplicity of potentates who dominated cities and highland strongholds, ports and passes . . . who might otherwise seek to benefit from assaults on imperial lands or from forging alliances with external powers."[31] For the most part the same principles seem to hold true for the empire's eastern frontier as well.[32] Much of the extension of imperial authority took place through the absorption of Georgian and Armenian princely families into the imperial aristocracy. Given this role of the frontier, the expansion of the empire would not have caused a great increase in the resources needed for administration and government.

---

[27] Haldon, *Warfare, State and Society in the Byzantine World*, 65.
[28] Jonathan Shepard, "Byzantium expanding, 944–1025," in *The New Cambridge Medieval History*, vol. III: *c. 900–c. 1024*, ed. Timothy Reuter (Cambridge, 1999), 604.
[29] Haldon, *Warfare, State and Society in the Byzantine World*, 65, 85.
[30] Stephenson, *Balkan Frontier*, 317.   [31] *Ibid.*, 318.
[32] Holmes, "Byzantium's eastern frontier in the tenth and eleventh centuries," 83–104. Holmes, "Basil II and the government of empire," 275–350.

The loss of revenues from territories that were conquered, coinciding with the exaggerated devaluation of the coinage, put the empire in a fiscal and military crisis at the accession of Alexios I Komnenos (1081–1118). He responded at first with any means possible, and later, as he proved successful, with a series of government reforms. A thorough reform of the coinage system was undertaken in 1091. The new system issued gold coins of stable value and nearly the same fineness as the tenth-century *nomisma*.[33] This monetary reform established a new and stable system of coinage that lasted through the twelfth century. That the reform of the coinage was possible indicates that Alexios was able to find ways of appropriating the wealth of the empire. He reduced the administration's need for cash by abolishing the traditional salaries that were paid to title-holders and by granting key supporters lands from which they could support themselves. He took steps to increase the revenue from taxation of the empire's remaining territory with new censuses of property and more rigorous tax assessments for religious institutions.[34] Alexios reorganized fiscal procedures by appointing two *megaloi logariastai*, or "grand accountants," to review and to enforce taxation decisions.[35] In the early twelfth century he rationalized the rates for assessing surcharges and customary gratuities on the land tax.[36]

Another significant change in administration was the creation of the office of the *logothete* of the *sekreta*, a general coordinator of administration that may have been established to help Alexios' mother, Anna Dalassene, with her task of managing domestic administration. This office quickly grew in significance and may have become "a supreme judge in fiscal affairs."[37] This would be the first time that fiscal cases could be heard by a court theoretically separate from the fiscal offices.[38] Alexios also established a significant institution for urban welfare, the *orphanotropheion*.[39]

---

[33] Michael F. Hendy, *Coinage and Money in the Byzantine Empire, 1081–1261* (Washington, DC, 1969), 14–15. Hendy, "Economy revisited, twenty years on," 38–41. Morrisson, "Byzantine money," 923–4.

[34] Alan Harvey, "Financial crisis and the rural economy," in *Alexios I Komnenos*, ed. Margaret Mullett and Dion Smythe (Belfast, 1996), 167–84. Alan Harvey, "The land and taxation in the reign of Alexios I Komnenos: the evidence of Theophylakt of Ochrid," *REB* 51 (1993): 139–53.

[35] Hendy, "Economy revisited, twenty years on," 34–7. Paul Magdalino, "Innovations in government," in *Alexios I Komnenos*, ed. Margaret Mullett and Dion Smythe (Belfast, 1996), 165.

[36] Cécile Morrisson, "La Logarikè: réforme monétaire et réforme fiscale sous Alexis 1er Comnène," *TM* 7 (1979): 419–64.

[37] Magdalino, "Innovations in government," 155.

[38] Paul Magdalino, "Justice and finance in the Byzantine state, ninth to twelfth centuries," in *Law and Society in Byzantium, Ninth–Twelfth Centuries*, ed. Angeliki Laiou and Dieter Simon (Washington, DC, 1994), 108–15.

[39] Magdalino, "Innovations in government," 165–6.

Imperial administration and political culture

By way of military recovery, Alexios I Komnenos was able to repulse the invasion of Robert Guiscard and reassert control over Bulgaria.[40] While the European crusaders did not prove to be the reliable and pliant helpers Alexios appears to have envisioned, they did help push the Seljuk sultanate out of Nicaea and western Anatolia.[41] By the end of Alexios' reign, the empire had regained the fertile western valleys and coastlands from the Seljuks and had stabilized relations with the sultan at Ikonion. The extent of Alexios' military recovery is in itself an argument in favor of those who would see Byzantine authority in frontier regions as dependent on maintaining the loyalty of key local potentates more than on an extensive military apparatus, which Alexios certainly did not have.

The administrative reforms undertaken by Alexios involved increasing the number of divisions of service and adding to the list of the government's responsiblities. This implies that at the end of the eleventh century the government grew either in numbers of administrators or in efficiency. The apparent increase in efforts to collect tax revenues also indicates that the administration was more effective in the 1090s than previously. This is important to keep in mind as we consider any changes in political culture that can give the impression of a decline of the service elite in the late eleventh century.

The period of greatest distress within the imperial administration in the eleventh century corresponds to the point of transition from one cultural understanding of proper imperial politics to another. As Byzantine culture changed, the ritual bonds that constituted the tenth-century government may have dissolved, leading to ineffective administration. Equally, as the imperial administration became less effective over the course of the eleventh century, the ceremonies that gave it authority may have become less awe-inspiring, leading to further shifts in political culture. The following describes two distinct eras of political culture. The first placed considerable importance on imperial ceremony and ritual exaltation of the emperor. For convenience this government culture may be called that of the "imperial centuries," after the title of Romilly Jenkins' *Byzantium: The Imperial Centuries, AD 610–1071*.[42] The second system, which emphasized aristocracy

---

[40] On Alexios' military organization see Armin Hohlweg, *Beiträge zur Verwaltungsgeschichte des ostromischen Reiches unter den Komnenen* (Munich, 1965). John Birkenmeier, *The Development of the Komnenian Army 1081–1180* (Leiden, 2002).

[41] On Alexios' relationships with the crusaders see Jonathan Shepard, "'Father' or 'scorpion'? Style and substance in Alexios's diplomacy," in *Alexios I Komnenos*, ed. Margaret Mullett and Dion Smythe (Belfast, 1996), 68–132.

[42] Romilly Jenkins, *Byzantium: The Imperial Centuries, AD 610–1071* (London, 1966). The phrase has been taken up by Magdalino to denote the culture that preceded that of the late eleventh

and kinship with the emperor, was that of the Komnenian dynasty. While a great simplification, this distinction may help in explaining a complex and gradual cultural evolution.

POLITICAL CULTURE OF THE IMPERIAL CENTURIES

The political culture of the Byzantine Empire in the tenth and at least the first half of the eleventh century insisted strongly on its imperial heritage and used grand ceremonial to exalt the emperor and empire. This government was constituted through the use of titles, salaries, robes, seals, processions, dinners, and ceremonies that both exalted the grand company of titled officials high above common humanity and bound them in a servile relationship to the far more august emperors. Byzantine imperial ideology placed the emperor and his servants in a mimetic relationship with God and the saints. The imperial court was modeled on the heavenly court: "Byzantines drew a subtle and profound analogy between the imperial court and the court of heaven, constantly enriching their conception of each one with their perception of the other."[43] Order, *taxis*, was the paramount virtue of imperial ceremonial because beautiful arrangement and order in imperial ritual allowed the emperor better to imitate God, who ordered and arranged creation. Constantine VII was the great spokesman of the imperial political culture, who through authorizing the compilation of the grand treatise on imperial protocol, known as the *Ceremony Book*, set out to make the beauty and grace in imperial ritual match that of heaven.[44] Constantine claimed that proper method in imperial ritual made his majesty appear more imperial and more fearsome.[45] This system of augmenting government authority through ceremony and ordered ritual is one of the most outstanding characteristics of medieval Byzantine civilization.

The ceremonies were performed by the servants of the palace, guards, circus faction cheerleaders, clergy, and people with imperial titles. These people were also the main audience for most ceremonies. Some ceremonies

---

and twelfth centuries. Magdalino, "Innovations in government," 146–7. Paul Magdalino, "Honour among Romaioi: the framework of social values in the world of Digenes Akrites and Kekaumenos," *BMGS* 13 (1989): 189.

[43] Magdalino, "Honour among Romaioi," 187. Henry Maguire, "The heavenly court," in *Byzantine Court Culture from 829 to 1204*, ed. Henry Maguire (Washington, DC, 1997), 247–58.

[44] Albert Vogt, ed., *Le Livre des cérémonies*, 2 vols. (Paris, 1935). Vogt's edition contains only the first half of the text. For the rest, the standard edition remains Johann Jacob Reiske, ed. *De ceremoniis aulae Byzantinae, Constantine VII Porphyrogenitus*, Corpus Scriptorum Historiae Byzantinae 9–11, edited by Barthold Georg Niebuhr, (Bonn, 1829).

[45] Reiske, ed., *De ceremoniis aulae Byzantinae, Constantine VII Porphyrogenitus*, 517.

like the "opening of the palace," performed each morning, were done entirely by servants and guards. Others, like processions to religious services, included more participants and had a wider audience.

The crowd of title-holders who gathered around the emperor had no routinely used name. In his treatise on titles and honors, completed in 899, Philotheos refers to his fellow companions concerned with proper precedence as a *diakonia*.[46] A text from the reign of Leo VI (886–912) gives prices of titles that could be purchased by one "wanting to become part of the grand company," the *megale hetaireia*. According to the same text one could pay less to become part of the "middle company," the *mese hetaireia*.[47] These companies evolved out of imperial bodyguard units.[48] Honorary titles of *protospatharios* and higher conferred senatorial rank. The senate was no longer a regular deliberative body. The references to people of senatorial rank and to those participating in the senatorial company do not seem clearly to distinguish one subset among the title-holders. In the *Ceremony Book*, the terms for the senate and senators "seem sometimes to encompass all ranking members of court; at others they seem to designate nonmilitary officials."[49] In the ninth century the emperors traveled on the Bosphoros in a small boat. Because Leo VI enjoyed the company of "magisters and patricians and familiars of senatorial rank" he began to travel habitually in a large galley so that more people could join him. Once that became the habit, a second galley was needed to carry the overflowing numbers of people who thought they should be at the emperor's side.[50] Estimates of the size of the imperial court suggest the number of male courtiers was in the order of 1000 to 2000.[51] This estimate is based both on the number of people who could fit into the galleries of Hagia Sophia on the occasions when all those with titles should assemble and on the lists of guests invited to imperial Christmas banquets.

Within the crowd of title-holders it is possible to distinguish some groups that may have had more to do with the work of government. The members of the "sandaled senate" have been identified as "middle-ranking bureaucrats" and "civil servants."[52] They were apparently named after the

---

[46] Nicolas Oikonomides, *Les Listes de préséance byzantines des IXe et Xe siècles* (Paris, 1972), 83.
[47] Reiske, ed., *De ceremoniis aulae Byzantinae, Constantine VII Porphyrogenitus*, 692.
[48] Nicolas Oikonomides, "Some Byzantine state annuitants: *Epi Tes (Megales) Hetaireias* and *Epi Ton Barbaron*," *Symmeikta* 14 (2001): 9–19.
[49] Alexander Kazhdan and Michael McCormick, "Social composition of the Byzantine court," in *Byzantine Court Culture from 829 to 1204*, ed. Henry McGuire (Washington, DC, 1997), 174 note 37.
[50] Moravcsik and Jenkins, eds., *De administrando imperio. Constantine VII Porphyrogenitus*, 246.
[51] Kazhdan and McCormick, "Social composition of the Byzantine court," 175–6.   [52] *Ibid.*, 180.

distinctive sandals they wore, which were described by the sixth-century antiquarian John Lydus.⁵³ The "sandaled senate" has been interpreted as referring to "functionaries subordinate to the *sekreta*."⁵⁴ *Sekreton* is usually a generic term for an administrative department. Philotheos wrote that the entire "sandaled senate" was to be invited to the first Christmas banquet and defined them as: "*asekretai, chartoularioi* of the great secretaries, imperial notaries of the said secretaries, such as are of the rank of *spatharokandidatos* and lower, *hypatoi, dishypatoi, kometes* of the schools, *silentiarioi, protiktoroi, euthychophoroi, skeptrophoroi, axiomatikoi*, and various *tagmata*."⁵⁵ For the most part these offices and titles are of the type one would expect the people in charge of imperial bookkeeping to have. Judging from the number of places reserved for this group in the Christmas banquets to which they were invited, the members of the "sandaled senate" "numbered fewer than 168."⁵⁶

People with imperial titles spent a significant amount of their time participating in imperial ceremonies. Officials in Constantinople were required to participate in ceremonial processions and other protocols that could be convoked on less than a day's notice.⁵⁷ Christian feast days and other regularly recurring anniversaries were celebrated ceremonially, as were promotions into various ranks and other court business. It has been noted that one could study the *Ceremony Book* for years without ever being able to visualize what these events were like.⁵⁸ The material in the *Ceremony Book* that seems to date from the ninth century gives specific instructions about which doors particular people should use, who should stand where, and what should be said. Groups of officials were needed to attend and to participate in acclamations that were part of most ceremonies. They were also important as the audience for whose benefit the ceremonies were enacted. These ceremonial obligations would have taken up a considerable amount of time. If these courtiers were also doing the business of administration, there would have to be a great many of them in order to get things done.

The imperial salaries and titles were a key element in creating and maintaining ties linking individuals to the emperor. Their function as a means of financial compensation and organizational labeling had a role whose importance is unclear and probably varied over time and by situation.

---

⁵³ Anastasius C. Bandy, ed., *On Powers, or, The Magistracies of the Roman State* (Philadelphia, 1983), 46–50.
⁵⁴ Oikonomides, *Listes*, 168 note 147.   ⁵⁵ *Ibid.*, 169.
⁵⁶ Kazhdan and McCormick, "Social composition of the Byzantine court," 180.   ⁵⁷ *Ibid.*, 196.
⁵⁸ McCormick, "Analyzing imperial ceremonies," 8–9.

Imperial administration and political culture

Formally there was a distinction between titles or dignities, called *axia* or *time*, and offices, called *offikion* or *arche*. In practice *axia* and *time* were used to designate both dignities and offices interchangeably. Even Philotheos, who draws the distinction between dignities and offices cleanly in his treatise on honors, occasionally uses *axia* for both.[59] Titles were granted either by the emperor through the ceremonial bestowal of a prize, *brabeion*, or through an oral pronouncement of the emperor or his subordinate. The titles granted through *brabeion* appear to have been honorary while those granted orally, *dia logou*, concerned offices. Philotheos described the process of receiving a title *dia brabeiou*:

> The gifts of imperial honors, given by the grace of God and as chosen by God, are bestowed upon the worthy by the divinely promoted emperors on the holy and wondrous imperial steps of the brilliant *chrysotriklinos* on auspicious days with the whole order of the imperial hall standing nearby and with their prizes lying near the imperial authority. They who are about to be honored are clothed in garnet cloaks and prepared outside of the curtain by the appointed imperial *protospatharios*. Before their entrance, three *spatharophoroi* of the same rank as those about to be honored enter with the imperial doorman, and making the customary reverence, they wait standing before the curtain for the presence of the candidate. And just as the curtain falls, the *protospatharios* of the imperials enters with the imperial doorman leading the one who is about to be received. [The *protospatharios*] urges him to make a prostration in three places. He stands him before the face of the emperor to take the prize of honor from the emperor's own hands. Soon after he gets it, the same *protospatharios* pulls him away backwards and adorns him with the prize given by the emperor and, immediately moving [the candidate] forward, makes him embrace the holy feet of the emperor. Then led down to those below, he is greeted by the men of the same rank as a friend of equal honor. Then, completing the reverence to the emperor, they shout thanks with a prostration and go out with [the candidate].[60]

The *brabeion*, prize, could be some sort of plaque, staff, diploma, or other decorative item of personal adornment.[61] The *Ceremony Book* describes officials as carrying particular items corresponding to their ranks, which probably were their *brabeia*.

The people who received titles gave gifts of money to certain palace officials. Philotheos recorded specific amounts to be given to particular palatine officials for the elevation to each dignity. For example the second rank is "that of the *silentiarioi*, whose prize is a gold staff given by the emperor's hand. He gives a gratuity of 6 *nomismata* to the *deuteros*, and

---

[59] Oikonomides, *Listes*, 281.   [60] *Ibid.*, 85–7.
[61] J. B. Bury, *The Imperial Administrative System in the Ninth Century* (London, 1911), 20–1, 121.

72 *nomismata* to the *praipositoi*."⁶² The *praipositoi*, eunuchs who arranged the ceremonies, would in turn distribute the money further:

> The *praipositoi*, in turn, reinforced their empire within the court by making, at no expense to themselves, a lengthy series of sub-gratifications extending from the imperial maître d's down to the palace bath attendants and through the personnel of the Hagia Sophia. Everyone in fact who participated in the promotion ceremony honoring the new patrician, and then some, received a share of the loot.⁶³

These donatives can be considered smaller versions of the imperial donatives that the emperors gave at their accession. Promotion into or within the company of title-holders was expensive. Once inside the organization, however, one would financially gain from every additional member.

Titles were not hereditary. Every member had to gain entrance through the bestowal of a title, regardless of how many of his kin were already there. Family names were generally not used in the ninth century. They appear with increasing frequency in the narrative histories of the tenth and eleventh centuries, and on seals only at the end of the tenth century.⁶⁴ The development of the custom of using family names is a cultural change that need not correlate to an increase in the importance of family connections. In fact, we know that even in the ninth century the leading families had strong networks that allowed them to dominate the top posts of the government. Imperial political culture, however, ignored these connections and placed the emphasis on the honorable service of individuals who were personally given titles. High status was defined through participation in the company of title-holders, even though family connections may have been the most common means of introduction to the palace.

The most frequently granted honorary titles derived from the actual offices of the Late Roman Empire. For example, *hypatos*, the Roman consul, became an honorary rank below its derivatives *dishypatos* and *anthypatos*. A *spatharios* in the late ancient empire was a member of the emperor's personal guard. *Spatharios*, *spatharokandidatos*, and *protospatharios* were granted as honors in the tenth century. The wives of title-holders seem to have taken the feminine forms of their husbands' titles. The *Ceremony Book* includes protocols for ceremonies involving female title-holders.⁶⁵

---

⁶² Oikonomides, *Listes*, 89.
⁶³ Kazhdan and McCormick, "Social composition of the Byzantine court," 189.
⁶⁴ Paul Stephenson, "A development in nomenclature on the seals of the Byzantine provincial aristocracy in the late 10th century," *REB* 52 (1994): 187–211. Werner Seibt, "Beinamen, 'Spitznamen' Herkunftsnamen, Familiennamen bis ins 10. Jahrhundert: Der Beitrag der Sigillographie zu einem prosopographischen Problem," in *Studies in Byzantine Sigillography 7*, ed. Werner Seibt (Washington, DC, 2002), 119–36.
⁶⁵ Vogt, ed., *Le Livre des cérémonies*, 61.

Imperial administration and political culture

The empress seems to have run a women's court with its own officials and ceremonies.

The people with honorary titles seem to have formed the pool of people who could be chosen for an actual office, although there are examples of individuals being given titles and offices at the same time. The following is a typical protocol for the promotion to an office by proclamation, *dia logou*:

> The emperor orders the *logothete* to introduce the one who ought to be promoted... and having come inside the swept curtain of the *chrysotriklinos*, he falls to the ground, prostrating before the emperor. Then the *logothete* stands and precedes him. [The candidate] comes forward and stands a little way from the emperor. The emperor exhorts him to manage and direct the service entrusted to him with truth, justice, and the fear of God, and to regard the subjects irrespective of gifts and persons, and to do all others things befitting those entrusted with such a charge. If he happens to be a *domestikos* of the *scholai* or a general or some other of the military officers, the emperor also exhorts him with rousing and stirring things about courage and nobility. After the proper things have been said, the emperor says to him, "In the name of the Father and the Son and the Holy Spirit, my God-given majesty promotes you *domestikos* of the God-guarded *scholai*." And immediately he falls to the ground and makes a prostration, then he kisses the feet of the great emperor and thus little by little he is led out by the *logothete* to the clock that is in the door of the *chrysotriklinos*. And the *logothete* hands him over to the *praipositoi* saying, "Our holy and God-led emperors promoted this one *domestic* of the *scholai*." And the *praipositoi* make the customary prayers for the emperors and they take him up and they lead him to the *Lausiakos* and the *protopraipositos* says to all, "Our holy and God-led emperors promoted this one *domestic* of the *scholai*." And everyone prays the "many-years."[66]

In Philotheos' list of titles, there were eighteen kinds of honorary titles for bearded men and eight for eunuchs.[67] He also lists sixty offices for bearded men and ten for eunuchs. Although many of the offices were held by only one person at a time, there were no limits on the number of people who could have an honorary title.

Those invested with offices had the right to put their office and title on their seal. Letters and other documents were sealed with lead blanks

---

[66] Reiske, ed., *De ceremoniis aulae Byzantinae, Constantine VII Porphyrogenitus*, 525–7.
[67] On eunuchs in Byzantium see Shaun Tougher, "Byzantine eunuchs: an overview, with special reference to their creation and origin," in *Women, Men and Eunuchs: Gender in Byzantium*, ed. Liz James (London and New York, 1997). George Sideris, "'Eunuchs of light': power, imperial ceremonial and positive representations of eunuchs in Byzantium (4th–12th centuries)," in *Eunuchs in Antiquity and Beyond*, ed. Shaun Tougher (London, 2002), 161–76. Margaret Mullett, "Theophylact of Ochrid's *In Defense of Eunuchs*," in *ibid.*, 177–98. Katharine Ringrose, "Living in the shadows: eunuchs and gender in Byzantium," in *Third Sex, Third Gender*, ed. Gilbert Herdt (New York, 1994), 85–109.

that were stamped with pincers, leaving an impression on both sides of the seal. Commonly one side bore a religious image and the other, the name, titles, and offices of the writer. As individuals were promoted they had new pincers made to reflect their new status.[68] A substantial number of known seals are anonymous or monogram seals. It is generally assumed that for official administrative business one would always use a seal that included one's titles and offices.

One could hold several titles and offices at the same time.[69] On seals and in documents the names of officials were organized so that the given name was followed by all the honors *dia brabeiou*, then all the offices in ascending order of importance, followed by a last name. For example, a tenth- or eleventh-century seal survives for "Pardos, imperial *protospatharios* and *strategos* of Thrace." Pardos' title was "imperial *protospatharios*" and his office was General of Thrace.[70] The eleventh-century seal of "John *patrikios, protospatharios, chartoularios* of the *dromos* of the West and *anagrapheus*" lists two titles and two jobs.[71] One could choose whether to include all of one's titles when signing a document or making a seal. In a document from the archives of Iviron from 975 Theodore Kladon made a cross at the head of the text and labeled it "Sign made by Theodore *protospatharios epi tou maglabiou* and *ekprosopou* Kladon." At the end of the same document he signed it "Theodore *protospatharios* and *epi tou maglabiou* Kladon."[72] Family names begin to appear on seals at the end of the tenth century and become standard by the 1030s.[73]

While offices granted *dia logou* were supposed to correspond to actual functions, the tasks people actually undertook did not always correspond to their formal office. For example, the *parakoimomenos* was technically the guardian of the emperor's bedchamber, but in the tenth century the *parakoimomenos* Basil was instrumental in creating and implementing imperial policy. Emperor Basil II ordered the *magistros* and *domestikos ton scholon* Nikephoros Ouranos to settle a boundary dispute between two monasteries on Mount Athos.[74] Such a judgment was not among his duties as a military officer. Rather, he was the person at hand capable of dealing with the problem. Throughout the history of the empire, emperors would

---

[68] Nicolas Oikonomides, "The usual lead seal," *DOP* 37 (1983): 148.   [69] Oikonomides, *Listes*, 284.
[70] John Nesbitt and Nicolas Oikonomides, *Catalogue of Byzantine Seals at Dumbarton Oaks and in the Fogg Museum of Art* (Washington, DC, 1991), vol. 1, p. 166, catalogue no. 71.33.
[71] *Ibid.*, p. 4, catalogue no. 1.6   [72] *Iviron I*, pp. 109–13, no. 2.
[73] Stephenson, "Nomenclature," 189–93. Jean-Claude Cheynet, "Du prénom au patronyme: les étrangers à Byzance (xe–xiie siècles)," in *Studies in Byzantine Sigillography 1*, ed. Nicolas Oikonomides (Washington, DC, 1987), 57–66.
[74] *Vatopedi*, pp. 67–76, nos. 2 and 3.

Imperial administration and political culture 21

1 Seal of Pardos, *c.* 950–1050. The inscription on the obverse reads: "Lord, help your servant." It continues on the reverse: "Pardos, imperial *protospatharios* and *strategos* of Thrace."

2 Seal of John, *c.* 1000–1100. The inscription on the obverse reads: "Theotokos help John *patrikios.*" The reverse continues: "*protospatharios, chartoularios* of the *dromos* of the west and *anagrapheus.*"

sometimes choose someone to play the role of chief executive for them. The title and office of this person did not change to reflect his status as the person in charge.[75] It seems that with this and other tasks the emperors delegated authority to someone of their liking without much regard for whether the person they chose had an office to match the task.

The holders of both titles and offices received their salaries in gold from the hand of the emperor in a ceremony lasting through Easter week. Yahya of Antioch described Romanos III as dying on Maundy Thursday after distributing salaries all day long. About five hundred imperial officials received their salaries from Romanos' hand.[76] A description of this ceremony was recorded by a European observer:

In the week before the feast of Vaiophoron, which we call the feast of Palms, the emperor makes a payment in gold coins to his vassals and to the different officers of his court, each one receiving a sum proportionate to his offices . . . The procedure

---

[75] Beck, "Theorie und Praxis im Aufbau der byzantinischen Zentralverwaltung," 23–4.
[76] Ignace Kratchkovsky, ed., *Histoire de Yahya ibn Sa'id d'Antioche*, Patrologia Orientalis 47.4, French trans. Françoise Micheau and Gérard Troupeau (Turnhout, 1997), 537.

was as follows. A table was brought in, fifteen feet long and six feet broad, which had upon it parcels of money tied up in bags, according to each man's due, the amount being written on the outside of the bag. The recipients then came in and stood before the king, advancing in order as they were called up by a herald. The first to be summoned was the marshal of the palace, who carried off his money, not in his hands but on his shoulders, together with four cloaks of honour. After him came the commander in chief of the army and the lord high admiral of the fleet. These being of equal rank received an equal number of money bags and cloaks, which they did not carry off on their shoulders but with some assistance dragged laboriously away. After them came twenty-four controllers, who each received twenty-four pounds of gold coins together with two cloaks. Then followed the order of patricians, of whom every one in turn was given twelve pounds of gold and one cloak. As I do not know how many patricians there are, I do not know the total amount that was paid; but every one received an equal share. After them came a huge crowd of minor dignitaries; knights of the sword of the first second and third class, chamberlains, treasury and admiralty officials. Some of these received seven pounds of gold, others six, five, four, three, two and one, according to their rank. I would not have you think that this all was done in one day. It began on the fifth day of the week at six o'clock in the morning and went on till ten and the emperor finished his part in the proceedings on the sixth and seventh day. Those who take less than a pound receive their share not from the emperor, but from the chief chamberlain during the week before Easter.[77]

In essence these accounts are corroborated by several Byzantine sources.[78] The leading officials of the empire would approach the emperor one by one to receive ceremonial silk robes and their salaries. The gold that was distributed in the spring was collected again in the fall in the form of taxes. In an economy that was not highly monetized, as seems to have been the case for at least some parts of the empire, the salaries put gold into circulation among people who would return it to the emperor half a year later as taxes: "The state appears as the main motor that puts money into circulation and collects it back through taxation."[79] Having a position with the imperial administration that paid a salary in gold made it far easier to pay taxes in gold. Those who received salaries, or who maintained gold reserves through other means, would be in an enviable economic position when people needed to convert their material resources into the imperial gold coins required for tax collection.

This passing back and forth of gold coins bearing iconographic images of the emperor and Christ also functioned as a ceremonial bond between

[77] Paolo Chiesa, ed., *Liudprandi Cremonensis: Antapodosis; Homelia paschalis; Historia Ottonis; Relatio de Legatione Constantinopolitana* (Brépols, 1998), 149. *Liudprand of Cremona: The Embassy to Constantinople and Other Writings*, trans. F. A. Wright (London, 1993), 155–6.
[78] Oikonomides, "Title and income," 201.   [79] *Ibid.*, 207.

Imperial administration and political culture

the servants of the empire and the emperor. The subsequent circulation of the coins in other contexts could have the effect of extending the lines of contact. Those who had gold coins had some relationship with the emperors, even if at several removes. The large salaries given to generals and other high-ranking officials were intended to cover their expenses.[80] We may presume that at least the more important people serving the general would then receive their payment from his hand. Those officers or supporters of the general would then have some of the emperor's largess mediated through the general. The practice of making payments in Easter week spread to monasteries and presumably to other contexts as well.[81] In the monastery of Gregory Pakourianos the distribution of stipends on Easter Sunday shared the ordered ranking of the imperial distributions:

> There should be three orders of brother and they should receive allowances. The superior of the monastery should receive 36 *nomismata*. The older priests along with the two administrators, the ecclesiarch, the sacristan, and as many as are notable among the brothers and of similar status to him – up to the number of 15 – will be called the first order and each of them should get 20 *nomismata*. The second order too should likewise be 15 men and each of these should get 15 *nomismata*. The third order should be made up of 20 souls and each of these should get 10 *nomismata*. The full amount of their allowance should be in standard *trachy* coinage.[82]

The *typikon* of Michael Attaleiates also distinguishes three levels of monks who receive different amounts of money, but the date of the payments is not specified.[83] Pakourianos explained that the allowances were given at Easter rather than in September, when the revenues were collected, because there was a fair available in the spring for them to spend the money with fewer distractions. Given his long career in imperial service and those of his companions who planned to join the monastery with him, it seems likely that they also considered a cash payment at Easter as appropriate and necessary. Certainly the need to distinguish a hierarchy within the monastery and enforce it with distinctions of wealth owes more to imitation of imperial customs than to ideals of monastic poverty and brotherhood.

One of the apparent paradoxes of Byzantine administrative history is that while the Byzantine economy became increasingly monetized over time, the activity of the imperial administration was most highly monetized in the eighth through tenth centuries and moved toward non-monetized

---

[80] *Ibid.*, 204.
[81] Michael F. Hendy, *Studies in the Byzantine Monetary Economy, c. 300–1450* (Cambridge, 1985), 192. *Typika*, 535.
[82] *Typika*, 535.   [83] *Ibid.*, 350.

means of direct exploitation and remuneration through granting privileges in the eleventh and later centuries.[84] The role of the state in circulating money seems to have diminished in importance as the size and general monetization of the economy increased. Perhaps the key to understanding this may lie with a greater appreciation of the role of coins in imperial political culture. Rather than being a monetized anomaly in an economy of exchange in kind, the ninth- and tenth-century government was constituted through a highly ceremonial circulation of wealth. Taxation and salaries were ritual exchanges of high-value coins that did as much to cement the government together as to participate in an economy.

While the formal distribution of salaries at the hand of the emperor looms large in our understanding of political practice in the imperial centuries, it does not seem to have been the sole means of remuneration of high officers at any time. A section of the *Ceremony Book* that appears to record practice under Leo VI (886–912) lists salaries for various generals and notes that one should:

Know that the generals of the west are not paid salaries on account of taking their own gratuities from their own *themata* every year. [They are] the general of the Peloponnesos, the general of Nikopolis, the general of Hellas, the general of Sicily, the general of Langobardia, the general of Strymon, the general of Kephalenia, the general of Thessaloniki, the general of Dyrachion, the general of Dalmatia, the general of Cherson.[85]

As these generals were officially empowered to support themselves out of the revenues of their territories, the imperial administration was ceding some of its sovereignty over taxation to the generals. It would be natural for these generals to assume more independence from the central administration. The same list indicates that the general of Chaldia would receive 10 rather than the usual 20 pounds of gold for a general of his rank because he received an additional 10 pounds from the *koumerkion*, which was a tax on trade. Likewise the general of Mesopotamia received no salary because he received all of the *koumerkion* for his region. Nineteen other generals and *kleisourarchs* (generals of border regions) were listed as receiving salaries in gold. This is clearly only a partial list of officers, but it puts roughly one-third of the high-level military staff of the empire outside of the formal salary system at the beginning of the tenth century.

---

[84] Metcalf, "Monetary recession," 114–15. Oikonomides, "Role of the Byzantine state," 979.
[85] Reiske, ed., *De ceremoniis aulae Byzantinae, Constantine VII Porphyrogenitus*, 697.

In addition to the official posts in the imperial administration that were remunerated by these salaries, salaries were also granted to the holders of imperial titles. Unlike the remuneration for the posts, in which case one received the salary for as long as one held office, the salaries associated with honorary titles were received for life.[86] Many of these titles were purchased for set fees. The initial charge was much more than the annual stipend.[87] One set of figures lists prices to be paid for dignities: "Imperial *mandator* 2 pounds; imperial *kandidatos*, 3 pounds; imperial *strator*, 4 pounds; imperial *spatharios*, 5 pounds; imperial *spatharokandidatos*, 6 pounds; imperial *protospatharios*, 12 pounds; and beyond this 18 pounds."[88] One could pay more to receive a higher annual stipend:

If one wants to become part of the grand company with a stipend up to 40 *nomismata*, one gives 16 pounds. If one seeks a greater stipend, one should raise the price in proportion to the stipend, i.e., one pound for seven *nomismata*. If one wants to become part of the middle company with a stipend up to 20 *nomismata*, one ought to give 10 pounds. If one seeks more than 20 *nomismata*, one ought to raise the price in proportion with the salary.[89]

There is considerable evidence for the practice of buying titles and treating such purchases as financial investments.[90] Michael Psellos purchased a dignity for his future son-in-law, Elpidios, as part of his adoptive daughter's dowry. We know about this case of patronage because Elpidios' poor conduct led to legal proceedings in which Psellos endeavored to have him demoted and recover some of his investment. Psellos worked to get the fellow both titles and positions:

He, the son of a *protospatharios*, was himself a *spatharios* and still without a post. Psellos obtained for him successively the offices of "lesser imperial notary" in the bureau of the Antiphon, judge of the Hippodrome, judge of the Velum, *thesmographos*, *mystographos*, and *exactor*; and on the other hand the high dignities of *protospatharios* and later *patrician*. An excellent example of a *cursus* of one who owed nothing to personal qualities, who is portrayed to us as ignorant, lazy, incompetent and debauched.[91]

---

[86] Oikonomides, "Role of the Byzantine state," 1008–10. Oikonomides, "Title and income," 202.
[87] Paul Lemerle, "'Roga' et rente d'état aux xe–xie siècles," *REB* 25 (1967): 99.
[88] Reiske, ed., *De ceremoniis aulae Byzantinae, Constantine VII Porphyrogenitus*, 692.
[89] *Ibid.*, 692–93.
[90] Lemerle, "'Roga' et rente d'état," 84–97; Oikonomides, "Some Byzantine state annuitants," 16–19.
[91] Lemerle, "'Roga' et rente d'état," 87–8.

The record of this episode leaves no doubt that titles were purchased with considerable sums and seen as significant financial investments. Once Elpidios fell from favor, Psellos worked not only to minimize scandal in reordering his personal relationships, but to recoup financial losses. The titles were seen as property that could be transferred. When Elpidios was made to return his patrician's diploma, Psellos kept it in order to give it later to "a less disappointing son-in-law."[92] It is clear that titles were held as a form of investment. In his seminal study of the issue Lemerle interpreted the stipends as interest paid on an investment:

We learn that in effect the officials of the State were able, at their discretion, to augment the rate of their pension against a proportional capital installment . . . a pension of 7 *nomismata* for a capital of one pound represents an interest of 9.72%. One must admit that the State, to attract private capital, made an offer with advantages comparable to those one was able to find elsewhere.[93]

If purchasing a title was in fact like buying a government bond, then as Lemerle concludes this rate of return would make it a fine investment. Unlike modern government bonds, however, the principal could not be retrieved. The stipend was given not for a period determined by the investment, but for the life of the title-holder. The title-holder who paid a pound for an augmented stipend that was 9.75 percent of his investment would need to live for another eleven years in order to recoup his investment. The basic prices for most titles, without the augmentation, were such that the annual return would be 2.5–3.5 percent.[94] Interest rates on loans hovered around 8.33 percent in the eleventh century and one estimate suggests that the annual return on an investment in agricultural land may have been approximately 3 percent.[95]

Titles seem to have been commonly purchased for fairly young children. In legislation that barred those less than twenty years old from receiving titles, Alexios Komnenos indicated that titles had been often transferred to children.[96] Men who seem to be quite young, such as Psellos' future son-in-law, are recorded as having titles already. It may be that titles were usually purchased early in life and that people commonly lived long enough for them to be a sound investment. Another compilation of information

[92] *Ibid.*, 88. [93] *Ibid.*, 82–3. [94] Oikonomides, "Role of the Byzantine state," 1009.
[95] On interest rates: Angeliki Laiou, "Exchange and trade, seventh–twelfth centuries," in *The Economic History of Byzantium from the Seventh through the Fifteenth Century*, ed. Angeliki Laiou (Washington, DC, 2002), 757; on profits from land: Lefort, "Rural economy," 302–4.
[96] Ioannes Zepos and Panagiotes Zepos, eds., *Jus graecoromanum*, 8 vols. (Athens, 1931), vol. I, pp. 349–50.

made under Constantine VII includes the following story from the reign of Leo VI:

> In the time of Leo, the Christ-loving and ever-memorable emperor, lived the late Ktenas, an aged cleric of great wealth, who was precentor of the New Church and was skilled in singing as was no other at that time. This same Ktenas besought the patrician Samonas, who was that time chamberlain, to intercede for him with the emperor so that he might be made protospatharius and wear the shirt and go in procession to the Lausiacus and take his seat as protospatharius and receive a stipend of one pound, and in respect of this remuneration might give the emperor forty pounds. But the emperor could not bring himself to do this, saying that it was out of his power, and "to the great disgrace of my imperial majesty if a cleric becomes protospatharius." On hearing this from the patrician Samonas, this same Ktenas added to the forty pounds a pair of ear-rings valued at ten pounds, and a silver table with animals on it in gold relief, also valued at ten pounds. And the emperor, besought by the request of the patrician Samonas, the chamberlain, took the forty pounds of gold and the pair of ear-rings and the table with its gold on silver relief work, so that the total gift of the same Ktenas amounted to sixty pounds. Then the emperor made him protospatharius, and he received a stipend on that occasion of one pound. After being honoured with the rank of protospatharius this same Ktenas lived two years and then died; and he received a stipend of one pound for each of the two years.[97]

Ktenas is presented as having made a bad investment because he only lived two years. This situation was odd in the first instance because Ktenas was a cleric. There were honorary titles given to priests, but Ktenas wanted one of the secular titles. Second, he was portrayed as acting out of vanity rather than good sense. Presumably had he been young enough potentially to earn money on the investment he would not have been remembered.

Another way to interpret this practice of paying for imperial positions is to assume that having the title put one in the position to earn money beyond the stipend:

> Bribery and fiscal extortions were a normal element of Byzantine state machinery and found their corollary in the practice of selling titles and offices. The fact that the price of a title was incomparably higher than the salary even for several years shows that the social prestige and additional income of an official were in excess of his direct material reward.[98]

Officials with certain duties presumably would be able to make bribes a significant source of income. Yet, as discussed above, not all the people paying for titles were paying for government jobs. Ktenas paid to become

---

[97] Moravcsik and Jenkins, eds., *De administrando imperio. Constantine VII Porphyrogenitus*, 244–5.
[98] Kazhdan and Constable, *People and Power in Byzantium*, 52.

a *protospatharios* without any indication that he would take up any administrative tasks. So while it seems highly likely that some functionaries made money through extortion, this cannot be the whole explanation.

The real value of titles was not in their economic worth, but in their ability to confer membership in the grand imperial company that mimicked the company of heaven. Titles meant that their holders were associated with the emperor, and hence were important people. Not everyone had to purchase titles. They were given freely to people whom the emperor wanted to associate with his rule in some way. Kekaumenos thought that one should not purchase titles.[99] Kekaumenos' sons should be important enough that the emperor would honor them freely in order to keep them as friends. If the emperor chose not to give his sons a title, they should work at being worthy of the honor: "If you have some title, honor this so that you may be honored, but if you do not, strive so that they honor you as much or more than those having titles."[100] Foreign rulers appear to have been regularly given titles and stipends as a tool of diplomacy. Granting titles to independent rulers was a way of expanding the empire's political authority, at least on paper. The administrative treatise *De administrando imperio* describes how some regions of northern Mesopotamia became part of the empire during the reign of Leo VI (886–912):

> Tekis belonged to Manuel ... Mesopotamia was not a province at that time. But Leo, the Christ-loving and ever-memorable emperor, brought the late Manuel out of Tekis upon a promise *of immunity*, and brought him to Constantinople and made him protospatharius. This same Manuel has four sons, Pankratoukas, Iachnoukas, Moudaphar and John. Pankratoukas the emperor made commander of the Hicanati and thereafter military governor of the Boukellarioi, and Iachnoukas he made military governor of Nicopolis, and to Moudaphar and John he gave crown land at Trapezus, and he honoured them all with dignities and conferred on them many benefits. And he made Mesopotamia a province ... all these being now beneath the dominion of the Romans.[101]

This type of imperial expansion by turning independent rulers into imperial subjects was not uncommon. The distinction between the high ranks of the Byzantine aristocracy and the independent or semi-independent princes appears to have been quite fine. Manuel's children were given titles, lands, and high-ranking military offices. Their children would then be high-ranking citizens of the empire as well as descendants of an independent ruler. It

---

[99] Kekaumenos, Litavrin, §60; Wassiliewsky, 59.
[100] Kekaumenos, Litavrin, §38; Wassiliewsky, 42.
[101] Moravcsik and Jenkins, eds., *De administrando imperio. Constantine VII Porphyrogenitus*, 238–9.

would be politically inept for an emperor to expect Manuel's grandchildren to pay for their titles.

Also from *De administrando imperio* we know that when Krikorikios, the ruler of Taron, was brought to Constantinople and invested as the *strategos* of Taron and given the rank of *magistros*, he received a house and a salary of 20 pounds. Krikorikios appears in discussions of officials' salaries and titles as if he were a typical civil servant, and scholars wonder whether this salary was given by virtue of his post as general or his rank as *magistros*.[102] Since he was already the ruler of Taron before he received anything from the emperor, neither the title nor the post changed his position in a practical way. It is clear from the account in *De administrando imperio* that his status was highly negotiated:

> The late Krikorikios, then, prince of Taron, at first bent and submitted himself before the emperor of the Romans, but from the first he seemed double-faced, and while in a word he pretended to esteem the friendship of the emperor, in fact he acted at the pleasure of the chief prince of the Saracens... However, he continually sent presents, such as appear valuable to the barbarians of those parts, to Leo, the glorious among emperors, and got in return more and better from the pious emperor, who also frequently urged him by letter to visit the imperial city and behold the emperor and partake of the bounties and honours bestowed by him.[103]

In time the emperor sent the *protospatharios* and *domestikos tes upourgias*, Constantine Lips, to Taron with letters and gifts. He first brought Krikorikios' illegitimate son to Constantinople, where "the emperor honoured him with the rank of protospatharius and richly entertained him."[104] Constantine then accompanied this son back to Taron and returned with Krikorikios' brother, who was similarly honored. On the third trip Constantine was able to persuade Krikorikios to come to Constantinople to receive his title, office, and salary. The association with the empire may have enhanced Krikorikios' standing with his local community or given him more authority over his rivals. If the salary was considered a payment for services rendered, then Krikorikios became a servant of the emperor when he accepted it. If the salary were considered an annual gift associated with a rank, Krikorikios could still claim an independent status, at least some of the time. His salary eventually excited the envy of other princes in the Caucasus who complained: "For what service – they said – is he performing more than we, or in what does he help the Romans more than

---

[102] Oikonomides, "Title and income," 203 and note 24. Lemerle, "'Roga' et rente d'état," 83–4.
[103] Moravcsik and Jenkins, eds., *De administrando imperio. Constantine VII Porphyrogenitus*, 188–9.
[104] *Ibid.*, 190–1.

we do? Either, therefore, we too should be stipendiary as he is, or else he too should be excluded from this largess."[105] The emperor, now Romanos I, negotiated with Krikorikios not for a reduction of his stipend, but for an increase in the gifts that Krikorikios sent to the emperor:

> He [Krikorikios] replied that he could provide neither gold nor silver, but promised to give, over and above the gifts he regularly sent, tunics and bronze vessels up to ten pounds in total value, and these he did give for three or four years. But thereafter he reported that he could not provide this tribute, and demanded either that he should receive the stipend gratis as in the time of the emperor Leo, of most blessed memory, or else that it should be cut off. And so, that it might not cause offence to Kakikios and the curopalate and the rest, the said emperor Romanus, of blessed memory, cut it off. But to console him, as it were, he afterwards honoured his son Asotios, when he came to Constantinople, with patrician rank and entertained him munificently before sending him home.[106]

Asotios' salary as a patrician and the gifts he received may have offset considerably the loss of his father's income as a *magistros*. This story also reveals that all the gifts did not flow from Constantinople eastward. Even though they may have been of token value, gifts from Taron were expected in Constantinople. While the official tax status of Taron is unknown, nothing suggests that the empire received any cash revenue from the region.

It is altogether unclear whether the princes who accepted titles thought of themselves as allies or servants of the empire. Lemerle would put these foreign princes in a different category altogether from the imperial elite.[107] One expects that in exchange for their salaries the foreign princes were supposed to refrain from attacking the empire. The distinction between tribute payments and stipend payments was fine yet ideologically strong. The boundary between salary for services rendered and tribute for quiescence was constructed so that people near the border could believe they were on the other side. The titles and salaries discussed in *De administrando imperio* have a great deal to do with maintaining and extending imperial authority in border regions and very little to do with government functionaries.

The relationship between payment, title, and function points out two boundary lines that are more permeable and vague than they are often supposed to be. On the one hand the boundary between powerful, aristocratic provincial subjects and independent princes is vague and malleable. The stipends allowed tribute payments to be interpreted as payment for services rendered, turning independent potentates into imperial servants. On the other hand the boundary between the government, in its human

---

[105] *Ibid.*, 194–5.   [106] *Ibid.*   [107] Lemerle, "'Roga' et rente d'état," 99.

incorporation, and the merely well-off is equally unclear. The system of imperial salaries meant that the whole of what can be considered the aristocracy was in the pay of the government.

KOMNENIAN POLITICAL CULTURE

The political system just described underwent profound changes in the course of the eleventh century, as did many other aspects of Byzantine culture and society.[108] The reign of Alexios Komnenos, 1081–1118, marks the break between two cultural styles of government organization. That of the ninth and tenth centuries has characteristics that have looked bureaucratic to some modern observers. The aristocratic political culture of the late eleventh and twelfth centuries has more characteristics in common with that of medieval Europe than its predecessor does. The empire of the Komnenoi therefore looks more medieval than the Byzantine empire of the "imperial centuries," which, especially as described in twentieth-century historiography, looks like a modern centralized state adrift in the Middle Ages.

Alexios responded to seven centuries' accumulation of ceremonial tradition in the imperial palace by moving across town. He moved the seat of his government to the Blachernai Palace in northwest Constantinople, away from the Great Palace which had been the residence of the emperors and the government since it was built by Constantine I.[109] The importance of the physical relocation of the imperial court away from the spaces that the imperial ceremonies were designed to fit cannot be underestimated. The relocation gave Alexios the ability to choose whether to have a ceremony for opening the palace. While he certainly maintained some traditional ceremonies, such as granting vestments to favored generals, Alexios refashioned the imperial government in a way that acknowledged that old political rituals and symbols had lost much of their power.[110]

---

[108] Alexander Kazhdan and Annabel Jane Wharton, *Change in Byzantine Culture in the Eleventh and Twelfth Centuries* (Berkeley, 1985); Alexander Kazhdan, "Aristocracy and the imperial ideal," in *The Byzantine Aristocracy, IX to XIII Centuries*, ed. Michael Angold (Oxford, 1984), 34–57; Paul Magdalino, "The Byzantine holy man in the twelfth century," in *The Byzantine Saint*, ed. Sergei Hackel (London, 1981), 51–66; Magdalino, "Honour among Romaioi," 183–218; Paul Magdalino, "Byzantine snobbery," in *The Byzantine Aristocracy, IX to XIII Centuries*, ed. Michael Angold (Oxford, 1984), 58–78.

[109] Steven Runciman, "Blachernae Palace and its decoration," in *Studies in Memory of David Talbot Rice*, ed. Giles Robertson and George Henderson (Edinburgh, 1975), 277–83; Raymond Janin, *Constantinople byzantine: développement urbain et répertoire topographique* (Paris, 1950), 125–6.

[110] Symbat Pakourianos mentioned imperial vestments given to him by Alexios in his will. *Iviron II*, pp. 154–5, no. 44.

The central element of the new Komnenian political culture was the reliance on the imperial family itself for managing the empire.¹¹¹ Alexios did not constitute his government through ritual exaltation of imperial servants, but by "bringing the empire's military command structure within the imperial *genos*, the extended imperial family, and by giving all who belonged to the imperial *genos* a vested interest in the imperial *oikos* and its domain, now less distinguishable than ever from the empire as a whole.".¹¹² Alexios bound his government together by applying the cultural rules that made the members of an aristocratic household into an effective force. This may have been more a matter of using whatever methods of gaining political support were available and effective than of creating a new theory of imperial government.

In the course of the eleventh century older titles were granted so widely they lost value.¹¹³ The prefix *proto* was added to a number of older titles, creating new tiers at the top of the hierarchy. According to our narrative sources Isaac Komnenos (1057–59) did not pay the salaries to the titles-holders and they were completely abandoned by Nikephoros Botaneiates (1078–81).¹¹⁴ Alexios made no effort to revive the tradition of paying salaries to those holding honorary titles.¹¹⁵ Kekaumenos' attitude toward imperial titles typifies an era when the erosion of the traditional culture of imperial titles and offices had progressed considerably. He would not turn down titles offered by an emperor, but they did not play a significant role in his cultural construction of prestige. Titles and honors are only valuable when people believe that they are, as Kekaumenos explained in his advice to emperors.¹¹⁶

An entirely new set of titles was created in the 1080s by Alexios Komnenos that used *sebastos*, the Greek translation of *augustus*, as a base term. The new titles were granted almost exclusively to members of Alexios' close family. The idea of precedence in title was replaced by precedence in kinship with the emperors. By the reign of Manuel Komnenos, designations of kinship such as "nephew" and "cousin" of the emperor took the place of titles.¹¹⁷ The older titles continued to be used by people of lesser prestige, the "subordinate functionaries, merchants, and the petty provincial elites."¹¹⁸ As

---

[111] Ralph-Johannes Lilie, "Des Kaisers Macht und Ohnmacht," *Poikila Byzantina* 4 (1984): 38–46.
[112] Paul Magdalino, *The Empire of Manuel I Komnenos, 1143–1180* (Cambridge, 1993), 187.
[113] Hohlweg, *Beiträge zur Verwaltungsgeschichte des ostromischen Reiches unter den Komnenen*, 34–9; Oikonomides, "L'évolution de l'organisation administrative," 126.
[114] Oikonomides, "Title and income," 208.   [115] Oikonomides, "Role of the Byzantine state," 1021.
[116] Kekaumenos, Litavrin, §81; Wassiliewsky, 95.
[117] Hendy, "Economy revisited, twenty years on," 27–31.
[118] Oikonomides, "L'évolution de l'organisation administrative," 128.

the importance of family connections grew, titles became less important and could be ignored. To take only one example of a well-known phenomenon, in 1112 Andronikos Doukas signed a ruling simply with his name "Doukas" instead of his title *pansebastos*. This was an "eloquent sign of the new mentality that prevailed under the Komnenoi, the relation or familiarity with the emperor swept away the importance of the office or dignity."[119] This is a matter of change in mentality rather than government. The changes in political style in the late eleventh century reflected the changing values of elite society generally. Military ability, personal honor, nobility, and ties of loyalty between extended family members became far more highly prized.[120]

As rank became a matter of degree of kinship with the emperor, Alexios' family assumed an unprecedented significance in the governing of the empire.[121] The rise of a new group of people was less significant than the new ways Alexios deployed his supporters to control the empire. The patterns of delegation that can be observed in the archival material indicate that in the later eleventh century personal ties between individuals operated more than formal lines of subordination. For example, the patriarch was represented in a dispute on Mount Athos by the most holy monk Ioannikios, grand *oikonomos*, first of the *protosynkelles* and the patriarch's "man."[122] The notary George was mentioned as the "subordinate" of Nikephoros Botaneiates, the *proedros* and *doux* of Thessalonike, in one document and as Nikephoros' "man" in another.[123] George's authority to intervene in this dispute was dependent on his ability to speak freely with the *proedros*, not his rank as a notary. The *protospatharios* Basil was called the "man" of the *sekretos*.[124] Even those with significant titles could also identify themselves as personal associates of someone more significant. For example, Stephen Chrysodaktylos was *magistros vestiarch* and "man" of the *caesar* Nikephoros Melessenos. John Melidones was *protovestes*, judge of the Hippodrome, grand *oikonomos* of Oikoprasteion and likewise "man" of the *caesar*.[125] In the Komnenian period important officials had their own staff associated with their person rather than any department of which they might be the head. The *sebastokrator* Isaac Komnenos had his own accountant, Spanopolos the *logariastes* of the *sebastokrator*.[126] The *panhypertimos*,

---

[119] *Docheiariou*, p. 63, no. 3.
[120] Kazhdan and Wharton, *Change in Byzantine Culture in the Eleventh and Twelfth Centuries*, 99–119; Magdalino, "Honour among Romaioi," 183–218.
[121] Magdalino, "Innovations in government," 148.
[122] *Iviron II*, p. 126, no. 40, lines 18–20. On forms of aristocratic service see Jean-Claude Cheynet, *Pouvoir et contestations à Byzance (963–1210)* (Paris, 1990), 287–301.
[123] *Iviron II*, pp. 94, 97, no. 34, line 14; p. 103, no. 35, line 22.   [124] *Ibid.*, p. 126, no. 40, lines 23–4.
[125] *Ibid.*, pp. 144–50, no. 43; p. 237, no. 52, line 323.   [126] *Ibid.*, pp. 159, 161, no. 45, line 5.

hypertimos, dikaiophylax, and *anagrapheus* George Xeros had the help of his man Michael, the *vestes,* and imperial notary.[127] From the third quarter of the eleventh century some seals also designate individuals as the emperor's men.[128]

The change in the system of titles was one of the ways Alexios made the government essentially coterminous with his kin. The transformation of the government limited who counted to Alexios' own closest supporters, to the exclusion of other families and the rest of those with imperial titles. That this created an effective government is shown through Alexios' successful reforms of imperial judicial, financial, and monetary systems.

BUREAUCRACY?

In the twentieth-century ideal, bureaucracy was defined by three main characteristics.[129] Authority is vested in offices or posts rather than in individuals. One has authority so long as one holds a particular post. Bureaucrats are anonymous replaceable cogs in a machine because the power is in the office. Second, the authority and duties of the offices are clearly defined. Bureaucrats cannot act on matters outside the purview of their department because their authority only extends as far as their mandate. Third, the actions of the bureaucracy are governed by forms, protocols, and precedents so that all situations that can be classified as examples of the same phenomenon are treated the same way. While no one would expect a medieval – or modern – government to conform completely to this ideal model of a bureaucracy, the model can help us identify those aspects of Byzantine political culture that have at times looked bureaucratic to scholars.

The highly ordered ranks of officials and title-holders can look like the clearly prescribed ranks of functionaries in modern bureaucracies. As Beck pointed out some years ago, the Byzantine system of titulature and precedence makes the imperial administration look like an ordered bureaucracy to modern observers.[130] Officials were arranged in strict order around the emperor and empress, and dependent upon the imperial will for their ranks. There were also actual administrative jobs. The correspondence between the ranks and the duties, however, is not always clear. Authority could be vested in individuals rather than offices. Basil the *parakoimomenos* did not rule the empire by virtue of his office. People of low office could wield great

---

[127] *Ibid.,* pp. 159, 167 no. 45, lines 94–6.   [128] Cheynet, *Pouvoir et contestations,* 296–7.
[129] Max Weber, *The Theory of Social and Economic Organization,* trans. A. M. Henderson and Talcott Parsons (New York, 1947), 329–41.
[130] Beck, "Theorie und Praxis im Aufbau der byzantinischen Zentralverwaltung," 4.

Imperial administration and political culture 35

power and those of high office could be ineffective. Salaries were paid in a highly ordered manner, but in many cases the payment was due to a person's rank and title rather than to the services rendered. There is no strong evidence that the imperial administration used forms and protocols to determine the treatment of various issues. The remaining fiscal documents – for all that they are documents – provide more evidence for deviation than consistency in form.

The lack of a system of hereditary titulature contributes to the sense that the emperor was surrounded by faceless bureaucrats, but a participant in the imperial processions and receptions would have been aware of the many kinship ties and legacies among the title-holders. Because these connections played no formal role in the protocols, we do not see them. To us, the titled crowd can look anonymous.

The sheer numbers of title-holders and officers described in the *Ceremony Book*, Philotheos' treatise, and the precedence lists give the impression of a vast array of individuals taking part in the government. The large numbers of title-holders seem to imply a large number of bureaucrats. But while the Byzantine title-holders were bound in a special relationship with the emperor, they were not necessarily working for the government. If it is correct to equate the "sandaled senate" with people actually doing paperwork, then about 160 people were employed in the central administration of the empire. The archival records indicate that the number of working officials would be in the hundreds rather than thousands at any given time. The documents in the archives of Iviron mention sixty-one individuals between 927 and 1100 with official titles, including people who signed documents as witnesses or whose lands were mentioned in boundary descriptions. The number of people who acted in official capacities was closer to thirty-eight. Some of the individuals mentioned in these documents were also recorded in the archives of other monasteries as well. The vagaries of preservation and the ideal of monastic detachment from the world are such that I would put little credence (and hence little effort) in an attempt to quantify the government through prosopography. All that can reasonably be observed is that the archives do not make a case for a government involving more than several hundreds of officials.

The thousands of lead seals also give the initial impression of a large government. By the early 1990s nearly 60,000 seals were attested in collections and more are continually found through excavation.[131] The study of Byzantine seals presents our best source for the individual imperial offices

---

[131] Nesbitt and Oikonomides, *Catalogue of Byzantine Seals at Dumbarton Oaks and in the Fogg Museum of Art*, vii.

and titles, prosopography, and developments in nomenclature.¹³² The seals inform us about titles and names that can be of great help in locating and dating people. The seals, however, are not in themselves informative about the strength of the government. The process of excavation and collection of seals has been a matter of such chance that we do not know whether the known corpus is a small or large percentage of the seals used. Many of the seals in collections are anonymous and indicate no connection to a government official. Were we to assume, contrary to reason, that every seal represents a lost government document, and that they were used at an even rate between 600 and 1200, the known corpus indicates a rate of production of just over eight letters a month. By multiplying this figure by whatever percentage of seals one thinks are uncollected and dividing it by whatever percentage of seals one thinks were from private correspondence, one could manipulate the rate of document production considerably. Yet without speculating wildly, it seems clear that the known seals do not constitute evidence of an unduly large amount of paperwork. More importantly, while every seal represents a lost document, paperwork does not simply mean authority or efficacy. The seals are manifestations of cultural attitudes about authentication of documents and self-presentation. They are another aspect of Byzantine political culture that can give a misleading impression of a bureaucratized government.

The protocols of Byzantine imperial ritual thus allow for an analogy of appearance, but not of function, between the titled crowd gathered around the emperor and the bureaucrats of a state machine. The culture that ennobled attendance upon the emperor in the Great Palace was underpinned by an ideology very different from that of modern civil service. Membership in the grand imperial company granted one the opportunity to imitate the company of heaven. Byzantine court ceremony, titulature, salaries, and vestments had substantial and varied significance. They do not seem to have had that much to do with the regular functioning of government administration.

The decline of this ceremonial political culture and the rise of an aristocratic political culture in the late eleventh century do not necessarily imply

---

[132] For an introduction to the study of sigillography see Oikonomides, "The usual lead seal," 147–58; Nicolas Oikonomides, *A Collection of Dated Byzantine Lead Seals* (Washington, DC, 1986); Cécile Morrisson, "Numismatique et sigillographie: parentes et méthode," in *Studies in Byzantine Sigillography 1*, ed. Nicolas Oikonomides, 12–26 (Washington, DC, 1987); Jean-Claude Cheynet and Cécile Morrisson, "Lieux de trouvaille et circulation des sceaux," in *Studies in Byzantine Sigillography 2*, ed. Nicolas Oikonomides, 105–36 (Washington, DC, 1990); Nicolas Oikonomides, "On sigillographic Epigraphy," in *Studies in Byzantine Sigillography 6*, ed. Nicolas Oikonomides, 37–42 (Washington, DC, 1999).

any change in the way the government actually worked. What changed was the way people described authority. Starting in the 1070s, archival documents acknowledge far more clearly that real authority moved through personal connections between individuals. This may be a new phenomenon and it may be true that previously authority ran through the formal system of imperial administrative appointments. I suspect, however, that the imperial appointments and promotions of the tenth and early eleventh centuries were every bit as subject to personal ties of patronage and recommendation. Beck's fundamental study of Byzantine *Gefolgschaftswesen* draws examples of personal ties of loyalty mainly from the ninth and tenth centuries.[133] The protocol of the era, however, was to find glory through anonymous solidarity with the grand company of people holding imperial titles. One who secured a good title for his protégé would be pleased to use that title rather than to say he was one's "man." It is not necessarily the case that ties of personal loyalty became more important in administration; rather the sense of honor gained through association with the palace officialdom lost its power. Any real change in administrative practice between 1000 and 1100 needs to be proven through more than reference to the changes in political culture.

Studies of Byzantine aristocracy have emphasized that civil service constituted the clearest path to aristocratic status in the eighth and ninth centuries and that the civil aristocracy was rivaled by an aristocracy of nobility, starting in the ninth century. In the middle of the twentieth century it was widely believed that eleventh-century politics were dominated by competition between the civil aristocracy and the military aristocracy.[134] The civil aristocracy owed its existence to its members' service in the imperial bureaucracy. It was Constantinopolitan, educated, and to some extent based on merit. The military aristocracy was provincial, was landed, and adhered to a system of nobility based on blood lines. In that narrative the accession of Alexios Komnenos marked the triumph of the military aristocracy, and the decline of the civil aristocracy and with it the bureaucratic forms of government that it had maintained since the age of Justinian. When the discussion turns to specific families, however, the distinction between a civil aristocracy and military aristocracy cannot be maintained because all major aristocratic families had members serving in both military

---

[133] Hans-Georg Beck, *Byzantinisches Gefolgschaftswesen* (Munich, 1965), 6–18.
[134] A. A. Vasiliev, *A History of the Byzantine Empire* (Madison, 1928), 426. George Ostrogorski, *History of the Byzantine State*, rev. edn (New Brunswick, 1969), 320. For a discussion of historiographical changes see Michael Angold, *The Byzantine Empire, 1025–1204: A Political History*, 2nd edn (London and New York, 1997), 15–18.

and civil capacities.¹³⁵ Actual families cannot be put into one camp or the other.

There may well have been tension between people who appreciated and found validation in the ceremonies and in the values of the "imperial" political culture and those who preferred the "aristocratic" culture of nobility. From the point of view of the working administration of the empire, however, few significant changes are apparent. Instead of several grand families vying for control of the top military and civil posts, Alexios' family occupied nearly all. The people who filled lower-level positions as judges, notaries, and fiscal paper-pushers likely continued to work with similar rates of efficiency, although perhaps with fewer numbers. On the one hand, Alexios' judicial reforms mandated that more work needed to be done by the civil administration. On the other, the decline in cultural prestige ascribed to imperial service may have meant that fewer people tried to look busy at the palace.

Initially it might seem that the central issue at hand is precisely the number of people working for the government at various times. But it must be remembered that, from the point of view of the strength and efficiency of the government, what matters is the accomplishment of tasks, not the numbers of people working on them. The number of employees at a given organization is not an indicator of the amount of work being done. Seals indicate paperwork, which of course is not to be confused with effective action. The number of officials could have been large without leading to a particularly powerful or pervasive government.

In short, the eleventh century was a time not when a bureaucracy gave way to aristocracy but when a political culture of ceremony and title gave way to a political culture of nobility and family. The use of ceremonies, titles, and salaries to augment imperial power may have been politically deft, but it had little to do with administration. To say that the changes in government in the eleventh century were largely reflections of changes in cultural values is not to say that they were unimportant. The shift in political style was part of a fundamental change in the Byzantine world. There were significant adjustments in the way some matters were administered and the government certainly *looked* quite different, but there is little evidence that the government became any more or less pervasive.

---

¹³⁵ Cheynet, *Pouvoir et contestations*, 191–8. Stephen Arnold Kamer, "Emperors and aristocrats in Byzantium 976–1081" (PhD thesis, Harvard University, 1983), 174–5.

CHAPTER 2

Activities of the imperial administration

The comparison between expressions of Byzantine imperial political culture of the tenth and eleventh centuries and modern images of governmental authority does not in itself make a statement about the efficacy or pervasiveness of the imperial administration. That the Byzantine administration has often seemed larger and more formalized than we have any reason to believe does not necessarily mean that the government was in fact ineffective. The strength and efficiency of the imperial government can be gauged by the actions of the imperial administration in the core provinces.

From such a practical, provincial point of view the imperial administration appears both apathetic in regard to regulating provincial society and determined in regard to maintaining a monopoly on sovereignty in Constantinople. The imperial administration intervened in the provinces to serve its own limited interests, not to regulate provincial life.

The chief government interest in the core provinces was the collection of revenue. The actions of the imperial administration in the core provinces first and foremost concerned wealth extraction, to the point that the entire civil administration may be characterized as a fiscal administration.[1] Until the late eleventh century, there were no provincial judicial officials separate from those with fiscal tasks. Aside from matters of taxation, the provincial administration appears largely to have been unconcerned with the ordering of provincial society.

The other interest of the imperial administration that could affect provincial life was the maintenance of the sole sovereignty of the emperor in Constantinople. Imperial sovereignty was protected primarily by maintaining the territorial integrity of the empire and by securing the loyalty of frontier princes. Within the core provinces it also appears that consistent efforts were made to ensure that only the emperor could be regarded as the legitimate ruler. Locally prominent individuals in the inner provinces were prevented

[1] Haldon, *Byzantium: A History*, 77.

from overtly governing their neighbors. Private fortifications seem to have been extremely rare. Prominent provincial individuals appear to have been afraid of accusations of disaffection and to have used such accusations to control their rivals.

SOVEREIGNTY

The military fortunes of the empire rose and fell with the efficacy of military leadership, foreign policy, and the strength of the opposition. The empire did experience great success at dealing with its foreign enemies. Tenth-century manuals on tactics indicate that the Byzantine military had exceptional organization and strategy in waging war.[2] The record, however, shows the military was not without serious failings. Invasions, raiding, and piracy were key influences on provincial freedom. Enemy incursions and raiding are presented in various sources as normal occurrences. St. Luke of Stiris' family was forced to leave its home in Aigina because of Muslim raids.[3] Luke's family settled in another seaside area that was then also attacked. They moved two more times before settling permanently in the village of Kastorion, north of the Gulf of Corinth. An estate of St. Nikon's monastery in Sparta was raided by a group of non-orthodox people who lived in neighboring mountains.[4] In 989 the Patriarch Nicholas gave a monastery to Athanasios of Athos that had been destroyed in a Bulgarian invasion.[5] The threat of Arab raids and pirates diminished as the political fortunes of the empire rose in the late tenth and early eleventh centuries. They were replaced in the eleventh century by new threats from Uzes, Pechenegs, Normans, and Seljuks. St. Christodoulos of Patmos left his monastery in western Asia Minor ostensibly under pressure of Seljuk attacks.[6]

The imperial administration expected that sooner or later cultivators would be driven off their land by enemy attacks. The *Marcian Treatise* explains a taxation method for dealing with regular movements of population caused by "perhaps some foreign incursion or some other wrath of God."[7] The administrators had special instructions for assessing the tax on villages where some of the population had abandoned their possessions. The taxation system formally included a process for reclaiming land that had been abandoned by its owners for over thirty years. Such lands were called

---

[2] Eric McGeer, *Sowing the Dragon's Teeth: Byzantine Warfare in the Tenth Century* (Washington, DC, 1995); John Haldon, *The Byzantine Wars* (Stroud, 2001), 89–108.
[3] *Life of Luke*, 160.   [4] *Life of Nikon*, 206–12.   [5] *Lavra*, pp. 115–18, no. 8.   [6] *Typika*, 580.
[7] *Marcian Treatise*, 116, lines 2–3.

"severed," *klasma*, because their records were separated from those of their original fiscal districts. The sale of *klasmata* marks the point when the fiscal administration gave up on the original owners ever returning. With this system the administration tacitly admitted that peasants were sometimes forced to flee. Further, when the officials sold *klasmata* to monasteries on Mount Athos they stipulated in the contract that the monasteries must allow refugees to shelter in that land as a refuge from enemy raids.

Imperial military tactics developed to combat Arab raids in Anatolia were grounded in the expectation of frequent raiding and incursions into Byzantine territory. The main idea was to track raiders that entered imperial territory and ambush them while they were returning through the mountain passes laden with plunder.[8] This was an effective strategy given the situation, and Byzantine control over eastern Anatolia increased through the tenth century.

The emperors transferred populations and settled hostile groups within the empire to increase stability. Several transfers of population in the seventh and eighth centuries are recorded.[9] In the tenth century John Tzimiskes moved Paulician heretics from Cappadocia to Macedonia.[10] The forced movement of population is a good example of government strength and ability to accomplish impressive tasks. The imperial army – the same organization that won campaigns – seems to have been largely responsible for effecting the transfers.

The empire had a worthy military record. On the whole, the emperors enjoyed considerable success in preserving the territorial integrity of an empire that had many enemies. The imperial administration's keen vigilance to keep the current dynasty in power checked the more threatening forms of private aggression that took place in the provinces. Yet, while the military effectively maintained the territory of the empire, it was not especially protective of individual security. The generals of the empire were charged with keeping the empire together and the emperor on the throne, not with maintaining peaceful circumstances in the provinces. Without chronicling every campaign and invasion one can say that during the period in question inhabitants of even the empire's inner provinces experienced warfare and its resultant disruption.

---

[8] Haldon, *The Byzantine Wars*, 67–8. George Dennis, *Three Byzantine Military Treatises* (Washington, DC, 1985), 143–239.
[9] Peter Charanis, "The transfer of population as policy in the Byzantine Empire," *Comparative Studies in Society and History* 3 (1961): 140–54.
[10] Diether R. Reinsch and Athanasios Kambylis, eds., *Annae Comnenae Alexias* (New York, 2001), 455–6, Book 14.8.

Building civic amenities and fortifications was one way the emperors asserted their sovereignty. Numerous inscriptions and literary references to imperial rebuilding of Byzantine fortified towns attest to the role of the imperial administration in building and strengthening provincial towns in the ninth through twelfth centuries. Rebuilding seems to have been primarily a matter of strengthening walls and fortifications.[11] Five medieval castles of the seventh through thirteenth centuries in the Meander region of Anatolia have been subject to an archeological survey. While the surveyors do not preclude the possibility that the local population worked communally to build their fortifications, they consider it most probable that the imperial administration was responsible for the construction of the fortifications.[12]

The imperial army may have provided the labor and expertise for the construction of town walls and other fortifications. Military manuals provide instructions about planning and execution of large-scale defensive structures. The army was a more efficient and skilled alternative to corvée labor, and given the scope of building projects described in the military manuals one can sensibly suppose that the army was the main workforce behind the construction of defensive structures.[13] Kekaumenos considered the fortifications of a city to be the charge of the presiding general.[14]

An example of a reconstruction project of considerable scale is provided by the excavations of Amorion, a major Anatolian town near modern Ankara. Amorion had been sacked by the Abbasid Caliph Mu'tasim in 838. The rebuilding involved demolishing and leveling the old defensive wall and other structures and filling in the ruins to a uniform height to create a new level building surface. It is estimated that "2,500,000 to 5,000,000 cubic meters of spoil were transported and dumped."[15] A new fortified city was built on the filled-in ruins of the old city. The height of the new city gave it a significant defensive advantage. Clearly the imperial administration was able to complete complex, labor-intensive projects when it needed to do so. There are numerous other examples of generals and emperors on campaign rebuilding fortifications.[16]

---

[11] Eric Ivison, "Urban renewal and imperial revival 730–1025," *BF* 26 (2000): 7.
[12] Hugh Barnes and Mark Whittow, "The Survey of Medieval Castles of Anatolia (1992–96): the Maeander region," in *Ancient Anatolia: Fifty Years' Work by the British Institute of Archaeology at Ankara*, edited by Roger Matthews (London, 1998), 356. This is a revision of their earlier opinion that one of the castles, Yilanli Kalesi, was built by the local community without imperial help, published in Hugh Barnes and Mark Whittow, "The Oxford University/British Institute of Archaeology at Ankara Survey of Medieval Castles of Anatolia (1993)," *Anatolian Studies* 44 (1994): 200.
[13] Ivison, "Urban renewal," 14.   [14] Kekaumenos, Litavrin, §32; Wassiliewsky, 29–30.
[15] Ivison, "Urban renewal," 15–16.   [16] *Ibid.*, 43–6.

Activities of the imperial administration

As significant as the imperial fortification of towns was for the maintenance of imperial sovereignty, the apparent absence of private fortifications was perhaps even more telling. The households even of prominent, wealthy, and militarily important families do not seem to have been fortified. In contrast to evidence from eleventh-century Europe, archeological evidence argues against a movement of prominent families into castles in Byzantine Greece. The towers, *pyrgoi*, that now dot the Greek countryside date from the late medieval and early modern periods.[17] In the tenth and eleventh centuries towers were very rare. The medieval castles surveyed in the Meander region do not appear to have been fortified houses.[18] The lack of archeological evidence for seigneurial castles is complemented by a lack of literary evidence for rebels using their houses as fortresses.[19] Kekaumenos held generals entrusted with towns or fortresses strictly accountable for maintaining their fortifications. Yet none of his advice for living privately suggests that he expected anyone to live in a fortress, unless he was either a general or a *toparch*, an independent frontier ruler.[20] The surviving title of a law issued by Michael VII (1071–78) indicates that fortresses could legally be held only for one lifetime. Apparently the aim of the law was to reinforce imperial ownership of fortresses that were granted to generals.[21] The implication of this admittedly fragmentary evidence is that the imperial administration insisted on maintaining ultimate control over all fortresses.

Some defensive structures were built by people who were not imperial military officers. An inscription found on the Athenian acropolis credits Leo, bishop from 1060 to 1069, with building a tower in Athens.[22] Gregory Pakourianos built two towers in the village of Stenimachos, next to his monastery in Petritzos.[23] In his foundation charter of his monastery, Gregory gave instructions for another tower to be built near the monastery's hospice: "They must build a tower on the mountain near the hospice and, if some cause for fear should arise there, they must provide protection for

---

[17] Mark Whittow, "Rural fortifications in Western Europe and Byzantium, tenth to twelfth century," *BF* 21 (1995): 61–3.
[18] Barnes and Whittow, "Survey of Medieval Castles of Anatolia (1993)," *Anatolian Studies* 44 (1994): 200.
[19] Whittow, "Rural fortifications," 63–6.
[20] Kekaumenos, Litavrin, §§48, 44; Wassiliewsky, 49, 46.
[21] Nicolas Oikonomides, "The donation of castles in the last quarter of the 11th century," in *Polychronion: Festschrift Franz Dölger zum 75. Geburtstag*, ed. Peter Wirth (Heidelberg, 1966), 413–17. Hélène Ahrweiler, "La concession des droits incorporels. Donations conditionnelles," in *Actes du XIIe Congrès international des études byzantines II* (Belgrade, 1964), 103–14.
[22] J. Travlos, *Poleodomike exelixis ton poleos ton Athenon* (Athens, 1960), 161. Georgos Soteriou, "Ta ereipia tou para ton Areion Pagon vyzantinou naou," *AD* 2 (1916): 139–42.
[23] *Typika*, 524.

the provisions in the tower so that if any violent person should come, his hand may not reach them."[24] Gregory also mentioned that his monastery was "situated in a strongly protected ravine."[25] He understood that he was responsible for providing adequate defensive structures to protect his foundation. Gregory's witness may not have been typical since he was writing in 1083, when imperial control was extremely tenuous and after he had lost several fortified cities and all his ancestral lands in the east to the Seljuks.[26] Gregory died fighting a rebellion not far from his monastic foundation.

On balance it seems that the imperial administration should be credited with maintaining a monopoly on fortification. There is no evidence that Byzantine people thought that they ought to live in castles or were frustrated that the imperial administration prevented them from fortifying their houses. Yet given the general state of insecurity owing to foreign incursions and the help castles could provide in controlling resources, it seems fair to assume that at least some prominent families would have fortified their houses if they could. Imperial control of fortifications was certainly one of the most significant differences between the empire and its European counterparts.

Imperial sovereignty was tested regularly by rebellions. Between 963 and 1100, 130 revolts of varying severity have been documented.[27] Byzantine political theory allowed the success of a revolt to be proof that the deposed emperor was a tyrant. The leader of a successful revolt was God's agent in removing a tyrant and would rule as God's regent on earth. The leader of an unsuccessful revolt, however, was a destroyer of peace who rose against God's regent on earth without justification.[28] Such a political theory greatly supported whoever was on the throne at Constantinople. At the same time, it did not discourage those who felt justified in their disgruntlement from attempting a revolt. Few revolts were successful in overthrowing the reigning emperor, but not every revolt was intended to change the regime. Rebellion was often a means of expressing dissatisfaction with the imperial administration. Kekaumenos associated rebellions with increases in taxation and inept military governors. Such rebels did not necessarily intend to overthrow the emperor as much as force the emperor to adjust policies.

The imperial administration often dealt with rebellious behavior through ritual punishment and appeasement because a combination of forgiveness

---

[24] *Ibid.*, 549.   [25] *Ibid.*, 523.
[26] Paul Lemerle, *Cinq études sur le XIe siècle byzantin* (Paris, 1977), 164–83.
[27] Cheynet, *Pouvoir et contestations*, 20–100.   [28] *Ibid.*, 177–90.

and threat best diffused tensions and restored order. Few people were executed for treason. Such was the importance of respect and public ritual performance that humiliation in triumphal processions was used in place of the death penalty for rebels.[29] The goal was to bring as many people as possible back into the imperial fold and to convince them to support the emperor. The leaders of revolts commonly were punished with confiscation of property, imprisonment, and sometimes blinding.

There are some indications that the confiscation of property as a punishment for rebellious behavior did not extend to all of a family's goods. Families that were involved in rebellions continued to be part of the empire's upper aristocracy. Kale, the wife of Symbat Pakourianos, received a dowry of 50 pounds of gold from her father some time after he had taken part in an unsuccessful revolt.[30] When the superior of Iviron was arrested for treason, many of the monastery's lands were confiscated or taken by other monasteries. The monastery had considerable support in regaining its lands in the decades following the superior's arrest.[31] Imperial confiscations would not necessarily finish off a prominent family altogether.

While they did not always entail the complete destruction of a household, ritual humiliation, confiscation of property, and imprisonment were sufficiently dire to make potential rebels hesitant and to fuel fears of false denunciations. The danger of false accusations was quite real. The emperors did not have enough accurate information about what was going on in the provinces to discourage provincial rivals from accusing each other of criminal actions. One of the dangers of opposing people who perpetrated injustice in the provinces, according to Kekaumenos, was that they would write to the emperor claiming that one was a rabble-rouser stirring up trouble.[32] He also cited the fear of being denounced to the emperor as one of the reasons a general in the borders could not punish improper behavior outright. Nikoulitzas claimed that he did not act immediately against the rebels in Larissa because he thought that the emperor would think that he was just slandering them as an excuse to seize their property.[33] This sort of situation was described in the *vita* of Paul of Latros. A family, the Mavroi, is described as repeatedly attacking the peasants living in imperial estates under the care of the *protospatharios* Michael. When Michael fought back

---

[29] Michael McCormick, *Eternal Victory: Triumphal Rulership in Late Antiquity, Byzantium, and the Early Medieval West* (Cambridge, 1986), 186–9.
[30] Jean-Claude Cheynet, "Fortune et puissance de l'aristocratie (x–xii siècle)," in *Hommes et richesses dans l'empire byzantin*, ed. Vassiliki Kravari, Jacques Lefort, and Cécile Morrisson (Paris, 1991), 211–12; Holmes, "Basil II and the government of empire: 976–1025," 257–63.
[31] *Iviron I*, pp. 45–59.   [32] Kekaumenos, Litavrin, §38; Wassiliewsky, 41.
[33] Kekaumenos, Litavrin, §74; Wassiliewsky, 67.

one of the Mavroi was killed in the fight and his relatives made an accusation against Michael in Constantinople. Michael was unjustly condemned to death, but after sending Paul a letter asking for his prayers, he was in fact released, as Paul predicted.[34] There is a strong presumption in the story that the officials in Constantinople would not have any idea who was the real aggressor. Both Saints Nikon and Luke assuaged the fears of local generals called to Constantinople on charges of treason. Pothos the *strategos* of Hellas received letters from his wife in Constantinople warning him to come to the city because he was being implicated in a plot against the emperor Constantine VII. Pothos was uncertain about whether it would be safer for him to stay away from the city until Luke's gift of prophesy reassured him that he could face the emperor safely.[35] In the *Life of Nikon*, slanderers told Basil II that John Malakenos was planning a rebellion. Basil sent two "legions" to Sparta to capture John and bring him to Constantinople. Once he reached the city, John was awarded more honors and titles.[36] Prayers in the name of St. Paul of Latros were credited with allowing the miraculous escape of prisoners who had been accused of treasonous behavior. Three villagers were arrested who had been slandered as being "disobedient, bold and ready for attacks."[37] Their chains were miraculously broken after one of them, John, insisted they spend the night praying to Paul. The fear of denunciation would not have been so strong had people not been falsely accused and condemned for treason. The imperial administration was portrayed as a frightening, uninformed force that could be expected to arrest the wrong people.

One effect of the administration's zeal in pursuing those accused of disaffection was to place a brake on independent action among provincial magnates. People who in the frontier provinces could become de facto rulers of their towns could not appear interested in such independence in the core provinces of the empire. The threat of denunciation thus appears in the cases described above to have been a method of social regulation in provincial society. Those who acted too aggressively ran the risk of having their neighbors accuse them of treasonous behavior. Households that themselves were acting with extreme aggression, such as the Mavroi, also used the threat of denunciation as a means of curbing their rivals.

The fear of denunciation draws attention to the two main features of the imperial administration in the provinces: it maintained a monopoly

---

[34] *Life of Paul*, 123. Hans Ditten, "Zu den Mauroi der Vita s. Pauli Junioris in Monte Latro (10 Jh.), dem Personennamen Mauros (um 700), der Maurousias der vita S. Petri Atroensis und den Athiopiern der Vita SS 42 Martyrum Amoriensium (9 Jh.)," *Klio* 72 (1990), 254–69.
[35] *Life of Luke*, 199–201.   [36] *Life of Nikon*, 148–53.   [37] *Life of Paul*, 135.

on sovereignty while being apathetic about governing. That people worried about accusations of treason means they both feared the power of the imperial administration and expected that the administration would not know what was really happening in the provinces. It was understood that acting like a ruler was highly dangerous but the lack of imperial intervention in regulating provincial society tempted prominent people to assume authority.

TAXATION

There is no question about the sincerity or tenacity of the imperial administration in trying to appropriate the wealth of Byzantine society. The imperial administration deployed substantial resources to maintain a methodical, centralized taxation system. Given the logistical and administrative difficulties involved in systematic taxation, as opposed to coarser methods of tribute extraction and direct exploitation, the Byzantine imperial administration should be credited with successfully making its fiscal systems work at all. The challenges, however, were considerable and the administration was not always successful. The Byzantine fiscal system was fundamentally formal and legalistic. Yet in practice the forms and protocols were compromised at nearly every turn by informal authority, by severe difficulties in making the system work, and by some formal policies that were not in the best interests of the fisc.

The system of tax registration gradually and continuously became more complex, to the point where it seems to have required more training and capacity for consistency than the officials had. Changing patterns of demography and landownership created constant exceptions to the geographically organized tax registers. Land changed hands far more quickly than those changes could be noted in the land-tax registers. Individual assessors had latitude in making decisions and arranging tax assessments, making them susceptible to the influence of the people being taxed. In addition, taxpayers did whatever they could either to ignore fiscal officials or to receive lenient treatment. Given the cumulative nature of these difficulties, the fiscal and monetary crisis of the eleventh century may be attributed, at least in part, to growing dysfunction in the imperial taxation systems.

The eleventh century appears to have been a period of change for the fiscal administration. At the end of the tenth century, taxes were collected using a system that had been in place since at least the early ninth century. Under that system, the land-tax was assessed in proportion to the property owned by each taxpayer. Tax assessments for individual households were listed in geographic order under the heading of the village containing those households. One group of administrators, the *epoptai*, created registers of the land of the empire, the people who owned it, and the tax burdens that were assigned to those individuals. Another group, the *dioiketai*, used those records to collect the taxes. Scholars have used the term *cadaster* to refer to the central land register that presumably was the foundation of the taxation system. Byzantine documents use the term *kodix* to refer to the land and taxation register.[38] By the twelfth century, a new system had developed using separate documents called *praktika* to register the taxes due from households with multiple properties. The *praktika* list all of the properties owned by a household and assess taxes on them as a whole. The household as well as the imperial administration would keep a copy of this record. There is no point at which one can say with confidence that the *cadaster* system fell out of use. The reforms of Alexios I Komnenos known as the *Palaea kai Nea Logariki* deal with additional charges added to the base land-tax in a way that suggests the means of assessing the land-tax had not changed from previous practice. While the use of *praktika* increased in the late eleventh and twelfth centuries, the two systems seem to have been used concurrently for some time.[39]

The process of tax assessment and collection was simplified in the eleventh century by the apparent decrease in the number of peasants who paid tax to the empire instead of rent to a landlord. The magnitude and date of this decrease, however, are fairly opaque. In the twelfth century and later all peasants seem to be called *paroikoi*. This term was used to refer to rent-paying as opposed to tax-paying peasants in the tenth century. So by the twelfth century either all the peasants had become renters or the meaning of the word *paroikoi* changed to include more kinds of peasants. Such a semantic shift may have accompanied the blurring of distinctions between renters and taxpayers caused by the common practice of *pronoia*. A *pronoia* was a method of remunerating people providing services to the empire by granting them the right to collect and retain the taxes from a

---

[38] Mark Bartusis, in Alexander Kazhdan, ed., *The Oxford Dictionary of Byzantium* (New York, 1991), s.v. "kodix." Nicolas Svoronos, "Recherches sur le cadastre byzantin et la fiscalité aux xie et xiie siècles," *BCH* 83 (1959), 19–22, 57–63. The term *cadaster* seems to owe its popularity to the work of Dölger, who in analyzing the *Marcian Treatise* associated the Byzantine land registers with that term. *Marcian Treatise*, 97 note 1.

[39] Oikonomides, "Role of the Byzantine state," 983–96. Nicolas Oikonomides, *Fiscalité et exemption fiscale à Byzance (IXe–XIe s.)* (Athens, 1996), 24–41. If Oikonomides' dating of the *Marcian Treatise* to the first half of the twelfth century is correct, it provides evidence of the continued use of the cadaster system into the twelfth century.

particular area.[40] The people who paid taxes to the holder of the *pronoia* were still proprietors, but because they did not pay their taxes to the state "it became the habit, in the second half of the eleventh century, to call these taxpayers '*paroikoi*,' even though they were still owners."[41] From a functional viewpoint therefore anyone called a *paroikos* was someone from whom the imperial government did not need to collect taxes directly. An increase in the number of people paying rent to landlords rather than land-taxes to the government would make the process of taxation simpler, if the state were able to collect taxes from the landlords reliably. The increase in grants of *pronoia* made the task of fiscal administration easier by delegating both the collection of revenue and remuneration.

Another development that is presumed to have taken place in the eleventh century was the increasing reliance on tax farmers.[42] "Tax farming" is a modern term that is applied to medieval situations when someone agrees to take on the work of revenue collection in the expectation of personal profit. Tax farming entails risk for the government because the contractors do not share the government's long-term interests in keeping peasantry healthy and populations quiescent. The evidence for the increase in tax farming is found in the narrative histories of Attaleiates and Skylitzes, where we see accusations of injustice and mismanagement that may not amount to significant changes in official policy.[43] Kekaumenos' anecdotes make clear that people expected to be able to profit from fiscal work, but this expectation was not out of place in any pre-modern government and is not evidence of a change in method. Kekaumenos advised against taking on fiscal responsibilities because local resistance made collection difficult and one would be held accountable for the money by the central administrators.[44] There may well have been an increase in tax farming in the eleventh century, but the evidence is more ambiguous than is frequently presented.

All of these changes – the development of *praktika*, the increasing numbers of indirectly taxed *paroikoi*, the possible rise in tax farming – can be seen as responses to economic changes in the empire and difficulties besetting

---

[40] Paul Magdalino, "The Byzantine army and the land: from stratiotikon ktema to military pronoia," in *Byzantium at War 9th–12th C.* (Athens, 1997), 35–6.
[41] Jacques Lefort, "Rural economy and social relations in the countryside," *DOP* 47 (1993): 112.
[42] Oikonomides, "Role of the Byzantine state," 1022–6.
[43] Oikonomides, "Title and income," 209–10. Ioannes Thurn, ed., *Ioannis Skylitzae Synopsis historiarum* (Berlin and New York, 1973), 404, 408–9, 422, 476; W. Brunet de Presle, ed., *Michaelis Attaliotae Historia* (Bonn, 1853), 80.
[44] Kekaumenos, Litavrin, §37; Wassiliewsky, 38–40. The story he told of a man who undertook the management of an imperial estate and was imprisoned when the revenues fell short does not provide evidence of tax farming.

the taxation systems established in the ninth and tenth centuries. The goal of the following discussions is to assess how the administration coped with change and explore the interface between the formal legal principles and their actual implementation.

The taxation system of the tenth and eleventh centuries was designed to encourage intensive use of land. The fisc's natural interest in maintaining as much land under cultivation as possible led the administration to have fairly flexible ideas about ownership and property rights. In Roman legal principle the rights of the owner over the use and deposition of property were fundamental and well defined. Roman law distinguished between *possession* and *ownership*, whereby a long-time possessor of land had some legal protection against the rights of the formal owner.[45] The formalities of the distinction between possession and ownership were blurred in the tenth and eleventh centuries by a fiscal administration that wanted to support people who were profitably using land they did not own. Fundamentally the state cared about bringing in tax money, not in upholding the property rights of citizens. Some fiscal policies, designed to encourage cultivation in times of uncertainty, supported the property rights of people who abandoned their land. In other cases the administration supported, over the theoretical owners, the rights of people profitably possessing land.

In theory the property rights of taxpayers who abandoned their lands were maintained for thirty years. Landowners were given incentives to return and no attempt was made to collect taxes on their lands. This policy of waiting for the original owners to return before selling their land only makes sense in an era of low population and labor scarcity. The practice of forgiving taxes of those who have fled apparently developed as a response to the late Roman system of forcing the neighbors of those who had fled to pay the tax burden for them. In late Roman times, if a landowner did not pay taxes his land was given to someone else who owned property in that area. A landowner with many estates would pay the tax on the abandoned

---

[45] In Roman legal tradition, possession, *nome* or *katoche*, was "the effective tenure of one's own or of another's object." Ownership, *despotia*, was legally defined as the "the full right to dispose of a thing at will... not only to have it and use it (as in possession) but also, unlike possession, to be able to dispose of it during one's lifetime or at death." Long-term possession brought the right to have ownership adjudicated: "a possession was protected against removal or interference by a so-called *interdictum* (parangelma)." Ownership would be given to the "better" owner. Maria Theres Fögen, in Kazhdan, ed., *The Oxford Dictionary of Byzantium*, s.v. "ownership," and "possession." On the use of Roman law in Byzantium see Alexander Kazhdan, "Do we need a new history of Byzantine law?" JÖB 39 (1989): 1–28; Bernard Stolte, "Not new but novel. Notes on the historiography of Byzantine law," *BMGS* 22 (1998): 264–79.

portion of his land from the revenues from his other estates.[46] From at least the tenth century the taxes on abandoned lands were given *sympatheia*, meaning that the taxes were forgiven, in order to prevent the other peasants in the village from fleeing as well to avoid the extra tax burden. Getting to take over the land of neighbors who leave would be advantageous for landowners with the resources to cultivate the land or otherwise pay the taxes. For those living in Byzantine villages comprised of small holdings, the requirement to pay the tax on neighbors' land was a burden. Under the Byzantine system, an inspector would make the abandoned lands tax-free for up to thirty years. If the original owners returned within thirty years, the tax on their lands would be gradually reinstated through the process called *orthosis*, or restoration. If they did not return, the fiscal administration would take those lands out of the fiscal district altogether and rent, sell, or give them away. Once they were removed from the fiscal district the lands were classified as *klasmata*.

This system only made sense in times when there was too much land for people to cultivate. If there had been people waiting and eager to take over abandoned land, the best fiscal policy would have been to let them have the land and then tax their produce. Holding land vacant for thirty years in the hope that the original owners would return would be a good policy for an era of depopulation, disruption, and peasant flight. Such conditions certainly were prevalent in at least some parts of the empire in the seventh, eighth, and ninth centuries. St. Luke of Stiris' grandparents abandoned their lands in Aigina because of attacks by Muslim pirates sometime in the ninth century. In such a case, there would be little chance of getting anyone else to farm that land and it was reasonable for the fiscal administration to leave the land available in case Luke's family decided to return.

The difficulty from the imperial standpoint was that this policy stayed in place after the demographic recovery. With increasing security and prosperity in the late tenth and eleventh centuries, the population so rose that the administration could put abandoned land to use immediately. In theory, however, the policy of waiting for the original owners to return remained in force and the civil administration was left with a formal policy that ran contrary to its own interests.

Not too surprisingly other procedures developed that forced households to give up land that they were not making sufficiently profitable. There is some evidence that if, in the eyes of the fiscal administration, a household

---

[46] Michel Kaplan, *Les Hommes et la terre à Byzance du VIe au XIe siècle: propriété et exploitation du sol* (Paris, 1992), 211.

did not pay enough tax for the amount of land it owned, the "extra" land was confiscated to be sold to others who could put it to better use.[47] Alexios Komnenos established a norm for the amount of tax to be paid for a given amount of land and pushed monasteries either to yield land or to pay more tax.[48] Land that was not being productively used by the owners could be awarded by imperial officials to a third party. The monastery of St. Hypatios fought with the monastery of Vatopedi over lands they claimed by virtue of a *sigillion* issued by the emperor Constantine Doukas allowing the monks of St. Hypatios to take over lands owned by Vatopedi because they were unused.[49] In selling land, imperial officials could impose considerable restrictions regarding the purchaser's rights of use and of disposal. In 941, for example, Thomas the imperial *protospatharios, asekretis, epoptes*, and *anagrapheus* of Thessalonike sold some parcels of abandoned land to Nicholas the son of Agathon. While Nicholas became the legal owner of the land, that ownership did not entail full control over the land and its resources:

None of those who have purchased land in the island of Pallene may hinder you from hewing lumber or firewood or from pasturage, similarly it is not possible for you to hinder those wanting to use pasture in the empty land you have purchased. For thus it is established and ordained [for you] to have authority over each privately sown field; all manner of pasturage of the island is to be altogether common, just as it has been stated, not only for those buying this land, but also for those not buying and fleeing from some assault and attack of gentiles.[50]

Clearly the interest of the empire was to have as much land cultivated, and therefore taxable, as possible. This land, as *klasma*, had once been taxed as cultivated land, but had been abandoned by the taxpayers for at least thirty years. By selling it Thomas was encouraging Nicholas to invest in its cultivation. At the same time, he did not want the sale to curtail the low-level exploitation of it that was already taking place. So long as Nicholas was not actually cultivating the land, he should not chase off people pasturing animals on the land. He had full control only over those areas that he actually farmed. These restrictions would provide Nicholas with a strong incentive to cultivate as much of the land as possible in order to solidify the legality of his sale.

---

[47] Oikonomides, *Fiscalité*, 26–8, 53–8. Nicolas Svoronos, "L'épibolè à l'époque des Comnènes," *TM* 3 (1968): 375–95. *Lavra*, pp. 70–1. Lefort, "Rural economy," 288.
[48] *Xenophon*, pp. 78–9, no. 2, lines 10–31. *Docheiariou*, pp. 54–9, no. 2, lines 22–6.
[49] *Vatopedi*, pp. 94–102, 99, no. 8, line 7. The lands were called *adespota*, "unowned."
[50] *Lavra*, p. 96, no. 3. A nearly identical sale was made to Euthymios the superior of the monastery of St. Andrew of Peristerai. *Ibid.*, pp. 91–4, no. 2.

The imperial administration also formally gave some rights to communities and neighbors over privately held land. The principle of *protimesis*, or the right of first refusal, gave relatives and neighbors the right to buy land adjacent to theirs before the sale was open to other buyers.[51] Romanos' law of 934 allowed for land sold in times of economic hardship to be retroactively reclaimed without payment.[52] Apart from its other possible roles, the land legislation weakened the binding power of legal sales and added to the restrictions on rights of deposition.

Fiscal registers did not always precisely record the owner of the land being taxed. The author of the *Marcian Treatise* explained that sometimes the land register listed "group for the heirs" instead of the name of an individual taxpayer. This meant that the heirs of the taxpayer were to divide the tax burden amongst themselves in proportion to the amount they inherited.[53] In the *Cadaster of Thebes* taxes are indeed listed for unspecified groups of people such as the "heirs of Leo Logaras" and the "heirs of *komes tes kortes* Strategios."[54] The tax collectors were concerned not with the way the land was divided up, but with collecting the same amount of money as previously. While the owner of land was free to divide it as he or she liked, the *Marcian Treatise* indicates that these decisions were subject to pressures from people with more resources to take what they could use. The tax collectors again were concerned with collecting the money, not upholding the testament of the deceased. Land could be divided either according to the previous owners' "desires and disposition" or according to how much the heirs were capable of cultivating.[55] In one sense this gave provincial people a great deal of freedom to do what they wanted with their land. In another it gave legal sanction to more aggressive and genetically successful brothers taking over lands given to their siblings.

The civil administration's support for taxing whoever happened to be cultivating land rather than observing the niceties of theoretical ownership is particularly understandable given the lack of distinction between fiscal and judicial roles in the civil administration.[56] Disputes over ownership of

---

[51] Eleutheria Papagianni, "*Protimesis* (Preemption) in Byzantium," in *The Economic History of Byzantium from the Seventh through the Fifteenth Century*, ed. Angeliki Laiou (Washington, DC, 2002), 1071–82.
[52] Nicolas Svoronos and P. Gounaridis, eds., *Les Novelles des empereurs macédoniens* (Athens, 1994), 72–92. Eric McGeer, *The Land Legislation of the Macedonian Emperors* (Toronto, 2000), 53–60. Paul Lemerle, *The Agrarian History of Byzantium: From the Origins to the Twelfth Century* (Galway, 1979), 94–5.
[53] *Marcian Treatise*, 121.   [54] *Cadaster of Thebes*, §§11c1, vd1.   [55] *Marcian Treatise*, 121.
[56] On the lack of such a distinction see Magdalino, "Justice and finance," 93–116; Magdalino, "Innovations in government," 146–66.

land would be heard by the judges whose duty it was to collect revenue. From the point of view of provincial communities, such administrative practice would have the effect of condoning aggressive behavior regarding the appropriation of land from households too weak to resist.

The lack of interest in strictly maintaining the Roman legal principles regarding ownership on the part of the imperial administration was matched by a concern with defining ownership, seen in acts of sale and donation.[57] The phrases describing ownership are far more elaborate in their medieval forms than in their classical predecessors. To some extent such phrases were formulaic, but their inconsistent use suggests that when they appeared they reflected real concerns of those writing the documents. Some documents explicitly mention the right of new owners to sell property to whomever they would like, whereas in Roman legal tradition the right of deposition was integral to the definition of ownership. In an act of sale written in 1007 the sellers explain that the land was transferred "with secure and complete ownership... And from now on you have possession of this farmland, to sell, to give, to plant vineyards in it, to give it as dowry, to leave to heirs and successors and to do in it as much as the divine and holy laws give permission and power to full owners."[58] Arrangements were made whereby an owner would control land but be restricted in its sale. For instance Theoktistos the superior of Esphigmenou gave a field of the monastery's land to his spiritual brother Nikephoros. Nikephoros was to have the field with its church, houses, and vineyards with full authority during his lifetime. He was to choose a successor, and the successor would choose a third monk to enjoy the field. After the third monk died, the field was to return to the monastery. Nikephoros was granted full power and control over the land. That full power did not include the right to sell it to whomever he wanted or to alienate the property from Esphigmenou.[59]

Some acts of sale place limits on the owner's authority over the property. When in 1033/34 Christodoulos the superior of Katzari and John his *hypotaktikos* sold land to their spiritual brother Euthymios, the superior of the monastery of Tryphonos, they made it a condition of the sale that Euthymios allow an elderly monk to remain in his retreat until his death. The old monk, Peter, had been given a small piece of land where he had grown a garden and vineyard. While Peter's land was part of the larger piece sold to Euthymios, Peter was to retain control of his hermitage until his death. The document included the formula that Euthymios was to own the

---

[57] For example: *Esphigmenou*, p. 41, no. 1.   [58] *Iviron I*, p. 181, no. 13, lines 11–16.
[59] *Esphigmenou*, pp. 43–6, no. 2.

land "in all power and lordship, to build, to plant, to leave to disciples, and to do all such things as the law ordains for private owners, hindered neither by us the monks Christodoulos and John, nor by our disciples and successors."[60] Euthymios' "complete lordship" did not include the ability to evict Peter. The hierarchical relationship between Peter and Euthymios was ambiguous. The elaborate definitions of ownership may have responded to the lack of a precise and consistently applicable legal definition of ownership.

The emperors' ability and willingness to confiscate lands to benefit the fisc have been interpreted as an indication that the state ultimately held supreme ownership over all the land of the empire. In this view the "entitlement" to confiscate lands was a consequence of the theoretical understanding of the state's supreme ownership.[61] Imperial confiscations need not be taken to indicate a particular legal understanding of the nature of private and state property, but may simply reflect the reality that, when they put their minds to it, emperors could do what they wanted.[62]

Throughout the eleventh century it appears that land increasingly came under the control of fewer people. The archives of the great monasteries on Mount Athos indicate a trend toward the steady accumulation of land into the hands of fewer wealthier people. For example, the village of Radolibos is well known through five documents preserved in Iviron's archives that allow for a fairly detailed history of property owning in the village. The entire village eventually became an estate of Iviron monastery on Mount Athos.[63] The development of the system of assessing taxes through *praktika* makes most sense as a response to the concentration of large amounts of property into the hands of particular households.

Other evidence suggests that land changed hands frequently. One fragmentary taxation register, the *Cadaster of Thebes*, seems to reflect a relatively rapid accumulation and fragmentation of property. At least in the small sample preserved in the *Cadaster*, some lands were being collected into substantial holdings while other substantial holdings were being split up among several individuals.[64] Even people with official titles seem to

---

[60] *Saint-Pantéléèmôn*, p. 34, no. 2, lines 14–17.
[61] Alexander Kazhdan, "State, feudal and private economy in Byzantium," *DOP* 47 (1993): 95–7.
[62] On the confiscations of Basil II see Holmes, "Basil II and the government of empire," 256–65. On the confiscations and aggressive fiscal policy of Alexios I see Harvey, "Financial crisis," 167–84, and Rosemary Morris, "Monastic exemptions in tenth- and eleventh-century Byzantium," in *Property and Power in the Early Middle Ages*, ed. Wendy Davies and Paul Fouracre (Cambridge, 1995), 200–20.
[63] Jacques Lefort, "Le Cadastre de Radolibos (1103), les géomètres et leurs mathématiques," *TM* 8 (1981): 269–313; Jacques Lefort "Radolibos: population et paysage," *TM* 9 (1985): 195–234.
[64] Some taxpayers were recorded in one place as paying tax on many properties. These people seem to have been accumulating land. *Cadaster of Thebes* §§vɪaɪ, vɪa2, ɪcɪ, ɪɪdɪ. While these people were

have gained and lost land in roughly equal numbers.[65] Based on this short fragment of the tax register, one would think that ownership of property was unstable and that major changes happened in each generation. Property is divided among heirs and brought together by the prosperous. The extant portion of the text may show more distribution than accumulation, but too many factors in the text are unknown or speculative to attempt any statistical analysis, and the sample size is too small to make such findings worthwhile. At least in this area, however, land was changing hands and people had the capacity for both gaining and losing property.

As the imperial administration was successful in its goal of bringing more land under cultivation, its job of updating the tax registers became more difficult. The basis of the *cadaster* system was a registration of all the cultivated land of the empire in geographic order and of the cultivators responsible for the tax on that land. Since land rather than people formed the basis of the registration, changes in what land was cultivated and the movement of people caused complications for the registration system. The *Cadaster of Thebes* shows people owning land in different villages and land changing hands frequently. Under these circumstances, village-by-village registration was not a simple matter.

While ideally the imperial cadasters were supposed to list the owner of every piece of land in the empire, the frequent fragmentation of landholding through inheritance and sales made this goal impossible. The author of the *Marcian Treatise* explained that inspectors could write "group for the heirs" instead of listing individuals.[66] The *Cadaster of Thebes* records taxes due by unspecified heirs of the previous owner. It would seem to be more difficult to collect the tax when looking for the "heirs of John" than for a specified individual. Presumably, therefore, inspectors resorted to writing "group for the heirs" only when listing each individual heir was not worthwhile either because there were too many heirs or because there was not enough land. The practice attests to the fundamental difficulty in maintaining the written records of landownership throughout the empire.

---

amassing holdings, other people were paying on fractions of land previously held by their parents or others: 11d1–11d4, 11f1–11f5.

[65] While the *Cadaster of Thebes* is routinely cited as evidence of aristocratic control over land, this conclusion is based on too cursory a reading of the text. Many of the people with titles are listed in several different places in the text, so simply counting titles leads scholars to exaggerate their presence. Leonora Neville, "Local provincial elites in eleventh-century Hellas and Peloponnese" (PhD thesis, Princeton University, 1998), 208–35.

[66] *Marcian Treatise*, 121–2.

Changes in what land was cultivated added to the complexity of the land registers. The author of the *Marcian Treatise* explained that some lands had a special fiscal status because they were not included in the initial land registration but later came under cultivation. Once the lands were cultivated, the inspector registered the possessors as taxpaying owners. As the amount of land under cultivation increased, the fiscal officials developed new categories of registering land that did not fit into the established scheme. The author explained that *agridia* were cultivated areas within the fiscal district of a village but separated from the main settlement:

> The *agridia* resulted from the fact that either some of the villagers did not settle in the center of the village, or they did not own equally with the others the so-called internal areas and on account of this they transferred their houses to part of the whole village and cultivated it and lived there. For perhaps some of their fathers who died with many children, to some he left the internal areas that they had in the village and to others he left the external areas. So those who received their paternal bequest in the external spaces were not able to remain and live far away from their bequest, they moved there and improving their houses and the place there, they made their bequest into an *agridion*. Or still others who happened to get wealthier in terms of herds and slaves or being harassed by wicked neighbors and not able to live in the center of the village, they relocated into some part of the whole fiscal district of the village and improving the land similarly they made the same things.[67]

These people moved out of the village center and established new settlements, *agridia*, on land that was not yet cultivated. These outlying areas were registered as *agridia* rather than as a regular part of the village because the initial registration was done before they were cultivated.

Theoretically the rate of taxation varied with the profitability of land. In reality, it varied with the profitability ascribed to the land by fiscal inspectors. Pastureland and uncultivated land used for foraging were taxed much less heavily than farmland. How one's land was assessed therefore depended on the periodic inspections. After land had been registered as pastureland or wasteland one would be free to start cultivating it and enjoying the extra profits for as long as it took for a new inspection to be made.

Newly cultivated land may have been effectively tax-free until it was entered into the state tax registers. The monks at Docheiariou were given a formal tax exemption for land that they had held for years without paying tax. It seems that this may have been land that was uncultivated at the time of the monastic settlement of Mount Athos and that it had never been

---

[67] *Ibid.*, 115, lines 24–38.

registered.⁶⁸ While the monastery was able to gain an official state exemption, households with less negotiating power in the same situation would have been entered into the rolls. The *Marcian Treatise* gave instructions for the enrollment of land that had been overlooked or left off the registers for a variety of reasons. The *Marcian Treatise* contains a vague indication that inspectors, *epoptai*, would survey the entire empire every thirty years. Even if the inspections did take place every thirty years, cultivators of new land would have a significant period of freedom from taxation. According to a story in the *Life of Basil I*, many people were not paying taxes for precisely this reason. The head of the fiscal administration, the *logothetes tou genikou*, wanted to reassess the land of the empire because people were enjoying profits from reclaimed land without paying taxes on them. Basil agreed that this was a good idea, but did not appoint anyone to do it on the grounds that it would be better for some people to gain illegally than for someone to be ruined.⁶⁹ The story is told as an example of Basil's loving consideration of his subjects. It may have been told in this way to preempt criticism of Basil's neglect of fiscal administration. It is highly significant for our purposes for indicating that, at least in the ninth century, basic tasks of fiscal administration required personal imperial approval. Even the thirty-year cycle of inspections implied by the *Marcian Treatise* would leave the administrators largely in the dark about who owned what much of the time. If inspections were actually undertaken even less regularly, we can assume that the registers were nearly always out of date.

The imperial administration was at a disadvantage in the mid-eleventh century because the economic and demographic reality of the empire changed more quickly than the fiscal systems in place for taxing the empire could keep up. The system of registering land for taxation had a logical foundation, but over time obsolete elements were maintained and exceptions accreted to the point that the author of the *Marcian Treatise* needed to relate lengthy anecdotes about the history of practices to explain what they were. This is not a stylistic choice, but a necessity imposed by the nature of the material. The various categories of land used by the fisc developed out of the past fiscal history of the land. As ownership and use of land shifted, the administration tried to keep up with changes by modifying the old system. The assorted patches make sense only in their context as adaptations.⁷⁰

---

⁶⁸ *Docheiariou*, pp. 49–53, no. 1.
⁶⁹ Immanuel Bekker, ed., *Theophanes continuatus*, Corpus Scriptorum Historiae Byzantinae 33 (Bonn, 1838), 346–8. Magdalino, "Justice and finance," 99–100.
⁷⁰ Neville, "Provincial elites," 165–72.

When we turn to the document that bears the most resemblance to the registration system described in the *Marcian Treatise*, we see manifestations of many of the difficulties the treatise leads us to expect. It is clear enough that the *Cadaster of Thebes* is a portion of the imperial land-tax register, following the principles laid out in the *Marcian Treatise*. The document is visually impressive, but on close inspection it proves to be practically unusable for the purposes of figuring out who owed what.[71] The surviving fragment is not sufficient to let the tax collector know the names of the people who owed tax. The increasing difficulties in making the cadaster system work, discussed above, led to the creation of taxation registers that were of little utility as repositories of information.

Consistency in form and practice is not found in our evidence of Byzantine fiscal practice. The fiscal sources indicate that officials were educated in the general principles of how the taxation system ought to work. In executing those principles, however, officials appear to have enjoyed fairly wide latitude. No two documents that exemplify imperial records of the cadaster system follow exactly the same form. The two documents that have come to be known as cadasters, the *Cadaster of Radolibos* and the *Cadaster of Thebes*, follow quite different forms.[72] The surviving sample of documents is admittedly minute, but it provides evidence for more variation and informality in administrative practice than uniformity.

The degree of variety in form seen in the surviving registers is also consistent with the degree of specificity in the instructions in the *Marcian Treatise*. The treatise would give one a general ideal about how to write up a tax assessment for an area, but would allow for the variations seen in the registers. The treatise provides several indications that officials were not expected to maintain a high level of uniformity. The author devotes a section of the treatise to explaining the meaning of various notes that could be written in the tax register books. He needs to list several different phrases and explain that they were different ways of saying the same thing before he could explain what they meant. For example, "These phrases, found among the register sections 'and for a detached place' or 'detached place' were written for this reason."[73] The people writing the tax register were following general guidelines for notation and wrote whatever they thought

---

[71] Leonora Neville, "Information, ceremony and power in Byzantine fiscal registers: varieties of function in the Cadaster of Thebes," *BMGS* 25 (2001): 20–43.

[72] *Ibid.*, 23–32. Three documents that preserve passages copied out of imperial land registers are *Lavra*, pp. 219–23, no. 39; *Iviron I*, pp. 262–70, no. 30; *Iviron II*, pp. 183–8, no. 48. The *Cadaster of Radolibos* is *Iviron II*, pp. 248–83, no. 53. Jacques Lefort, "Le Cadastre de Radolibos (1103), les géomètres et leurs mathématiques," *TM* 8 (1981): 269–313. Lefort, "Radolibos: population et paysage," 195–234.

[73] *Marcian Treatise*, 121.14–15, 21–2.

made the matter clear. In explaining how to read the registers, the author of the *Marcian Treatise* coaches readers to expect variation.

The generally low level of training officials received and the variations in practice made it possible for fiscal records to be misunderstood fairly significantly. The author deals at length with a problem in the central archive caused by inconsistent work done by administrators in the provinces. The surcharges and customary gratuities paid directly to the tax collectors were assessed in proportion to the amount of land-tax due, but were not supposed to be counted as part of the taxpayer's land-tax.[74] Some assessors did calculate the surcharges as part of the land-tax while others did not.[75] When the assessors submitted this information to the central administration the officials were unable to tell whether the numbers for the total of taxes included the surcharges or only the land-tax. In response to the problem the author makes the stunning recommendation that, for the purposes of calculating the tax rate of an area, administrators should work with the old registers rather than newly submitted information.[76] One of the biggest problems facing the fiscal administration was the lack of up-to-date information about provincial landownership. Yet the newly written information was not considered trustworthy because it was not consistently recorded.

The author of the treatise describes differences of opinion within the imperial administration about what was proper procedure. He gives an example of the thinking employed by officials in his discussion of the status of the so-called "standing exemptions":

Now then, the standing tax exemptions are considered by some to be inactive and no longer remaining as exemptions, by others they are considered to be steadfast and authorized. The second interpretation appears to be more accurate. For those who have researched say, "If they stopped being exemptions they ought to be classified with the payments. Since this is not so, but they are still today kept with the exemptions, it is obvious that the standing exemptions are called those that received ratification from very long ago." And thus is the opinion regarding the standing exemptions. But an imperial order authoritatively commanded this not to be accepted at all.[77]

The author's position is based on the classification and storage of information rather than the actual disposition of the land and revenue involved. The emperor's decision came down clearly on the side of collecting more

---

[74] Morrisson, "La Logarikè," 419–464; Oikonomides, *Fiscalité*, 76–79.
[75] *Marcian Treatise*, 122.25–31.
[76] *Ibid.*, 122.31–123.1. Leonora Neville, "The Marcian Treatise on taxation and the nature of bureaucracy in Byzantium," *BF* 26 (2000): 48–50.
[77] *Marcian Treatise*, 118.12–20.

tax revenue. The imperial intervention may mean that this was a matter of importance or that imperial decisions were necessary to resolve issues of fiscal policy.

As well as a fairly natural variation in ideas about how to implement the principles of fiscal practice, officials were subject to a perhaps equally natural tendency towards incompetence and helping their friends. The author mentions the techniques used by "accurate notaries" and inspectors "who care for the truth," letting slip evidence for inaccurate and careless officials.[78] In Kekaumenos' advice about how lower-level officials should act to get promoted, he recommends that they should not deprecate their superior for any mistakes he makes with the taxes, even if they have to pay the difference themselves. Rather they should try to hide his secret completely, "since if you make it known from then on everyone will flee from you as from a snake."[79] The implication is that officials would not want to work with someone who held them to a high standard of accuracy. The author of the treatise describes a practice specifically done to correct inaccurate work. The note "detached place" is entered in the fiscal record book in order to correct errors made by other officials:

Perhaps when someone was buying or taking land as a gift . . . the inspector making the transfer [of ownership], transferred not as much as he should have but more than was necessary. Then another inspector, coming and recognizing this from some accusation or declaration, did not demand back the price for the excess land, but he separated the excess land and returned it to the proper place.[80]

Acting in favor of a particular landowner was sufficiently commonplace to have standard systems for rectification. Whether the land was repossessed by the fisc or paid for by the new owner was left to the personal discretion of the second official, who was likely subject to the same pressures and incentives as the first.[81]

Even the most general of principles were not followed by imperial tax assessors. In the middle of the tenth century the boundary between the inhabitants of Hierissos and the monasteries on Mount Athos was disputed at length because the assessor for Thessalonike had sold *klasmata* to people of Hierissos without specifying the boundary between their land and that of the Holy Mountain. Neither party had the documents to support their testimony of where the boundary was, because the administrator had not

---

[78] *Ibid.*, 114.31, 122.2.   [79] Kekaumenos, Litavrin, §4; Wassiliewsky, 5.
[80] *Marcian Treatise*, 121.15–21.   [81] *Ibid.*, 121.15–23.

written them.[82] The author of the *Marcian Treatise* reiterates emphatically that land given *sympatheia* should not be sold or rented to a new owner by the fisc before thirty years have elapsed for the original owners to return.[83] His insistence suggests that sometimes officials confiscated the land before the thirty years were up. The author also points out that lands with *sympatheia* frequently were not relabeled as *klasma* after thirty years as they should have been.[84] The thirty-year limit on *sympatheia* was so commonly ignored that, in effect, it may have become a method of simply lowering taxes.[85] In 996 some villagers acted as witnesses in a dispute involving the monastery Polygyros, over land that was acquired by Iviron. They explained that they had fled their native villages because of foreign invasions. They were currently living on land of the monastery Polygyros, but continued to pay tax on their old villages because they intended to return.[86] They were clearly not trusting that the fiscal administration would wait for them to return. They continued to pay taxes on lands that were scarcely within imperial control in order to maintain their ownership rights. Either they did not know that the fiscal administration was supposed to preserve their title to their lands for thirty years, or they never expected the formal fiscal procedures to be followed.

Another highly significant obstacle in the path of the imperial administration was provincial households' tenacious resistance to being taxed. The methods provincial people used to befriend and influence the administrators will be explored in chapter 4. At least as seen in the archives of grand monastic households, these methods met with considerable success.

If it is true that the taxation registers were not always clear repositories of information, they could still have been worthwhile aids in the process of tax collection. The *Cadaster of Thebes* presents the possibility that much of the effort of the imperial administration to maintain extensive written records was just for show. Documents and books played a significant ceremonial role in the ritual of tax collection. When tax collectors had registers that contained fairly accurate information about landownership in a region, they may well have relied heavily on those registers to ascertain who should pay what. At times when the registers were hopelessly inaccurate, the mere existence of a book purporting to be a universal register of all the people and

---

[82] Rosemary Morris, "Dispute settlement in the Byzantine provinces in the tenth century," in *The Settlement of Disputes in Early Medieval Europe*, ed. Wendy Davies and Paul Fouracre (Cambridge, 1986), 132–5.
[83] *Marcian Treatise*, 119.   [84] *Ibid.*, 120.8–10.   [85] Kaplan, *Les Hommes et la terre*, 402–4.
[86] *Iviron I*, pp. 163–72, no. 10.

land in the empire may have eased the process of taxation by impressing people with the awesome authority of the empire. A tax collector would have tried to make onlookers think that the empire knew exactly what they owed, even if his records on them were a mess. The important ceremonial role that the tax registers had in the process of taxation gave them a utility beyond that of simple record keeping.[87] Given the concern of the administration to get as much revenue as they could without driving off the cultivators, it would make sense to key the amount of material extracted to what was available, regardless of written tallies.

The difficulties in collecting revenue through taxation were offset in the early eleventh century by the revenues gained through direct exploitation of imperial estates. Some of the land conquered from the Arabs in the tenth century may have been directly converted into imperial estates that supplied important revenues. The imperial administration may have received more revenue from imperial estates in the early eleventh century than it did from land taxes.[88] The loss of the imperial estates in eastern Anatolia to the Seljuks in the 1070s forced the imperial administration to return vigorously to the task of collecting revenue through taxation. As with other aspects of government, Alexios Komnenos responded with new methods. He seems to have taken the immediate expedient of treating the empire like a private household, granting sections to his close supporters from which they could draw their own revenues.[89] He also undertook to measure more carefully the territory claimed by great proprietors, such as the Athonite monasteries, and conclude reasonable tax agreements with them. Alexios did not trust the books as he received them, but sent inspectors to check the monasteries' records against reality. A series of assessments and concessions to the great monasteries on Mount Athos attest to Alexios' concerted efforts to hold the monasteries responsible for a reasonable assessment of their taxes.[90] Alexios' efforts to make the fiscal administration more effective produced an "anguished reaction" from monasteries on Mount Athos with extensive holdings.[91] The correspondence of Theophylakt of Ochrid also attests to new pressures to increase tax yields.[92]

---

[87] Neville, "Information, ceremony and power," 40–3.
[88] Lefort, "Rural economy," 287–8. Oikonomides, "L'évolution de l'organisation administrative," 136–7. The extent of direct exploitation may not have been as great as has been suggested. Holmes, "Basil II and the government of empire: 976–1025," 256–74.
[89] *Iviron II*, pp. 244–7, no. 52; pp. 255–9, no. 53.
[90] *Vatopedi*, pp. 115–18, no. 11. *Esphigmenou*, pp. 54–8, no. 5. *Docheiariou*, pp. 54–9, no. 2. *Lavra*, pp. 247–51, no. 46; pp. 263–9, no. 50; pp. 271–5, no. 52; pp. 282–96, no. 55; pp. 300–4, no. 58.
[91] Rosemary Morris, *Monks and Laymen in Byzantium, 843–1118* (Cambridge, 1995), 284.
[92] Harvey, "Land and taxation," 139–53.

While there is no point at which we can say that the cadaster system of tax registration fell out of use completely, the increasing numbers of extant *praktika* suggest that these individualized tax agreements became the empire's dominant method of tax assessment in the twelfth century. The increasing use of *praktika* should be seen as part of Alexios' efforts to rationalize the revenue system. The progression from a system based on a universal registration in geographic order to a system based on tracking the possessions of individual households is perhaps the strongest evidence for the increase in large-scale landholding. The *praktika* represent a shift in the fundamental fiscal organization, away from tracking all the land of the empire with the people who happen to work it, to tracking individual taxpaying entities and all the land that they control. An increase in the amount of land held by individuals and a decline of smallholders may have motivated this transition. If most of the revenues came from independent peasant landowners, it would make sense to tax them village by village. If most of the production was done by peasants paying rents to a landlord, it would make sense to tax the landlords.

The switch to the *praktika* system made a great deal of sense because it tracked in writing the holdings of the sort of person or organization who could both read texts and dispute their contents with the fiscal administration. Rather than trying to keep accurate records for thousands of illiterate peasants, administrators concentrated on accurately recording all of the property held by the wealthy people with education, or educated assistants, who would spend far more time working on their tax status than the administration ever could. The systems that the imperial administration established to assess and to collect revenue were all too easily manipulated by people with legal ability or friends in the administration. The new system acknowledged the negotiating ability of prominent landowning households by making an individual agreement, a *praktikon*, between the imperial administration and each significant landowning household. What was given up in this change was the attempt to rule in the manner of Caesar Augustus, whom the Evangelist Luke described as registering the whole world for taxation.

For imperial political history, the conclusion to be drawn from this study so far is that the military and fiscal crises of the second half of the eleventh century may be attributed in part to the malfunction of the taxation systems. The difficulties described above were sufficiently significant to cause the imperial administration to run out of money. Komnenian rebuilding included the increasing use of a new method of recording taxation, the *praktika*, and vigorous efforts to extract taxes from the empire's grand households.

The imperial administration was generally effective at achieving its goals, but defined those goals narrowly. The emperors, through their military organization, protected the territorial integrity of the empire, built and strengthened fortifications, and even settled conquered populations. In most periods the civil administration extracted sufficient surplus revenue to maintain the military organization, pious donations, and the palace life. This admittedly impressive set of achievements leaves many aspects of life outside the purview of the imperial administration. The consequence for people living in the hinterland was that imperial authority did not intervene in their lives for good or ill. Provincial people were simply able to ignore formal authority and laws, because they knew the imperial administration did not care what happened so long as they paid their taxes and did not stir up rebellion. How people in the core provinces regulated their society in light of this strong yet apathetic rule is the subject of the remainder of this book.

CHAPTER 3

Provincial households

Byzantine writers described their society in terms of relationships between people rather than with absolute, classifying names. The habit of avoiding names that categorize has usually been treated as a literary peculiarity or a stylistic preference. The preference for relational description, however, is a systemic aspect of Byzantine culture that needs to be engaged rather than worked around in order to understand what Byzantine authors were saying about their world. Periphrastic description was valued as a mark of good rhetorical training and consequently many Byzantine authors avoided precise nomenclature as a matter of course.[1] Beyond this common practice of periphrastic writing, when Byzantine writers did name things they used terms that set one object or person in relation to another. Documentation with little literary pretension also defined people in relation to other people and things.[2] The terms used to describe people and things depended on the relationships in that particular context and so could vary as contexts changed.

The argument is not that the Byzantines had no unified sense of personhood, but that most of the time they chose to describe themselves and

---

[1] This is a well-known phenomenon. For example, in 1057 the *protos* of Mount Athos selected a committee of notable monks to adjudicate a dispute between two monasteries. The monks chosen for the committee were referred to as "a capable gathering of chosen fathers." Their signatures at the end of the document reveal their identity as *hegoumenoi, presbyteroi*, monks, and one *oikonomos*. The group is not given a precise name such as "committee on adjudications." *Saint-Pantéléèmôn*, pp. 57–9, no. 5. In the *Life of Nikon*, a certain Stephen is designated as the one "always entrusted with public affairs and community services." *Life of Nikon*, 228. St. Luke was delayed by "the one in charge of the harbor." *Life of Luke*, 184. These people probably had more precise titles, which the authors chose to ignore.

[2] For example, documents discussing the Byzantine taxation system described people in relation to their property. Those who owned a yoke of beasts were called *zeugarioi*, or "yokers," while those who owned an ox were *boidion*, or "oxers." Angeliki Laiou, *Peasant Society in the Late Byzantine Empire: A Social and Demographic Study* (Princeton, NJ, 1977), 69; *Iviron II*, pp. 206–11, no. 51; pp. 232–47, no. 52. Byzantine units of measurement are also conditional. The *schoinion* was a measure of length used in boundary delimitations. In areas with poor growing conditions a *schoinion* was 12 *orgyiai* long. In more fertile areas the *schoinion* was 10 *orgyiai* long because it measured land in relation to productivity. Lefort, "Rural economy," 300.

others in terms of relationships rather than with discrete labels. Byzantine writers avoided proper names and definite nomenclature, not only because of their rhetorical training, but also and more fundamentally because they perceived reality in terms of model relationships and they tried to act in accordance with those models. The Byzantine method of patterning behavior on ideal models crafted certainly the descriptions of behavior, and to some extent the behavior itself. An explanation of the causes for this cultural characteristic falls far outside the scope of this project. It seems clear, however, that it is at least partially a consequence of participating in a philosophical and theological tradition that posited the imitation of ideals and patterns, *mimeseis*, as the fundamental method of moral and spiritual cultivation.

While many models of behavior are visible in Byzantine provincial society, one extremely pervasive set of relationship ideals were those of the *oikos*, the household. The relationships within the *oikos* formed a fundamental Christian metaphor for the relationships between God and creation. *Oikos* was an economic metaphor for the relationships between a landlord and those on his estates. It was a political metaphor for the relationships between the emperor and other rulers, and a monastic metaphor for the relationships between spiritual fathers or mothers and monastic brothers or sisters. The relationships within the *oikos* were used to describe relationships between teachers and students. The terminology of the *oikos* was of course also the standard language for describing relationships between the head of an actual household and its members: parents, children, siblings, familiars, servants, tenants, and slaves. Metaphorical or literal *oikoi* could be allied or connected through various ties of kinship, friendship, or geographic proximity. Houses could also form hierarchical associations through ties such as economic dependence. Nearly every relationship seen in our evidence for provincial society can be explained in terms of *oikos* in either its literal or metaphorical uses.

The terminology of *oikos* established relationships between individuals that, to a greater or lesser degree, were patterned on ideal relationships in a harmonious family. In all of its metaphorical uses and frequently in its literal uses the terminology of the *oikos* was hortatory. Calling someone "brother" metaphorically invoked a relationship with that person and could have the force of calling that person to act in accordance with the ideal of brotherhood. Calling the rulers of Bulgaria "sons" of the emperor not only established a relationship in which they were subordinate to him but implicitly called on them to act as *good* sons.

Oikos is a category of analysis that cleaves closely to the terminology of our source material. Taking the *oikos* as an analytical model for understanding

Byzantine society not only has the virtue of using the same terminology as our sources, but also – and more importantly – proves to be explanatorily fruitful. The patterns of competition and collective action seen in provincial society can be explained satisfactorily in terms of the relationships within a household and competition and alliances between households. The hortatory aspect of *oikos* terminology illuminates the habits of competition and the methods of attaining authority in Byzantine society. This chapter both explains some of the ways the vocabulary of the *oikos* was used in describing human relationships and presents it as a model for understanding provincial society.

In proposing that provincial society be conceived as consisting of alliances and hierarchies of houses, I am calling for a change in emphasis more than revealing anything new. *Oikos* already has proven to be an important category for understanding Byzantine aristocracy.[3] The immediate family has been identified as the primary element of Byzantine social organization.[4] The goal here is to emphasize how the different uses of the terminology of *oikos* mentioned above were consonant with each other and together form a coherent paradigm for understanding provincial society. The relationships within and between *oikoi* may prove to be more salutary than the two categories that dominated discussion of Byzantine society in the twentieth century: the powerful (*dynatoi*) and the village community.[5] Both of these

---

[3] Paul Magdalino, "The Byzantine aristocratic oikos," in *The Byzantine Aristocracy, IX to XIII Centuries*, ed. Michael Angold (Oxford, 1984), 92–111; Magdalino, "Honour among Romaioi," 183–218; Paul Magdalino, "'What we heard in the Lives of the saints we have seen with our own eyes': the holy man as literary text in tenth-century Constantinople," in *The Cult of the Saints in Late Antiquity and the Middle Ages: Essays on the Contributions of Peter Brown*, ed. James Howard-Johnston and Paul Anthony Hayward (Oxford, 1999), 96–9.

[4] Kazhdan and Constable, *People and Power in Byzantium*, 26–36. Alexander Kazhdan, "Small social groupings (microstructures) in Byzantine society," in *Congrès international des études byzantines: Actes 16* (Vienna, 1982), 3–11. Kazhdan understood the primacy of the nuclear family as a consequence of the absence of other horizontal or vertical social ties. Hence the primacy of individual families was a mark of an atomized and individualistic society. Here the primacy of families is interpreted within the context of relationships within and among *oikoi* that are seen as more complex and thus far less atomistic than Kazhdan's nuclear families. The means of forming associations among households through metaphorical or actual kinship ties could lead to a rich network of horizontal and vertical social ties.

[5] A classic statement of the mid-twentieth-century theory of Byzantine rural society is found in George Ostrogorski, "Agrarian conditions in the Byzantine Empire in the Middle Ages," in *Cambridge Economic History of Europe*, vol. 1: *The Agrarian Life of the Middle Ages*, ed. M. Postan (Cambridge, 1966), 205–34. The origins of this paradigm are explained by Alexander Kazhdan, "Russian pre-Revolutionary studies on eleventh-century Byzantium," in *Byzantine Studies: Essays on the Slavic World and the Eleventh Century*, ed. Spyros Vryonis Jr. (New Rochelle, NY, 1992), 111–24. The first attempt to see the *dynatoi* as designating a relationship rather than a class was made by Rosemary Morris, "The powerful and poor in tenth-century Byzantium: law and reality," *Past & Present* 73 (1976): 3–27.

categories appear in Byzantine sources, but they are not the most helpful organizing rubrics for analysis. The prominence of these categories arose from the historiography on the tenth-century legislation on landownership, which restricted the ability of the powerful to buy lands in communities where they did not already own land. The notion of the village community derived from the categories of fiscal jurisdiction that the land legislation tried to protect. This fiscal category has been taken as reflecting cohesive social organization in village communities. Information about Byzantine society can be made to fit into the categories of *dynatoi* and village communities, but they are not explanatorily helpful, because Byzantine society vigorously resists classification and they are effectively substitutes for the class vocabulary of aristocracy and peasants derived from historiography of Western Europe.

An aristocratic *oikos* and a peasant *oikos* were the same with respect to many of the roles. This means not that Byzantine society was egalitarian but that similar relationships existing at distant levels of the social hierarchy were described with a terminology that emphasized their similarities. The markers of status that clearly distinguished an aristocratic *oikos* from a peasant *oikos* to members of Byzantine provincial society are frequently difficult for us to identify. When a text describes an interaction with reference to an *oikos*, we know that a set of relationships was in play but we do not always know where on the social scale of power that particular set of relationships might be.

Familial households were fundamentally structured around physical kinship, in particular around a nuclear family. The nuclear family emerges as one of the clearest social units visible in Byzantine sources.[6] The head of a household was its owner or *despotes*. *Despotes* was a proper form of address for the emperor, but any owner of a thing was its *despotes*. In our fiscal information the head of a household was the *oikodespotes*, the house-owner. The author of the *Marcian Treatise* saw the countryside as inhabited by *choroikodespotai*, village house-owners/lords, and "simple villagers." We cannot tell from the *Marcian Treatise* whether the *choroikodespotai* included petty aristocracy or grand aristocracy or merely anyone with a house. The *oikodespotes* was the father of the core family of the household. An ideal father was providential and charitable toward his children and cultivated their character through proper correction. These characteristics are appropriate for other men in positions of leadership. The head of a monastic

---

[6] Kazhdan and Constable, *People and Power in Byzantium*, 26.

household was the spiritual father of the brothers. The emperor should govern the empire as a father governs his house.

The wife of a male head of household was the *despoina*. Women could be heads of household in their own right as widows. The *Cadaster of Thebes* records property tax due from a number of households headed by women.[7] It appears that women would also act as head of the household when their husbands were absent. The models for the mistress of a household were the empresses and the Mother of God. In a significant departure from earlier models of female sanctity, Byzantine housewives were able to become saints in the tenth century.[8] Perhaps the positive and important role of the mistress of a household helped make it possible for non-celibate women to achieve sainthood.

In our sources we see the *oikodespotai* more often than we do their wives, daughters, sons, and servants because a household was identified through the name of its *despotes*. The head of household necessarily represented a larger collection of people. When fiscal assessors counted *paroikoi*, they counted male heads of household and listed their names. The work involved in coming up with the cash to pay rent or tax fell on other members of the household as well. Wives, children, and servants were less visible but active members of households.

Byzantine sources frequently talk about good birth and its importance. Yet *eugeneia* does not seem to have been an absolute category. All the saints of the period were from "well-born" families. This can be explained in part by the financial requirements of participation in monastic life.[9] Anyone from a truly poor house would have to keep working. It equally may be that any family that could produce a saint was a good one. In the context of the epic of Digenes Akritas it has been suggested that nobility was a matter of membership in a powerful family: "*Eugeneia* may imply the prestige of an illustrious pedigree, but what it actually denotes throughout the poem is something more tangible: the solidarity of a powerful kin group."[10] The well-born have the support of an effective household. To be well-born was to participate in a household that could supply the relationships and resources needed for an honorable life. Honorable conduct need not correlate with wealth.

The same vocabulary of caring familial relationships between fathers and mothers, brothers and sisters, was used for the spiritual monastic family.[11]

---

[7] *Cadaster of Thebes*, 57–63.
[8] Alice-Mary Talbot, ed., *Holy Women of Byzantium: Ten Saints' Lives in English Translation* (Washington, DC, 1996), 239–322.
[9] Morris, *Monks and Laymen*, 76–7. [10] Magdalino, "Honour among Romaioi," 195.
[11] Alice-Mary Talbot, "The Byzantine family and the monastery," *DOP* 44 (1990): 120–1.

Monasteries have been called "the alter ego of the secular oikos."[12] In monastic households, physical kinship was considered a hindrance. Rather, one's spiritual brothers were supposed to be more important than one's brothers according to the flesh. An ideal characteristic of holy men was detachment from worldly relationships and familial affections, yet not many Byzantine saints, let alone ordinary monks and nuns, were able live up to this ideal.[13] When Lazaros returned to his homeland after many years of wandering asceticism in the Holy Land he was reunited with his mother.[14] Later his mother and brothers became prominent in his monastic foundations. The hagiographer of Luke of Stiris received information for his story from Luke's sister, who was a nun.[15] Luke's sister had regular contact with him while he was living in ascetic seclusion.[16] Paul of Latros fell into extreme poverty after the death of his parents. His brother, who was already a monk, found Paul working as a pig herder and helped him join his monastery.[17] Nikon was unusual in making a strong break with his family. The hagiographer makes much of this break, with a highly dramatic narration of the saint's escape from his physical family. Nikon's father and kin ransacked the monastery where Nikon had taken refuge, forcing Nikon to part tearfully from the true, spiritual father who tonsured him. Nikon's fleshly father and family, who were hunting him on horseback with hounds, were just about to catch him when the Mother of God miraculously carried him across a river.[18] The story of Nikon's separation from his family became a prominent element in his *vita* precisely because few of his contemporaries made such complete breaks with their kin. The narrative makes clear the ideal that a monk's spiritual relationships with the fathers and brothers of the monastery were supposed to be more significant than the relationships with physical kin.

The metaphor of the house extended to include the entire empire. The emperor was the providential father: "Not only the reality but also the formality of imperial power tended to cast the emperor in the patrimonial role of a head of a universal household."[19] The vocabulary of the fiscal administration was that of careful parenting and husbandry. *Sympatheia*, literally "sympathy," was a technical term for a kind of tax relief. The abrogation of that relief was *orthosis*, "correction" or "restoration." A kind of provisional landholding granted to people helping the government was a *pronoia*, "providence," connoting the emperor's providential care for his

---

[12] Magdalino, "The Byzantine aristocratic oikos," 92–111.
[13] Bernard Flusin, "L'hagiographie monastique à Byzance au IXe et au Xe siècle," *Revue Bénédictine* 103, no. 1–2 (1993): 47–50; Talbot, "The Byzantine family and the monastery," 119–29.
[14] *Life of Lazaros*, 115.   [15] *Life of Luke*, 162.   [16] Ibid., 196.   [17] *Life of Paul*, 106–7.
[18] *Life of Nikon*, 58–74.   [19] Magdalino, "Honour among Romaioi," 186.

helpers and their care for the territories they were granted.[20] All these terms place the emperor in the role of a caring father for his people. This also places him in the role of God, who is the father of creation. Byzantine foreign relations also were modeled famously on family relations, with foreign rulers being placed in the role of sons, brothers, and cousins of the emperor.[21] Such terminology accorded respect to foreign rulers while reinforcing the emperor's authority as the head of the family.

The Confraternity of Thebes was another context in which relationships were defined through metaphoric kinship. The members of the Confraternity became brothers and committed themselves to the familial tasks of prayer and burial. When the members of the Confraternity spoke about brotherhood, they were referring to a set of behaviors associated with an idealized fraternity: care, respect, help in trouble, etc. The charter specified that the role included praying for each other when sick and burying each other. Just as monastic brotherhood was an ideal abstraction of a human relationship, so the Confraternity drew on a common set of assumptions about what proper brotherly behavior was. The ties of brotherhood among the members created a full complement of relationships for others in their households.

The gender integration of the Confraternity of Thebes makes the most sense when regarding Byzantine society as consisting of households. Seen as individuals rather than as members of households, the women in the Confraternity appear incongruously as a few feminist pioneers in an all-male club. When individuals are understood as members of households, the signatures on the charter do not represent an exclusive list of the individuals participating in the association. Rather they indicate the heads of household who signed as representatives of their *oikoi*. Similarly when "villages" made legal agreements, all the members of the community were represented by the few male heads of household who signed the documents.[22] The women who signed the charter of the Confraternity of Thebes acted as the heads of their households. Other women probably participated in the activities to a comparable degree but were included silently as the wives of male members. When the *despoina* was the head of the household, because either she was widowed or her husband was absent, she

---

[20] The term has traditionally been understood as referring to the emperor's provision for his helpers. It may also refer to the care the holder of the *pronoia* had for the territory he nominally administrated. Magdalino, "Army and the land," 35–6.
[21] Alexander Kazhdan, "The notion of Byzantine diplomacy," in *Byzantine Diplomacy*, ed. Jonathan Shepard and Simon Franklin (Aldershot, 1992), 14–15. Evangelos Chrysos, "Byzantine diplomacy, A.D. 300–800: means and ends," in *ibid.*, 37.
[22] *Iviron I*, pp. 117–34, nos. 4 and 5.

signed the document.²³ The women whose husbands were "brothers" in the Confraternity were naturally also "sisters" to the other people in the organization.

Another kind of brotherhood was fostered within military units. The handbook on strategy written by the emperor Nikephoros Phokas emphasized the importance of arranging men in a unit, *bandon*, according to "kinship and friendship." These bonds of trust and affection would be strengthened by having the men in each *bandon* work, camp, and fight together all the time.²⁴

The household was the category used to organize relationships of service as well as of family.²⁵ Prominent households contained slaves, servants, and supporters under varying degrees of subservience.²⁶ Throughout the period under discussion some people were enslaved to others.²⁷ As prisoners of war formed the most common source of slaves, it is not surprising that they appear more common in the late tenth and early eleventh centuries when the empire was winning battles than in the late eleventh and twelfth centuries. Slaves could not own property but could possess and use personal property granted to them by their owners. Leo VI (886–912) issued a law making the wills of imperial slaves valid, which implies that slaves commonly held personal property.²⁸ It seems that, at least in the urban context of Constantinople, slaves could be entrusted with significant financial and managerial responsibilities.²⁹ The *Book of the Eparch* allowed slaves to be members of the guilds of Constantinople.³⁰ Judging from surviving testaments, it was fairly common to free slaves upon one's death.³¹ Leo VI also legislated that the testimony of a slave who was to be freed upon his owners' death was valid, even if the slave did not know that he was to be

---

[23] The women who joined were Maria Kamateros, the wife of Theodore Kamateros, Irene Skardos, Maria Mardanros, and Manacho Phegellete. John W. Nesbitt and J. Witta, "A confraternity of the Komnenian era," *BZ* 68 (1975): 360–84.
[24] McGeer, *Sowing the Dragon's Teeth*, 38–9.   [25] Magdalino, "Honour among Romaioi," 185.
[26] Cheynet, *Pouvoir et contestations*, 287–301.
[27] Rosemary Morris, "Emancipation in Byzantium: Roman law in a medieval society," in *Serfdom and Slavery: Studies in Legal Bondage*, edited by Michael Bush (London, 1996), 130–43; Ludwig Burgmann, "Sklaven in der Peira," *Fontes Minores* 9 (1993): 1–33; Christina Angelide, "Douloi sten Konstantinoupole tou I' ai.," *Symmeikta* 6 (1985): 33–51.
[28] Pierre Noailles and Alphonse Dain, eds., *Les Novelles de Léon VI, le sage* (Paris, 1944), 150–3.
[29] Gilbert Dagron, "The urban economy, seventh–twelfth centuries," in *The Economic History of Byzantium from the Seventh through the Fifteenth Century*, ed. Angeliki Laiou (Washington, DC, 2002), 420–2.
[30] Eleutheria Papagianni, "Byzantine legislation on economic activity relative to social class," in *The Economic History of Byzantium from the Seventh through the Fifteenth Century*, ed. Angeliki Laiou (Washington, DC, 2002), 1087.
[31] Morris, "Emancipation in Byzantium," 135–9.

freed.³² Christian marriages of slaves were made legally valid under Alexios Komnenos, but seem to have taken place before then.³³

When St. Luke was a young man, still living in his parent's household but adopting an ascetic lifestyle, he was captured by a group of soldiers hunting for runaway slaves. They took his shabby clothing as a sign of slavery. Luke greatly annoyed them by claiming to be the slave of Christ.³⁴ The ideal of complete service to a master was powerful and adopted by a wide range of people who were not legally owned by others. The distinction between servants and slaves may have been stark in legal terms, but is glossed over and obscured in our sources. People who were manifestly wealthy and powerful called themselves the slave, *doulos*, of the Theotokos or of Christ. This designation is frequently found on seals. Members of the Confraternity of Thebes used it in their signatures. With increasing frequency in the eleventh century, those in imperial service called themselves the *douloi* of the emperor as a mark of honor.³⁵ *Doulos* was also the standard term for a person literally enslaved and owned by another. When the soldiers who captured Luke wanted to know whose *doulos* he was, they took his claim to be Christ's *doulos* as wild effrontery and beat him senseless. Another standard word for a slave, *oiketes*, derives from the word *oikos* and denotes specifically one in a menial role within a household.

There are some cases in which it is difficult to tell the real extent of a person's enslavement. After his mother died Paul of Latros fell into poverty and worked as a swineherd for a village. When Paul's older brother, who was a monk, sent someone to find Paul, the villagers refused to let Paul go. They demanded payment for Paul's release from their service, although he worked for wages.³⁶ Often there is no way to determine precisely the legal status of subordinate members of household. The servants simply are present without further elaboration. To take one example, in the *Life of Thomaï of Lesbos*, Thomaïs and her husband lived without parents or children. They are not described as having servants or slaves yet Thomaïs gave death-bed instructions to those she "lived with."³⁷ Thomaïs' household would be expected to contain more people than simply herself and her husband.

Some members of households held the vaguely defined position of familiars and "men."³⁸ Kekaumenos wrote that it was "a great thing to have

---

³² Dagron, "The urban economy," 148–51.
³³ Zepos and Zepos, eds., *Jus graecoromanum*, vol. 1, p. 343–6.   ³⁴ *Life of Luke*, 165.
³⁵ Cheynet, *Pouvoir et contestations*, 288–99.   ³⁶ *Life of Paul*, 119.
³⁷ Talbot, ed., *Holy Women of Byzantium*, 316.
³⁸ The Byzantine use predates the period of western influence. Cheynet, *Pouvoir et contestations*, 289.

3 Ring of Michael Attaleiates. This gold and enamel ring of the late eleventh century bears the inscription "Mother of God, help your servant Michael Attaleiates."

a faithful slave or free man" but that they should not get too friendly with one's daughters.[39] Given Kekaumenos' rigorous attitude regarding keeping his household private, anyone given the opportunity of seeing his daughters would have to be a member of the household. Kekaumenos seems far less concerned with the legal status of his faithful man than with the proper relationship of respectful service. Alexios Komnenos sent Theodore Senachereim to Mount Athos as an envoy. Theodore was described as Alexios' *oikeios*, literally his "domestic."[40] Senachereim was a servant, but were we to speculate about who Alexios felt affection for, Senachereim would figure among the principal candidates. Those in one's household could occupy a position as both friend and servant. Kekaumenos recounted the advice of Bishop John of Larissa regarding attachment to worldly things:

To someone he had said, "If you take joy in a friend or slave, remember that he is a man and will die as a man, and do not be troubled at his end. For it will not benefit you. If you take pleasure in an object of gold or silver or perhaps glass, reckon when having it that one may be lost and the other broken."[41]

The bishop placed both friends and slaves in the same category as transient pleasures. Some grand aristocratic households also included *syntrophoi*,

---

[39] Kekaumenos, Litavrin, §56; Wassiliewsky, 55.   [40] *Xenophon*, p. 71, no. 3.
[41] Kekaumenos, Litavrin, §62; Wassiliewsky, 60.

who were children of another family, sometimes captives, who were raised along with the sons of the *despotes*.⁴² The combination of affection born of childhood companionship with complete dependence on the *despotes*' household seems to have produced relationships of considerable trust.

Just as the ideal set of behavior for a father was appropriate for a general or a monastic superior, the ideal set of behavior for a servant was appropriate for any relationship involving service. For example: "If you work for an *archon*, serve him not as an *archon* or a man, but as a king or God."⁴³ Kekaumenos' point was that the role of dutiful respectful service should be used regardless of the *archon*'s actual rank and abilities. If one was subordinated to another, one should properly play the role of a subordinate: "If he is ignorant and incompetent, while you are full of knowledge and wisdom and capabilities, do not disdain him and hurt yourself."⁴⁴ His advice for how to deal with subordinates mirrored his advice for dealing with superiors.⁴⁵ Both sets of advice outline an ideal relationship characterized by mutual respect and care. The roles of provident father and faithful children were proper and useful for describing, and ideally playing, the head of department and subordinates.

As was explained in the first chapter, imperial honorary titles were granted that did not have any corresponding duties. These honors, however, derived from titles that once corresponded to services in the late Roman period. The *spatharioi* had been imperial bodyguards in late antiquity. The salaries that the *spatharioi* of the tenth and eleventh-centuries received were in some sense still payments for servants. While those holding imperial honorary titles did not necessarily provide services for the emperor, they participated in a relationship of service with the imperial household. The titles exalted and honored the recipient by allowing him to be a member of the imperial household, broadly conceived.

In the eleventh century fiscal documents begin to record peasant tenants as *paroikoi*. The *paroikoi* paid rents to a landowner rather than tax to the fisc. Although the apparent rise in number of *paroikoi* in the tenth and eleventh centuries has been associated with the "feudalization" of the empire in mid-twentieth-century historiography, it is unclear what if any rights of citizenship were lost to the *paroikoi* or if the *paroikoi* were at an economic disadvantage compared with peasant proprietors. The landlords were not granted any formal jurisdiction over them. In the cases of monasteries that

---

[42] Cheynet, *Pouvoir et contestations*, 290.   [43] Kekaumenos, Litavrin, §4; Wassiliewsky, 5.
[44] Kekaumenos, Litavrin, §4; Wassiliewsky, 5.
[45] Kekaumenos, Litavrin, §§4, 34; Wassiliewsky, 5, 35.

were granted a certain number of *paroikoi* tax-free, the kinds of corvée labor imperial officials could extract were limited. *Paroikoi* could benefit from their association with households that were able to gain exemptions and other favorable fiscal treatment.[46]

Paroikoi were the members not of a distinct social class, but of an economic relationship with another house. Etymologically *paroikoi* are those who live "beside the house." The term was used in theological contexts to mean sojourners in a foreign land such as Israel in Egypt. The terminology of the *oikos* had been applied to estates since the late Roman period.[47] In the middle Byzantine documents, the *paroikoi* were "beside the house" in that they were associated with but not part of the household whose land they worked. A family of *paroikoi* was a small household that was associated with another larger familial, monastic, or imperial household. Only one son inherited the status of being a *paroikos*.[48] This was because only one peasant household needed to continue the economic relationship with the larger house. In 975 an inspector, Theodore Kladon, separated the taxpaying peasants, the *demosarioi*, from the *paroikoi* who were to work on the estates of the monastery Kolobou. Theodore established that the monastery was entitled to thirty-six *paroikoi*.[49] He referred to them as both *paroikoi* and *oikoi*. Clearly he was not counting individuals, but households that were fiscally subordinate to the monastery. The monastery was entitled to have a certain number of peasant "houses" working for them tax-free. Another document granting Iviron forty *paroikoi* referred to them once as *paroikoi* and twice as *stichoi*.[50] A *stichos* was a single entry for a head of household in the tax registers. Counting *stichoi* was another way of counting households.

The vocabulary of an *oikos* was thus used to discuss a variety of human relationships in Byzantine society. While essentially familial, this vocabulary was applied metaphorically to wide-ranging experiences. *Oikos* terminology is precise about the nature of the relationships at hand, at least ideally, but vague about the status of the participants relative to the rest of society. While this discussion has emphasized the common elements of various kinds of provincial households, the following attempts to illuminate the ways status was differentiated between households.

---

[46] Lefort, "Rural economy," 236–41; Laiou, *Peasant Society*, 144–58.
[47] Kaplan, *Les Hommes et la terre*, 136–49; Jean Gascou, "Les grands domaines, la cité et l'état en Egypte byzantine," *TM* 9 (1985): 4.
[48] Laiou, *Peasant Society*, 155.   [49] *Iviron I*, pp. 109–13, no. 2.   [50] *Ibid.*, pp. 152–4, no. 8.

STATUS DIFFERENTIATION

The similarity of roles and relationships can mask differences in status and hierarchical distinctions between houses. There was a definite pecking order in Byzantine society, and individuals and households strove vigorously to improve their status. The relative openness in Byzantine society to social mobility meant that people actively engaged in social climbing at all levels of the social hierarchy.[51] Prosopographical studies of the Byzantine aristocracy have identified the most important families of the empire and increased our understanding of composition and evolution of the Byzantine aristocracy.[52] The following does not attempt to repeat that work, but rather outlines some of the main factors involved in differentiating status among provincial households. Community perception and judgment of honorable conduct, wealth, and the ability to call on the help of a more significant household appear in our sources as the three most important markers of social status for provincial society. These factors seem to have established the hierarchy among modest villagers as well as among aristocratic households.

Social status other than slavery was not juridically defined in Byzantium.[53] Based on their merits, people were able to move from houses lacking in prestige to grand houses, and whole houses could rise and fall rapidly.[54] Kekaumenos thought that the emperor Michael the Paphlagonian was a great man even though he was from a humble family:

For thus the blessed one did not have glorious parents – rather his parents were undistinguished and extremely lowly – but he had great virtue. Some of the unlearned started the rumor that he was well-born and from a great stock, but he was ignoble and humble. I say that all men are the children of one man, Adam, both those kings and rulers and those begging for bread. For I have seen great-seeming

---

[51] Hélène Ahrweiler, "Recherches sur la société byzantine au XIe siècle: nouvelles hiérarchies et nouvelles solidarités," *TM* 6 (1976): 99–124; Jean-Claude Cheynet, "Le rôle de l'aristocratie locale dans l'état," *BF* 19 (1993): 105–7; Kazhdan and McCormick, "Social composition of the Byzantine court," 169–72.

[52] Alexander Kazhdan, *Sotsial'nyi sostav gospodstvuiushchego klassa Vizantii XI–XIIvv* (Moscow, 1974); new edition and translation: Alexander Kazhdan, *L'aristocrazia bizantina: dal principio dell'XI alla fine del XII secolo*, trans. Silvia Ronchey (Palermo, 1997); Cheynet, *Pouvoir et contestations*, 207–377; Stephen Kamer, "Emperors and aristocrats in Byzantium 976–1081," PhD thesis, Harvard University, 1983; Spyros Stavrakas, "The Byzantine provincial elite: a study in social relationships during the ninth and tenth centuries" (PhD thesis, University of Chicago, 1978); Michael Angold, ed., *The Byzantine Aristocracy, IX to XIII Centuries* (Oxford, 1984).

[53] Kazhdan, *L'aristocrazia bizantina*, 167. The absence of legally defined social classes has been interpreted as the basis of fundamental differences between Byzantine and western European societies of the thirteenth century. David Jacoby, "From Byzantium to Latin Romania: continuity and change," *Mediterranean Historical Review* 4 (1989): 3–5; David Jacoby, "The encounter of two societies: western conquerors and Byzantines in the Peloponnesus after the Fourth Crusade," *The American Historical Review* 78 (1973): 879–82.

[54] The biography of Michael Attaleiates in his *typikon* provides just one example. *Typika*, 333–4.

ones turn to theft and divination and magic. I say these are the ill-born. For a man, being reasonable, may become god, if he wants, through God's grace. Thus was the blessed emperor lord Michael.⁵⁵

Byzantine guilds, as seen in the *Book of the Eparch*, were restricted not by heredity, but by qualifications.⁵⁶ Such qualifications were certainly most easily acquired by growing up in a family engaged in the guild activity. Nonetheless, the openness to new people is significant. Kekaumenos frequently ends his worst-case scenarios by saying, "and you will be ruined." His opinion of the ease with which one could lose social status may have more to do with the reality of downward social mobility than any personal pessimism.

The clearest indication of the lack of defined social status in Byzantine society is provided by the attempts of the tenth-century emperors to legislate the activity of the "powerful." The emperors needed to define who they were talking about. In Romanos I Lacapenos' first law to proscribe the actions of the powerful they are defined entirely by their ability to intimidate others: "Let them be considered powerful who are capable of terrifying sellers, if not by themselves then by the power of others with whom they had familial access, or on the assured promise to provide beneficence to them."⁵⁷ Romanos' second law on this matter provided a more precise list of who the powerful were. The definition still did not delimit a classification but gave examples of some of the kinds of people who could frighten their neighbors:

Famous magistrates or patricians, or those having ruling, military, or civil, or strategic honors, or those numbered in the senate, or the rulers and overlords of the provinces, or the God-loving metropolitans or archbishops or bishops or abbots or ecclesiastical rulers or those having the management and oversight of pious or imperial houses, either privately or as a representative of the imperial or ecclesiastical power, either by themselves or through an agent for such a person.⁵⁸

Since the definition was fundamentally based on actions rather than a classification, one could make the definition inapplicable by modifying one's behavior. Someone with little power could still be intimidating to poorer neighbors and hence deserve to be counted among the powerful. Yet that same person could be intimidated in turn by many other people who were more powerful. The administrators entrusted with applying the legislation

---

⁵⁵ Kekaumenos, Litavrin, §83; Wassiliewsky, 98–9.
⁵⁶ Papagianni, "Legislation on economic activity," 1086–7.
⁵⁷ Svoronos and Gounaridis, eds., *Les Novelles des empereurs macédoniens*, 70–1.
⁵⁸ *Ibid.*, 84, lines 50–7.

certainly were themselves highly intimidating to many. By including anyone who could credibly claim the protection of someone who could be terrifying, the definition could expand to fit people who by any quantifiable standard were not well off. The emperors thus were unable to develop a juridically satisfying definition of a segment of the population.

The vocabulary of our sources consistently describes prominence in terms of its public perception. In the *Life of Luke*, when an imperial official passing through Corinth suffers from the theft of imperial gold in his charge, he is comforted by the "brilliant and distinguished."[59] Luke brings about the healing of one of the "the distinguished" people of Thebes."[60] St. Nikon was met by "the chief men and the rest of the people."[61] Paul of Latros was mistakenly cornered by hunting dogs owned by a man called the *protos* of Samos.[62] These authors use a visual vocabulary in which important people are distinguished, brilliant, notable, famous, radiant, or admirable. The words focus attention on the way prominent people were seen by others. When Luke was mistaken for a runaway slave, it was because his shabby physical appearance made him look like one. The soldiers released Luke after he was recognized by people who knew him and attested who he was and "what sort."[63] People did, in fact, come in different "sorts," but those categories were defined by variable human perception.

Kekaumenos described his characters as above and below others, leaving precise placement on the social scale vague. The emperor, who was above everyone but still below God, is the only character whose rank can be fixed securely. He had advice for one who lived privately and had someone "higher-up" as a neighbor and for one who lived privately but to whom "the people of the country are subordinate."[64] He advised three different courses of action for dealing with the same scenario based on whether "you have the power to judge," "you are of the middle ones," or "you are one of those completely lowly."[65] This vocabulary of verticality is echoed in other sources. Estates were defined in the *Marcian Treatise* as lands on which the owners did not live: "Now then, the estates (*proasteia*) have the same manner of foundation as these [the small fields]. But they differ in the fact that the owners do not have their abodes in the estate but some people under them, slaves or hired hands or others."[66] Absent in the discussions of social hierarchy is any sense that distinctions in prominence were due to or dependent on qualitative differences in kinds of people, or that poor people were defective or particularly different from well-off people.

[59] *Life of Luke*, 188.   [60] *Ibid.*, 203.   [61] *Life of Nikon*, 110.   [62] *Life of Paul*, 119.
[63] *Life of Luke*, 165–6.   [64] Kekaumenos, Litavrin, §§38, 58; Wassiliewsky, 40–1, 56–7.
[65] Kekaumenos, Litavrin, §2; Wassiliewsky, 2–3.   [66] *Marcian Treatise*, 115.

Public perception seems to have had a real role in creating social status. Jews in Byzantium were marginalized not so much by imperial law or Church canons as by their image in the eyes of their Christian neighbors.[67] Performance in public spaces was considered highly significant. Regarding the concept of nobility in Byzantine society one scholar has remarked, "In the final analysis, we may have to accept that rhetoric and bluff *were* the real norms."[68] In a Constantinopolitan context, bluff and posturing did much to help create status: "Status was created not only by establishing rights and securing assets, but also by scoring points in public encounters."[69] In provincial settings, social events and gatherings became arenas of competition. In Sparta local men were joined by the *strategos* in *tzounganon*, a ballgame played on horseback. According to both the *Life of St. Nikon* and Nikon's foundation charter, Nikon's church abutted the field used for the game. The game was loud enough to disturb the church services and Nikon had a row with the *strategos*, who had been losing.[70] The game provided a forum for competition not only among the players on the field but also between the general and Nikon. Kekaumenos wrote that if the reader became a corrupt provincial administrator the local people would "make the day of your transfer an extraordinary annual holiday."[71] Having a party in honor of someone's departure would display grandly that the departed was despised. When the members of the Confraternity of Thebes finished their processional, it would make sense for them to relax and to share a meal together. While such a shared meal would be a friendly occasion, it also would provide an opportunity for competitive entertaining. Other community events such as weddings and feast days would similarly be opportunities for gaining and losing the respect of one's neighbors.

Public humiliation could cause a considerable loss of prestige. The threat of public humiliation could be a powerful tool for getting people to respond to one's claims. One who fell into debt risked being publicly reprimanded by the lender:

Then finding you in the market or in the *praetorium* or in church on a feast day, wanting to show himself before the people to be above you and wealthy he will say to you "Man, how have I treated you that you hold onto my property? Do you want me to damage you?" He says these things for the sake of damaging you and he knows that he damaged you. And if you are silent, everyone will say, some in private and others openly: "The debtor has no nerves" and "Evil is the day of being

---

[67] David Jacoby, "Les Juifs de Byzance: une communauté marginalisée," in *Oi perithoriakoi sto Byzantio (Marginality in Byzantium)*, ed. Chryssa A. Maltezou (Athens, 1993), 137–8.
[68] Magdalino, "Byzantine snobbery," 63.   [69] *Ibid.*, 69.
[70] *Life of Nikon*, 134–40. *Typika*, 317.   [71] Kekaumenos, Litavrin, §20; Wassiliewsky, 19.

in debt." But if you answer him, then everyone will laugh saying to you, "How are you not ashamed, to thus act shamelessly against one doing good for you?" And he will turn to them saying, "Do you see, my lords, such shamelessness?"[72]

It is not altogether clear who Kekaumenos thought counted as "everyone" and "the people." But he seems to have been concerned with general public opinion. The creditor could use public humiliation and the fear of humiliation as a key means of enforcing repayment of loans. A number of different sources repeat the method for correcting a friend's behavior taught in the Gospel of Matthew, where one who is behaving badly should be corrected privately and then, if unrepentant, in increasingly public circumstances.[73] Public humiliation appears to have been a significant deterrent to improper behavior. For example John Xenos' testament is mostly comprised of injunctions to his survivors to obey his decision to give his property to the church of Mary Myriokephala. Those who disobey are to be anathema, and blessings are called on those who preserve the testament.[74] Having his curses written down and made public was considered worthwhile because public opprobrium, if not the curse itself, would help deter those who might be tempted to disregard John's testament.

While humiliation caused loss of prestige, participation in admirable roles and actions enhanced social standing. One became brilliant and radiant through performing public ritual well. When the members of the Confraternity of Thebes processed through town with their icon, they were reverencing the Mother of God and also presenting themselves before their community as her servants. Their procession would have been akin to other liturgical and imperial ritual processions. Members of provincial communities could reinforce their status through participation in ceremonial rituals:

> Ritual was anything but a monopoly of church and monarchy. Law students, guilds, confraternities, freshly baptized children and criminals projected their discrete social identities and received public honor or blame by means of processions or other rites. It is sometimes overlooked that emperors, patriarchs and saints' relics were not alone entitled to the ancient honors of an *adventus* ceremony. Bishops, generals, medieval faction officials and even legendary magnates of Digenes Akritas' ilk enjoyed them. In one sense, imperial ceremonial was but the apex of a pyramid of rituals dispersed through society and anchored in the fundamental values of ancient and medieval culture.[75]

---

[72] Kekaumenos, Litavrin, §35; Wassiliewsky, 37.
[73] Matthew 18:15–17. Nesbitt and Witta, "A confraternity of the Komnenian era," 365, lines 56–7. Rule of Christodoulos for the Monastery of St. John the Theologian on Patmos, in *Typika*, 589.
[74] *Typika*, 146.
[75] McCormick, "Analyzing imperial ceremonies," 14–15.

Such ritual encounters raised the prestige of the participants in the eyes of the community audience. Community observers were constantly judging proper behavior and giving respect to those who behaved well.

The Confraternity of Thebes was formed in part "in order that also we might receive the praise of men and deserve the manifold gifts of God."[76] Divine approval was undoubtedly foremost in the minds of the brothers, but they were open about their desire for human praise as well. The praise of men was important not only for the gratification of ego but to ensure the social standing of one's household.

Wealth is rarely mentioned explicitly as an indication of social status in our sources, but was implicitly a fundamental determinant of what people were able to do with themselves. While high social status in Byzantium was not defined by wealth, wealth was almost always a sign of high status.[77] The impression arising from our information about the economic underpinnings of Byzantine provincial society is that there were economic disparities among peasant cultivators as well as among trades-people and those who lived off fortunes in land. We have evidence for grand fortunes and middling fortunes, proprietors of workshops and commercial properties, comfortable peasants and poor peasants.

Byzantine fiscal documents make a fundamental distinction between villages in which the cultivation was done by the residents and estates whose owners were not themselves cultivators. The owners of estates frequently lived elsewhere, either in Constantinople or in provincial towns, leaving a representative resident on the estate. Estates could vary tremendously in size: some were vast and others hardly bigger than peasant holdings. The *Cadaster of Thebes* lists individuals paying taxes on dozens of discrete tracts of land that, judging by the amount of tax due on them, were far too small to justify a steward.[78] Presumably these parcels were rented. Cultivators of the soil could work land they owned, work land owned by another for wages, or rent that land. They could owe tax to the empire, or rent or labor services to a landowner. Not everyone who labored on an estate lived there and not everyone in a village owned land.[79]

While being a landowner must have carried some prestige, it is not at all clear that landowning was necessarily financially better than renting. In theory rents were twice as high as the land-tax, although there does not seem to be any mechanism for regulating how much rent landowners

---

[76] Nesbitt and Witta, "A confraternity of the Komnenian era," 366, lines 84–7.
[77] Kazhdan, *L'aristocrazia bizantina*, 175. Cheynet, *Pouvoir et contestations*, 253.
[78] *Cadaster of Thebes*, 57–63.   [79] Lefort, "Rural economy," 239–42.

charged. Estate owners could receive fiscal privileges that exempted some of their *paroikoi* from corvée labor and some taxes. They may have passed on some of the benefits of other tax exemptions to those who worked their land. Families may have chosen to rent land on an estate because the local landowners could provide better protection than the distant imperial government.[80]

Regardless of the legal relationship between the cultivators and the land they worked, the work itself seems to have been undertaken by individual households.[81] Such households certainly enjoyed varying levels of economic success. Villages could include households in a fairly wide range of economic health.[82] There was also money to be made in provincial society from manufacturers, most notably in pottery and silk production.[83]

The two main sources of income for the aristocracy were land and salaries for imperial service. Landowning brought fairly steady but relatively low returns on investment.[84] The yearly incomes from rents on urban commercial property were somewhat higher.[85] The annual rate of return on an investment in an imperial honorary title ranged from roughly equivalent to an investment in land, to slightly more than standard interest rates on cash.[86] While there is some evidence that titles were transferred between parties, they were certainly less fungible than real estate and they were not heritable. As a means of raising social status, imperial titles must have been of great value, at least until the middle of the eleventh century. Imperial salary incomes that were payments for actual services were an extremely significant source of wealth for most of the people who held such offices

---

[80] Ibid., 237–8. [81] Ibid., 243–8. Kaplan, *Les Hommes et la terre*, 484–522.
[82] *Marcian Treatise*, 115.
[83] A brick factory was sold to the monastery of Iviron in 1001. *Iviron I*, p. 178, no. 12, line 14. The variety and quality of ceramics in use in Corinth increased dramatically at the end of the eleventh century. G. D. R. Sanders, "Corinth," in *The Economic History of Byzantium from the Seventh through the Fifteenth Century*, ed. Angeliki Laiou (Washington, DC, 2002), 651. The silk industry of Thebes became famous in the twelfth century, and seems to have developed by the middle of the eleventh century. David Jacoby, "Silk in western Byzantium before the Fourth Crusade," *BZ* 85 (1992): 481.
[84] A recent, very approximate, estimate put yearly income from agricultural real estate at 3 percent of the value of the land. Lefort, "Rural economy," 302–4.
[85] As calculated from one tenth-century text recording the sale of five shops, income from urban rents was 5 percent of the value of the property before a tax of between 0.17 and 0.81 percent. Dagron, "Urban economy," 424–5.
[86] Most annual salaries for honorary titles were 2.5–3.5 percent of the price of the title, but could reach 9.72 percent in the tenth century and 8.33 percent in the first half of the eleventh through a further investment. Oikonomides, "Role of the Byzantine state," 1008–21. The interest rate in the eleventh century "seems to have fluctuated around a norm of 8.33 percent." Laiou, "Exchange and trade," 757. See also Angeliki Laiou, "God and Mammon: credit, trade, profit and the canonists," in *Byzantium in the 12th Century: Canon, Law, State and Society*, ed. Nicolas Oikonomides (Athens, 1991), 266–85.

and one of the main avenues for new families to enter the aristocracy.[87] Our admittedly meager information about private fortunes suggests that the income from salaries associated with imperial offices was less important the higher a family was on the social scale. The families on the highest level had fortunes in real estate, livestock (especially horses), and cash that far exceeded the income they may have received from titles and offices.[88] The emperors could elevate their chosen beneficiaries to the highest level of richness through grants of land, salaries, and tax exemptions. The greatest fortunes we know of were created by imperial favor. While imperial service allowed fortunes to be made quickly, such accumulations seem to have been fairly fragile. The emperors seem to have regularly confiscated the property of their very richest citizens, ostensibly to preempt treasonous behavior. These confiscations also gave the emperors the land with which to reward their new supporters.[89]

The third major element in creating social status was the ability to get the assistance of others. This ability was gained through forging connections and associations between households.

ASSOCIATIONS BETWEEN HOUSEHOLDS

Associations between households had the potential to help all the participants gain in prestige, wealth, and power. One of the best ways to increase one's prominence was to become part of a better household. The terminology of household lies behind Romanos' first definition of who the powerful were: "Let them be considered powerful who are capable of terrifying sellers, if not by themselves, then by the power of others with whom they had familial access."[90] The powerful were those who could frighten their neighbors or who had a household connection to those that could. "Familial access" translates the phrase *peparresiasmenos oikeiontai* which more literally means "those speaking freely, having been made part of one's household."[91] The point is that freedom of access and speech came with

---

[87] Kazhdan, *L'aristocrazia bizantina*, 140.
[88] Cheynet, "Fortune et puissance de l'aristocratie (x–xii siècle)," 205.   [89] *Ibid.*, 205–10.
[90] Svoronos and Gounaridis, eds., *Les Novelles des empereurs macédoniens*, 70–1.
[91] *Ibid.* Ἐκεῖνοι δέ νοείσθωσαν δυνατοὶ οἵτινες, κἂν μὴ δι' ἑαυτῶν, ἀλλ' οὖν διὰ τῆς ἑτέρων δυναστείας πρὸς οὓς πεπαρρησιασμένως ᾠκείωνται, ἱκανοί εἰσιν ἐκφοβῆσαι τοὺς ἐκποιοῦντας ἢ πρὸς εὐεργεσίας ὑπόσχεσιν τὴν πληροφορίαν αὐτοῖς παρασχεῖν. Svoronos and Gounaridis, eds., *Les Novelles des empereurs macédoniens*, 70–1. McGeer translates: "Considered to be dynatoi are those who, even if not personally but through the influence of others with whom it is common knowledge that they are connected, are capable of intimidating sellers or satisfying them with a promise of some benefaction." McGeer, *Land Legislation*, 46. Brand translates: "Let those be

being part of a household. Where the precise boundary around a household lay is unclear: "as regards the coterie of friends, neighbours and hangers-on, there are no fixed criteria for deciding who was or was not thoroughly 'at home' in the aristocratic household."[92] This is partly why Romanos was not able to define the term more clearly. Everyone knew what he meant, but that common knowledge did not translate into a juridically satisfying definition.

Having access to wealthier and more prestigious households than one's own was an important way of increasing one's social standing. Individuals could rapidly change their social status by switching from one household to another. The great value of imperial honorary titles was that they made the title-holder to some degree a member of the extended imperial household. We can assume that people routinely claimed to have familiar access to households more important than their own. A study of social climbing in Constantinople has identified entering a relationship of service to a prestigious household as the crucial first step in an enterprising young man's career.[93] Even a subordinate role in a prominent household would allow the young man access to the people he needed to impress. The aspirants were accepted and promoted by those households because it was thought that they could add to the prestige of the house. Once launched on a brilliant career, the young men would be useful allies for their supporters. When the young shining light of a provincial household became a servant in the Constantinopolitan household of his parent's best contact, his ego may have taken a beating, but his new position greatly increased the importance and authority of his kindred back home.

The power of the kinship bond to access a household is illustrated well by a story Kekaumenos told of a man who was able to gain access to a judge's house in Constantinople and seduce the judge's wife by claiming to be her kinsman.[94] The man was admitted to the household and became a companion to the judge on the basis of his claim to be a member of the wife's family, although she apparently did not recognize him. The same woman had previously been propositioned by the emperor but had turned him down despite offers of wealth and advancement. Presumably therefore she was not looking for an affair and would have denounced the man as

considered powerful who are capable of terrifying sellers, some not by themselves but by the authority of others, with whom they are conversationally intimate, or who on the excuse of beneficence offer them full security." Charles Brand, ed., *Icon and Minaret: Sources of Byzantine and Islamic Civilization* (Englewood Cliffs, NJ, 1969), 78–81.

[92] Magdalino, "The Byzantine aristocratic oikos," 97.
[93] Kazhdan and McCormick, "Social composition of the Byzantine court," 190–5.
[94] Kekaumenos, Litavrin, §39; Wassiliewsky, 42–4.

an imposter if she had trusted herself to recognize her kinsmen. He was trusted on the basis of being a relative even though he was in fact a perfect stranger.

Marriage was the primary method of creating an alliance between two households. Beyond uniting a husband and wife, marriage expanded networks of brothers, sisters, and kin by uniting two households. For Kekaumenos it was as bad to fight with a son-in-law as with a son.[95] Disputes about marriages and dowries demonstrate that a marriage was an alliance of two households. The efforts of ecclesiastical leaders to ban marriages within seven degrees of kinship helped to create a common understanding that in-laws were fully kin.[96] Marriage alliances among the aristocracy were political and economic arrangements of great importance. Byzantine practice of partitive inheritance and dowry gifts meant that, for all families, marriages were important times for gaining and dividing property.[97] Marriage provided familial access to anyone associated with the household into which one's kin was marrying.

Standing as godparent for another created a strong connection between two households. As with marriage, everyone in each household was placed in a new relationship with those of the other. Usually one person was godparent to all the children of a marriage.[98] Ties of spiritual kinship created through baptism were regarded as physical kinship and counted as impediments to marriage for both sets of parents and children involved. The kinship established in baptism, however, was not considered to extend beyond the two nuclear families for the purposes of calculating affinity. Baptismal sponsorship was thus a way of connecting households that had fewer ramifications than marriage.[99] While gaining access to another's household was not commonly admitted to motivate the choice of a godparent, it is clear that it did.[100]

Spiritual kinship could also be constituted through the custom of *adelphopoiia*, or "sibling-making." Ritual brotherhood is attested in all periods of Byzantine history and, along with marriage and baptismal

---

[95] Kekaumenos, Litavrin, §51; Wassiliewsky, 51.
[96] Angeliki Laiou, *Mariage, amour et parenté à Byzance aux XIe–XIIIe siècles* (Paris, 1992), 13–15, 21–66.
[97] Angeliki Laiou, "Marriage prohibitions, marriage strategies and the dowry in thirteenth-century Byzantium," in *La Transmission du patrimoine: Byzance et l'aire méditerranéenne*, ed. Jöelle Beaucamp and Gilbert Dagron (Paris, 1998), 132–51; Jean-Claude Cheynet, "Aristocratie et héritage (XIe–XIIIe siècle)," in *ibid.*, 53–80.
[98] Ruth Macrides, "The Byzantine godfather," *BMGS* 11 (1987): 146.
[99] Claudia Rapp, "Ritual brotherhood in Byzantium," *Traditio* 52 (1997): 325–6.
[100] Macrides, "The Byzantine godfather," 152.

sponsorship, was an important method for formalizing relationships.[101] While solemnized through a religious liturgy, ritual brotherhood was canonically suspect and became increasingly castigated by theologians and canonists from the twelfth century onward.[102] *Adelphopoiia* was a more flexible way to create kinship than baptismal sponsorship, first, because it did not rely on the birth of a child, and second because it did not create barriers of affinity between the participants' families.[103] According to the eleventh-century legal compilation, the *Peira*, persons who undertook vows of *adelphopoiia* could not be married, but their vows did not affect their kin.[104] While the ritual kinship created through *adelphopoiia* was not considered to extend to other family members in a sufficiently material way to prevent intermarriage, the adoptive brothers certainly enjoyed familial access to each other's households.[105]

In some cases, the adoption of a child could create kinship bonds between the child's physical family and adoptive family.[106] The members of the physical and adoptive families sometimes knew each other and maintained contact. Unlike adoption in classical Roman law, which was seen as dissolving when the *patria potestas* ended, Byzantine adoption formed a life-long Christian relationship established through ecclesiastical liturgy and recorded through legal contracts. The vocabulary of adoption mirrors that of baptismal sponsorship to the point that it is "difficult to distinguish an adopted child from a godchild, unless a qualifying phrase is added."[107] The inheritance rights of an adopted child were not automatically assumed but were defined in the contracts. Leo VI, whose laws on adoption reinforced the Christian understanding of the bond, prohibited marriage between adopted and physical siblings.[108] In the twelfth century the canonist Theodore Balsamon argued that marriage prohibitions should be fully extended to members of the child's adoptive and physical families because

---

[101] Rapp, "Ritual brotherhood in Byzantium," 285–326; Elizabeth A. R. Brown, "Introduction: ritual brotherhood in ancient and medieval Europe, a symposium," *Traditio* 52 (1997): 261–8; Brent Shaw, "Ritual brotherhood in Roman and post-Roman societies," *Traditio* 52 (1997): 327–56.

[102] Evelyne Patlagean, "Christianisation et parentes rituelles: le domaine de Byzance," *Annales Economies, Sociétés, Civilisations* 3 (1978): 625–36.

[103] Rapp, "Ritual brotherhood in Byzantium," 303.

[104] Zepos and Zepos, eds., *Jus graecoromanum*, vol. IV, p. 201.

[105] In the *Life of Euthymios* the Patriarch Nicholas is described as having been the ritual brother of Leo VI and as having visited Leo's mistress Zoe Karbonopsina every day in the imperial palace when she was pregnant. Nicholas "enjoyed the same liberty with the women of the imperial household as a family member, most likely by virtue of being Leo's ritual brother." Rapp, "Ritual brotherhood in Byzantium," 299.

[106] Ruth Macrides, "Kinship by arrangement: the case of adoption," *DOP* 44 (1990): 114.

[107] *Ibid.*, 111–12.

[108] Noailles and Dain, eds., *Les Novelles de Léon VI, le sage*, 92–5.

spiritual relationships ought to take precedence over physical ones. While this evidence suggests that adoption was used to forge alliances between households, the majority of adoptions by far were acts of charity toward individuals bereft of their natural family, and hence brought only spiritual benefit to the adopting household.[109] Given the ease of creating fictive kinship ties through baptismal sponsorship and *adelphopoiia*, it seems that adoption was only used to create associations between households in unusual circumstances.

Adoption also played a role in high-level Byzantine politics. For example, the empress Maria of Alania adopted Alexios Komnenos shortly before Alexios' coup.[110] His status as the empress' "child" gave him daily access to the palace at a time of great political uncertainty. Alexios in turn is described as having adopted a number of western noblemen during their passage through Constantinople in the course of the first crusade.[111] Differences in the ways Alexios and his "sons" understood their bond eventually caused considerable ill-will between them.[112] It is conceivable that the westerners misunderstood the Byzantine metaphoric use of kinship terminology. It would have been entirely fitting from the Byzantine perspective for Alexios to call respected foreign noblemen "sons" without implying any literal adoption of them. Whatever was said or done led the westerners to expect more support from Alexios than he endeavored to supply. In light of multiple competing obligations created by spiritual kinship, Byzantines may not have expected a father to be equally responsive to all of his physical and metaphorical sons.

The members of the Confraternity of Thebes had familial access to each other because by becoming brothers they joined in a relationship that created lines of association among their households. They met at a different member's church each month and processed together to the church of the member who was to care for the icon the next month. The churches that housed the icon may have been neighborhood churches or chapels associated with the members' households. This implies a degree of physical access to each other's houses. We do not know how tight the bond between the members became, but they certainly had some claim on each other.

Another way to move up to a better household was to join a monastic household. Monasticism has been interpreted as an effort to achieve complete atomism and detachment from society: "In the end even the family

---

[109] Macrides, "Kinship by arrangement," 114–15.
[110] Reinsch and Kambylis, eds., *Annae Comnenae Alexias*, 61, Book 3.3.
[111] Shepard, "'Father' or 'scorpion'?," 81.   [112] *Ibid.*, 109–32.

appeared insufficiently atomistic. The ultimate aim was celibacy, the disruption of family links, detachment of the self from society."[113] The chief aim of monastic celibacy may have been to detach oneself from society, but that ideal was rarely met. Monastic celibacy also allowed one to move from one household to another, from ties of fleshly kinship to ties of spiritual kinship. Given that joining a monastery did not in fact mean breaking all ties to one's physical family, it meant that a new connection was forged between one's physical and monastic households. Monks and nuns formed alliances between two houses, as did marriage. To take one example, Theodosios, a monk in St. Luke's monastery, was frequently visited by his brother, the *spatharios* Philip. The hagiographer tells us about the spiritual advantages Philip enjoyed through his brother's membership in the monastery.[114] We can assume from the grandeur of the churches built at Luke's monastery after his death that the monastery also benefited from its alliances with families such as Philip's.

Marriage, spiritual kinship, fraternities, and monasteries all offered ways to create links between households and hence gave the members of the respective houses access to each other. Friendship offered another way to access a household. Margaret Mullett has argued that friendship in Byzantium was of vital importance and has offered the following definition:

And so *philos* can mean ally, supporter, spy, backer, useful friend, patron and client. But all were recognizable as participants in a single relationship, heavily instrumental and with its own ceremonial. Friends ate, drank and talked together, stayed in each other's houses, wrote letters and sent gifts to one another, and undertook obligations of ritual kinship with one another.[115]

To this definition we may add that a friend was not a member of one's own household. Ties of friendship created links between different households. I would not attempt to distinguish firmly between a person's "friends" and "familiars." Yet the core of the distinction seems to be that a friend held loyalty primarily to a different group.

As seen in collections of letters, friendship appears to have been highly instrumental. So many of Psellos' letters involved recommendations of friends for offices and requests for promotions that one scholar surmised that eleventh-century bureaucrats were poorly paid and suffered from job insecurity.[116] Theophylakt of Ochrid cultivated an extensive network of

---

[113] Cutler and Kazhdan, "Continuity and discontinuity in Byzantine history," **448**.
[114] *Life of Luke*, 204–6.
[115] Margaret Mullett, "Byzantium: a friendly society?," *Past and Present* 118 (1988): **18**.
[116] Gunter Weiss, *Östromische Beamte in Spiegel der Schriften des Michael Psellos* (Munich, 1973), 38–41.

friends whom he called on to help with various difficulties. Many of Theophylakt's letters petition people who were not formally subordinate to him for "concrete and tangible action."[117] Theophylakt's correspondence has many concerns besides trading favors, but all the letters helped him cultivate his friendships. Through letters, gifts, and visits Theophylakt maintained familiarity with the members of his network. Friendship was crucial for creating connections and alliances between different households.

Friendship is one of the relationships that we see most easily in our sources because it took the most effort. Brothers and cousins could presume upon each other's help whereas friends, as members of different households, needed to be cultivated. Theophylakt "worked hard at his friendships and all his relationships."[118] While Kekaumenos had reasonable advice for maintaining oneself in a number of different household roles, the ones he knew best and advised most were the heads of households: fathers, generals, governors, princes, emperors. He considered equality odd and difficult: "I never loved to have another either sharing the table or being equal with me, unless by necessity."[119] Kekaumenos was not a misanthrope. He greatly appreciated spousal relationships and expressed affection for children and servants. Equality was unpleasant for him because, as the *oikodespotes*, his equal would be the *oikodespotes* of a different household and hence in a position of natural competition. Situations of equality for those in the head of household roles were at best cordial diplomatic summits. Kekaumenos' frequently quoted negative sentiments regarding friends stem from the way he saw friendship as an alliance between houses that were potential competitors.

Kekaumenos relates numerous stories of people deceitfully pretending to be friends in order to improve their own position. One general was befriended by a border prince, or *toparch*, who offered to provision the castle. The *toparch* hid armed men among the sheep and barrels of grain. Once inside the castle walls they attacked and took the castle.[120] Kekaumenos advised those living next to border princes to seduce them by pretending to be friends:

If your neighbor *toparch* undertakes to harm you, do not be rash against him, but hide your hostility to him and feign peace and simplicity. Then guard your country and make friends, if you can, in his country. Send them gifts privately so

---

[117] Margaret Mullett, *Theophylact of Ochrid: Reading the Letters of a Byzantine Archbishop* (Aldershot, 1997), 201.
[118] *Ibid.*, 204. [119] Kekaumenos, Litavrin, §65; Wassiliewsky, 61.
[120] Kekaumenos, Litavrin, §30; Wassiliewsky, 26–7.

that you may learn his plans through them. Further hiding your hostility, send gifts openly to the *toparch*. For having relaxed him completely with the gifts and feigned love, he will be free from care. And then gather up your army secretly and with eagerness, attack him and his army unexpectedly and you won't go wrong. You will obliterate and remove him.[121]

Kekaumenos even told a story of two generals who both simultaneously pretended to be friends while plotting treachery:

Katakalon Klazomenites was general of Raousios. The general wanted to win a victory through false friendship. There was a *toparch*, Vojislav the Dukljan, in the castles of Dalmatia in Zeta and Stamnos. Katakalon wanted to capture him. And what did he do? He made friends with him, sending him gifts most frequently, wanting to deceive him through these. But, even though the *toparch* was a gentile, he had wisdom by nature and from experience, and he took the gifts and he pretended to be the slave of the emperor as if from the general's goodness and presents. When the *toparch* had a new-born child, the general informed him that he would receive the child at holy baptism. The *toparch* joyously said, "by your bidding, also come to my house." The general did not want to. They both arranged then, that they would have the adoption between the province of the general and the land of the *toparch*. The general had warships ready in the sea (the place was by the sea) so that when he nodded they would throw the *toparch* onto the boat capturing him. The *toparch* also had this plan and he had brave men ready in hiding so that when he made a sign that they had arranged, they would attack and capture the general and those with him; which is what happened. They came together, embraced, and sat down. As soon as they were sitting, at the sign the *toparch's* men encircled the general and binding him hand and foot they led him bound with his son and all of those with him and the warships to Stamnos.[122]

This is a particularly frightening story because, next to marriage, baptismal sponsorship was the primary way to create a kinship bond between two houses. One needed to be able to trust one's kin. Kekaumenos told many other stories of treachery perpetrated through false friendship. He certainly believed that friends were worth cultivating and treating well. He gave advice about how best to help friends in various situations. As Mullet has observed, "Kekaumenos is not afraid of friendship in the abstract; he is afraid of what bad friends do to you."[123] Kekaumenos "has strong views on what one should or should not do for a *philos*, but that one should do something is not in doubt."[124] Kekaumenos thought it was proper to

---

[121] Kekaumenos, Litavrin, §29; Wassiliewsky, 25.
[122] Kekaumenos, Litavrin, §30; Wassiliewsky, 27–8. On Vojislav, see Stephenson, *Balkan Frontier*, 123–30, 133–5.
[123] Mullett, "Byzantium: a friendly society?," 12. [124] *Ibid.*, 14.

respond kindly and as a friend even to an enemy professing neediness, so long as one did not actually trust him.¹²⁵ Friends could have every good intention, but when situations became tense, their primary loyalty lay elsewhere.

Households could also share a simple connection of geographic proximity and common neighborhood. There is evidence both that people moved from one village to another and that full assimilation took time. Some of the taxpayers listed in the *Cadaster of Thebes* seem to have moved from one village to another. For example, "widow Poletiane, daughter of Basil, the son of Chage, from Anysos," is listed under the heading for the village of Tache. Her father, "Basil, son of Chage, from Anysos" is listed under the heading for the *topos* Kyberiate.¹²⁶ Kyberiate had previously been owned in its entirety by Baanos the notary who gave Basil a portion of the *topos* as dowry for his daughter, presumably Poletiane's mother. Hence we can deduce that Basil and Poletiane were not recent newcomers from Anysos.¹²⁷ It seems that Poletiane's grandfather Chage came from Anysos and the identification with Anysos was passed on for two generations. This small family history may display the movement of population as members of the same family owned land in at least three different villages over the course of three generations. Another taxpayer registered in the village of Tache was George "from Douchos, son of John Kampos, lives in Thebes."¹²⁸ George lived in Thebes and owned land in Tache, but was still "from" Douchos. Villages therefore could form a lasting part of a household's identity. When "George from Douchos" met another person from Douchos while living in Thebes, it is likely that they acknowledged some common association. The geographic proximity that made people neighbors therefore served as a means of forging connections between households.

The strength of the bond between neighboring households within villages has been a matter of debate. In the first half of the twentieth century evidence for villages having a particular tax status, especially mutual responsibility of villagers for tax payments, was elaborated into more general theories of community solidarity and collectivity. Byzantine rural villages were seen as forming cohesive "communes." The interest of nineteenth- and twentieth-century historians in historical precedents for communism made the Byzantine village community a subject of considerable study.

---

¹²⁵ Kekaumenos, Litavrin, §41; Wassiliewsky, 45.
¹²⁶ *Cadaster of Thebes*, §§vf9 and 11f4.   ¹²⁷ Neville, "Local provincial elites," 222–7, 256–63.
¹²⁸ *Cadaster of Thebes*, §vf3.

Evidence for the fiscal solidarity of the villages is ambiguous, however, and does not necessarily imply collectivity. Kazhdan's assessment was that:

> Village solidarity did exist, but it did not consist . . . in collective sovereign rights to the soil. The salient feature of Byzantine agrarian relations was the peasant's perpetual possession of his allotment, of which the economic independence was marked by a surrounding brick wall. The common rights of the villagers consisted primarily of neighbors' rights *in re aliena*, such as making hay and collecting chestnuts on the neighboring lands. They had the right of pre-emption, if neighboring land was sold, and were liable for the taxes of their impoverished or absconding neighbors by virtue of the law of "common responsibility" . . . In general, however, the individualist marks of the Byzantine village community seem to have predominated.[129]

Kazhdan's views have been influential, to the point that a recent treatment of rural economy noted that "while the community aspect of the village has previously been exaggerated, it is now probably underestimated."[130]

For the imperial administration, "village," *chorion*, was both a technical term for a particular kind of fiscal district and a general term for rural settlements.[131] The village fiscal district was a paper community that did not need to have any correspondence to a community of people bound by some sense of common identity. In the *Marcian Treatise* the technical fiscal meaning coexists with the more common-sense definition of a village as a place where people live together and whose houses are "situated in a neighborly fashion near each other."[132]

A reasonable way to make sense of the information indicating both competition and community feeling in rural villages is to see those villages as collections of households. The households were independent and competed for resources. At the same time they provided mutual help for those tasks that required cooperation and they were natural allies. Individual exploitation was the primary mode of operation among peasant cultivators and all endeavors were individual when they could be.[133] One of the healing miracles that took place at Luke's tomb involved a young man who hurt himself by trying to pull a heavy stone out of a storage pit he was digging. The man knew that the stone was heavy but did not want to ask his neighbors for help.[134] The author of the *Marcian Treatise* described the expansion of settlement in the fiscal district of a village as a matter of the growth and competition between families. Large families had the opportunity to divide

---

[129] Kazhdan and Constable, *People and Power in Byzantium*, 31.
[130] Lefort, "Rural economy," 279.   [131] See Kaplan, *Les Hommes et la terre*, 95–101.
[132] *Marcian Treatise*, 115.15–16.   [133] Kaplan, *Les Hommes et la terre*, 203–5.
[134] *Life of Luke*, 217–18.

Provincial households 95

property into two or more households. Not all neighbors would have equal claim on the common areas of village. There is a strong presumption of inequality among the villagers.[135]

While the man in the *Life of Luke* who injured himself rather than ask for help testifies to the desire for independent action, he also serves as a reminder that mutual help was essential. Neighbors in rural communities naturally helped each other with those tasks that benefited from collective action. Neighbors also celebrated weddings and festivals together. Familial households in close geographic proximity would provide natural allies for each other.

A group of neighboring households could ally to bring suit against a mutual enemy. In collectively bringing suit, the neighboring households of the village became "a legal entity, de facto if not de jure."[136] The surviving legal material makes clear that even when a village formed one legal party it consisted of individual households acting in mutual interest. The legal party of the village was defined in the documents by the signatures of the *oikodespotai*, the heads of household.[137] An act of exchange between the monastery of Kolobou and the village of Hierissos opened with seven signatures and twenty-one signs of inhabitants of Hierissos. The declaration of intent in the document was made by twenty-three specifically named individuals and "the remaining inhabitants of our *kastron*."[138] Some of the twenty-three people listed in the body of the document are not among the twenty-eight people who signed and marked it. Neither the group that signed the document nor the group that was listed in the body of text can be considered a precisely selected delegation. There seems to have been considerable latitude regarding who was able to sign and how they would define themselves.[139] The officials making up the document were comfortable writing down twenty-three specific names and leaving the rest of the members of the village vague. Another document was signed by

---

[135] *Marcian Treatise*, 115.   [136] Lefort, "Rural economy," 279–80.
[137] For example, the inhabitants of Siderokausia were one party, *meros*, in their fight with Iviron. The list of *oikodespotai* varied slightly in two documents regarding the fight with the monastery. The villagers are also called the "crowd" and described as rustic and all talking at once. They are called a crowd in a quite formal context of dividing up the taxes owed by the monastery and the villagers. The villagers are called a community, *koinotes*, only once. *Iviron I*, p. 162, no. 9.
[138] *Ibid.*, pp. 129–34, no. 5.
[139] The signatories included five presbyters, one reader, two deacons, two clerics, one *protos*, one *deuteros*, and two *oikodespotai*. Loiveanos called himself an *oikodespotes* in his signature and simply Loiveanos in the text. Some men have surnames and others not. Some identified themselves as brothers of other people. Some of the heads of household who signed the act of exchange between Hierissos and Kolobou had descendants who are known from other acts to have made significant donations to Iviron and Lavra. *Iviron I*, p. 132, no. 5.

a much larger group of seventy-four men representing the inhabitants of Hierissos.[140] These seventy-four men may have been nearly all of the heads of household in the village. In other legal acts, when members of a "village community" had to provide testimony, they were listed as individuals.[141]

In a dispute between the monastery of Roudabon and the village of Radochostas over the monastery's mill, the village similarly was treated collectively as one party. This guarantee was written in 1008 and recorded the payments previously made by the monastery for the land and a firm boundary description. The document opens with the signatures and marks of fourteen men who must have been acting as representatives for the rest of the village: "We the inhabitants of the village Radochostas, made clear above, making the sign of the honored and life-giving cross with our own hands, guarantee to you the monks of the most holy monastery of Roudabon..."[142] The monks had purchased village land at two different times, paying first 40 *nomismata* and then two more. That the land was purchased from the village as a whole through the representation of fourteen members means that the villagers must have had some confidence in the judgment of their representatives. The arrangements affected a river whose water may have been an important resource for many different households. The text contains no information about how the money was distributed among the villagers. It may have been a contentious process. While the sale and the agreement were made between the monastery and the villagers, it is unclear whether all the villagers shared in the decisions and benefits of the agreement. From the point of view of the monastery, the implementation of the agreement was an internal village problem. The men who signed the agreement must have had some authority to act as representatives for the other villagers but we do not know how they achieved their status as representatives.

According to the *Marcian Treatise*, typically some neighbors in a village did not possess the enclosed areas, *enthuria peribolia*, equally with the other villagers.[143] The "enclosed areas" seem to have been either some sort of common pasture used by all or nearly all the villagers, or the central land of the village. It is unclear why some villagers would be excluded from use of the common land. Perhaps a group of families living together for many generations did not want to share their resources with newcomers.

---

[140] *Ibid.*, pp. 117–29, no. 4.   [141] *Ibid.*, pp. 169–72, no. 10.
[142] These fourteen men were not the only inhabitants of the village. Twelve of the fourteen signatures were written by the scribe. Three of the villagers identified themselves as *oikodespotes* and two as *presbyteros*. Lavra, p. 135–9, no. 14.
[143] *Marcian Treatise*, 115.26.

Perhaps use of the common areas required a maintenance contribution that some people were too poor to make. Those who did not equally possess these enclosed areas may not have been much poorer than their neighbors, but they had a different kind of membership in that community. In legal decisions the enclosed areas naturally would be referred to as lands that the village held in common. So when we read of a village collectively buying land or bringing suit, we may assume that not every member of the village in fact shared in that land or assented to that decision.

Sharing a common neighborhood therefore could prove to be both a strong bond between households when they acted for mutual defense and a weak bond when those houses were in competition. The bond between houses created by neighborliness varied greatly, depending on the task at hand. Proximity may have been a relatively weak way of connecting households when compared to friendship, marriage, godparenting, and monasticism. On the other hand, for the great majority of people, neighbors formed the natural pool from which to choose friends, spouses, god-children, and spiritual fathers.

A final way of entering into an association with another household was to form an economic relationship by renting land or working for wages on the property of a landowning household. As mentioned above, it may have been beneficial for families to become the *paroikoi* of a landowning household. Rents may have been less burdensome than land-taxes and a local landowner could provide increased security.[144] This kind of association had a far greater hierarchical disparity than associations formed by marriage and fictive kinship. Members of the *paroikoi* households would certainly not have full familial access to the landowning household, but they could expect the landowner to listen to their complaints. Michael Choirosphaktes responded forcefully to complaints made by the peasants on his estates that their fields were being damaged by the livestock on an estate belonging to Nikon's monastery.[145] Michael gathered his men and burned down the fences and sheepfolds of the monastic estate. In the conflict between the Mavroi household and the *protospatharios* Michael, described in the *Life of Paul of Latros*, Michael fought on the pretext of protecting the peasants on the estates he administered.[146] The landowner could also provide powerful advocacy for the *paroikoi* in their dealings with the fiscal administration. Prominent provincial households could call on alliances of kinship or friendship with members of the central imperial administration to alleviate

---

[144] Lefort, "Rural economy," 237–8.   [145] *Life of Nikon*, 194–200.   [146] *Life of Paul*, 123.

the fiscal burdens that ultimately fell on the peasant *paroikoi* associated with their households.

These means of forming associations between households allowed individuals to have fairly expansive networks of people whose assistance they could draw on. Such connections could be fairly horizontal, as when the village households acted together to bring suit against the grand monastic households, or strikingly vertical, as when provincial landowners petitioned important officials in Constantinople for relief from the fiscal demands on their *paroikoi*. Most of the associations formed by marriage and fictive kinship would have been contracted by households of roughly equal prominence. Making an advantageous match was the goal of everyone's marriage policy, but for that very reason one could not hope to marry into a household much more prominent than one's own. The associations of baptismal sponsorship, *adelphopoiia*, and friendship may have allowed for somewhat greater disparities in prestige. The relationships of service were the ones that created strong vertical links between households. As we shall see, authority was created in part by being associated with people in high places and so such vertical ties could be of great importance.

CHAPTER 4

Provincial households and the imperial administration

The imperial administration was embodied in individuals who, as titled imperial servants, had roles as subordinates in the imperial household. They also had roles within their own households as sons, brothers, or *oikodespotai*. The natural desire of the people in the administration to participate well in all of their roles made the imperial administration malleable. Some provincial households had numerous points of approach for interacting with officials and crafting their relationship with the imperial administration. Pressures of friendship, social obligation, and bribery were commonly and effectively brought to bear on officials. The authority of provincial officials could be circumvented by informal appeals to people with ties to the central authorities in Constantinople. Prominent provincial households frequently made use of personal relationships with people who far outranked the local provincial administrators in terms of access to the emperor, and hence real power. The central administration's essential ignorance and apathy about provincial matters, combined with the ability of some provincial parties to seek intercession and to make accusations, allowed provincial people to manipulate their relationship with the administration and their provincial rivals.

This chapter aims to illuminate the options open to provincial households to negotiate with imperial officials with a view to understanding how authority was actually exercised in provincial society. Obviously, not all provincial households enjoyed this ability to resist and negotiate with imperial officials. The ideal relationships and vocabulary of the *oikos* could be applied with equal suitability to grand and humble households. Yet, most of our sources for provincial society display households in unequal relationships of status and authority. The great majority of households at the lower end of the scale would not have opportunities for interacting with imperial officials. The few households at the very top end of the hierarchy would not avail themselves of the methods described below because they would call directly on the emperor. This examination for the most part, therefore, is of provincial households with at least some ability to articulate a position to an official and to make arguments that could sway official opinion.

Many of the officials in question seem to have become enmeshed in the power politics of local provincial settings, if they were not members of provincial society already. The centralization of power in Constantinople meant that the authority of provincial officials depended on the strength of their position in the capital more than on their formal rank and office. An official who was going to return immediately to Constantinople had far more coercive power in the provinces – so long as he was there – than one who was required to stay. Once officials became resident in provincial settings they became part of provincial society and subject to the local pressures modulating imperial authority. Kekaumenos clearly acknowledged the distinction between holding imperial office and living privately. His advice for those with imperial posts and those living privately, however, deals with identical pressures and dynamics of power. He had no sense that holding an official position allowed one to behave with impunity in provincial settings. On the contrary, the further away from the capital the more circumspect one needed to be. In the hagiographical sources it is frequently difficult to determine whether powerful and important characters held any formal imperial offices.[1] The system of honorary titles of course meant that a great many people had a formal association with the imperial government without any functional role in the administration. In interactions between provincial officials and prominent provincial households frequently the officials were also heads of provincial households and often they did not hold a monopoly on the personal contacts with the imperial court that bestowed effective power.

The officials' dual responsibility for both judicial and financial administration formed another important element in their relationship with provincial society. Despite the continuity of the tradition of Roman law in Constantinople, provincial justice was inherently compromised by the multiple tasks of the provincial administration. Judges were provincial administrators who had a variety of responsibilities.[2] Until the reforms of Alexios

---

[1] Did, for example, the "*protos* of Samos," whose hunting dogs cornered Paul, have an imperial office, or was he simply considered the most important man on the island? *Life of Paul*, 119. Did Stephen, who was "always entrusted with public affairs and community services" by the people of Sparta, have a position recognized by the emperors? *Life of Nikon*, 228. Both men probably had imperial honorary titles.

[2] Saradi, "The Byzantine tribunals," 170–4. Roman law, while formally in effect until the end of the empire, can by no means be assumed to have been applied rigorously in the tenth and eleventh centuries even in Constantinople. Kazhdan, "Do we need a new history of Byzantine law?," 1–28.

Komnenos, there was no distinction between the fiscal and judicial administration in the provinces.³ In the ninth and tenth centuries the *strategos*, or general, of a province had military, judicial, and administrative functions. In the eleventh century the judicial and administrative functions were given to provincial judges. One set of civil officials had jurisdiction over both financial and judicial civil matters. For the most part, legal education was acquired privately along with grammar and rhetoric. Specialized legal training was not required for judges, although general competence in reading and writing formal documents was appropriate. Judges seem to have had prior appointments either in the imperial chancellery or as private secretaries and notaries.⁴ Imperial sponsorship of a school of law in Constantinople in the middle of the eleventh century increased the sophistication and specialization of legal training.⁵

The lack of division between judicial and fiscal administration created a natural conflict of interests. One official could have a duty both to "augment imperial revenue" and to "administer impartial justice."⁶ The interests of provincial justice and imperial wealth extraction frequently did not correspond. Michael Psellos recommended a candidate for a post as a provincial judge because "he will not only distinguish himself justly in his appointed theme, but if there is any opportunity for increasing the emperor's treasure, he will increase it and add it to the treasury."⁷ Fines assessed in civil lawsuits were due to the fisc, which also profited from confiscations resulting from criminal or treasonous activity. The fiscal administration maintained the paperwork that was used to judge disputes over land and the fisc itself was frequently a party in such cases.

In Byzantine tradition, judgmental righteousness was commonly tempered by gracious accommodation. Judges were not obliged to adhere to the dictates of imperial law absolutely in every case because of the Byzantine legal concept of *oikonomia*.⁸ *Oikonomia* literally means proper household

---

³ Magdalino, "Justice and finance," 93–116.
⁴ In the letters of Psellos, Weiss found that men were appointed as judges who had previously served in the chancellery as *asekretai, hypogrammatoi, chartoularioi,* and *grammatikoi*; and in the "notariat" as *taboullarioi, symboularoigraphoi,* and *nomikoi*. Weiss, *Ostromische Beamte in Spiegel der Schriften des Michael Psellos*, 24–8. Morris, "Dispute settlement in the Byzantine provinces in the tenth century," 137–40.
⁵ Wanda Wolska-Conus, "Les écoles de Psellos et de Xiphilin sous Constantin IX Monomaque," *TM* 6 (1976): 223–43. Saradi, "The Byzantine tribunals," 192–9.
⁶ Magdalino, "Justice and finance," 93.
⁷ K. N. Sathas, ed., *Mesaionike Bibliotheke*, 7 vols. (Venice and Paris, 1872–94), vol. v, pp. 399–400. Quoted and translated in Magdalino, "Justice and finance," 94.
⁸ John H. Erickson, "Oikonomia in Byzantine canon law," in *Law, Church and Society: Essays in Honor of Stephan Kuttner*, ed. Kenneth Pennington and Robert Somerville (Philadelphia, 1977),

management, or husbandry. It is the key term in Orthodox theology for describing God's action in the history of salvation in the Incarnation. As a righteous judge, God recognizes human sinfulness, but through *oikonomia*, God responds with grace and forgiveness. Because of human sinfulness, the proper management of creation calls for God to be gracious and forgiving. *Oikonomia* became a legal concept through the influence of ecclesiastical leaders who endeavored to imitate God's grace in the face of human failings in dealing with political and theological opponents. Those desiring *oikonomia* acknowledged their guilt and asked for an abrogation of legal penalties. Proper management of the Orthodox household required, for example, that repentant iconoclast bishops be received into communion. The rigor of law could be relaxed to accommodate human moral failings when such a relaxation would bring greater benefit to the household of the Church, empire, or creation.

The pervasiveness of *oikonomia* made rigorous application of legal dictates more or less optional for Byzantine judges. The theological and canonical idea of *oikonomia* seems not infrequently to have become a justification for relaxing law at the judges' discretion.[9] The character of Byzantine law was such that the virtues of a good judge did not necessarily depend on accurate knowledge or application of written law.[10] In one assessment:

> Byzantine law was not rigid but flexible, and its results depended on various extrajudicial principles: Christian mercy, imperial command, social conditions, and – last but not least – *philia* that by no means was concealed or disguised; the judges were supposed to act under the pressure of personal relations.[11]

One consequence of this concept of law was to increase the importance of lines of friendship, contact, and solidarity at the expense of legal standing. One's experience of the judicial system would be entirely dependent on whom one knew and what favors one was owed.

The importance of personal connections was made even more pronounced by the reactive and responsive nature of the Byzantine administration. The administration could respond to appeals for judgment, if

---

225–36; Gilbert Dagron, "La règle et l'exception. Analyse de la notion d'économie," in *Religiöse Devianz: Untersuchungen zu sozialen, rechtlichen und theologischen Reaktionen auf religiöse Abweichung im westlichen und östlichen Mittelalter*, ed. Dieter Simon (Frankfurt, 1990), 1–18. Carolina Cupane, "Appunti per uno studio dell'oikonomia ecclesiastica a Bisanzio," *JÖB* 38 (1998): 53–73.

[9] Dagron, "La règle et l'exception," 17.

[10] Alexander Kazhdan, "Some observations on the Byzantine concept of law," in *Law and Society in Byzantium, Ninth–Twelfth Centuries*, ed. Angeliki Laiou and Dieter Simon (Washington, DC, 1994), 206; H. J. Scheltema, "Byzantine law," in *The Cambridge Medieval History*, vol. IV: *The Byzantine Empire*, Part II: *Government, Church and Civilization*, ed. J. M. Hussey (Cambridge, 1966), 70.

[11] Kazhdan, "Some observations on the Byzantine concept of law," 212.

people in the provinces were able to excite the interest of an official. Those who were able to call on friendships or other associations with officials would be better placed to motivate the administration to act in their favor. Aside from cases in which the fiscal branch of the government stood to profit, however, the administration was not proactive in settling disputes or regulating behavior. In the tenth century, imperial laws frequently were issued in response to legal questions brought to the emperor's attention by imperial officials.[12]

The judiciary's role in mediating local conflicts was effectively undercut by the circumstance that most fines for misconduct were paid to the fisc and the mandate of the judiciary to increase revenues. It was frequently advantageous to let imperial officials remain in the dark about one's landholdings. This would create a natural reluctance on the part of at least some provincial parties to engage the official authorities. Because the provincial judicial administration was not proactive, people who wished to settle their disagreements outside of the formal provincial courts were welcome to do so. Rather than a source of adjudication, the judiciary became an arena where accusations of misconduct or threats of accusations were used by provincial rivals to manipulate each other. The episode in the *vita* of Paul of Latros about the conflict between the Mavroi family and the *protospatharios* Michael illustrates the use of judicial accusation in provincial disputes. When one of the Mavroi was killed, they made an accusation against Michael in Constantinople, and Michael was condemned to death.[13] While the Mavroi are portrayed as the instigators of the conflict, they were able to use the imperial administration against Michael by making a false accusation. Paul's biographer thought it plausible for the Mavroi to act lawlessly and violently in the provinces without fear that the imperial administration would know about their behavior.

Another case in which someone tried to involve the judicial administration in a local dispute is preserved in the archives of the Great Lavra of Athos. A retired military officer, the *droungarios* John, appealed to the judicial administration to take his side in a property dispute by invoking the imperial legislation on preemption. He is described as having violently attacked the monk Stephen and contrived through various machinations to nullify Stephen's purchase of land. When he and Stephen were brought before the judge, he claimed to be acting on behalf of imperial interests.

---

[12] Marie Theres Fögen, "Legislation in Byzantium: a political and bureaucratic technique," in *Law and Society in Byzantium, Ninth–Twelfth Centuries*, ed. Angeliki Laiou and Deiter Simon (Washington, DC, 1994), 63.

[13] *Life of Paul*, 123.

John's argument was not accepted because "no advantage would be brought to the fisc and there would be a cause of great damage to the poor neighbors."[14] Scholarship on this case has tried to determine whether John was correct in appealing to the laws of preemption.[15] Regardless of whether the laws should have applied in this case, it is clear that John was trying to enlist the interests of the fiscal officials on his side of the fight. One of the stated reasons for dismissing John's accusation was that finding in his favor would not benefit the fisc.

Provincial officials could of course make decisions based on what would benefit themselves as well as the fisc. Kekaumenos' advice to provincial judges suggests that officials were commonly bribed and that he considered judicial corruption a serious moral failing:

> If you are a provincial judge, do not reach out with your eyes and hands to take gifts. He who gapes after gifts wanders in darkness of ignorance, even if he is educated and full of wisdom and full of knowledge. Rather be satisfied with what you have from the [salary] agreement. They did not send you to reap money, but to judge the unjust. Be partial to no one in judgment out of affection, but if it is some dear friend of yours you are about to condemn, decline this case and do not judge unjustly. For in the end you will be ashamed and your friend will be condemned by the city judges. If you look for gain, they who do not give you gifts will not appear good in your eyes, even if they are very worthy. And those who do give will appear good to you and your spirit will be lenient with them, even if they are murderers . . . For hear what Habukuk shouted to the Lord "There was a judgment from my enemy," he said, "and the judge took gifts and because of this the law was scattered and not brought forth to a perfect judgment, so that the impious oppressed the just one. For the sake of this a twisted judgment will be brought forth."[16] And if someone should come to you giving you gifts without a reason and saying, "Take these, I give these to you out of love for you," do not take them. For even if he does not ask anything of you then, after you have taken them he will ask to you to make some irregular document for him. And if you do this, you will be condemned by God and by the emperor and by the city judges. But if you do not do this, when summoned by him you will return the things given to you with shame.[17]

While Kekaumenos' quotation of the prophet Habukuk serves as a reminder of perennial corruption of judicial systems, there are aspects of his attitude that reflect the peculiarities of his own society. The concern with

---

[14] *Lavra*, pp. 97–102, no. 4, lines 16–21.
[15] Lemerle, *Agrarian History*, 157–60. George Ostrogorski, "The peasant's pre-emption right: an abortive reform of the Macedonian emperors," *Journal of Roman Studies* 37 (1947): 119–22.
[16] Habukuk 1.3-4. Kekaumenos' quotation is reasonably close to the Septuagint text. He added "gifts."
[17] Kekaumenos, Litavrin, §5; Wassiliewsky, 6.

the city judges, *oi politikoi dikastoi*, indicates that provincial judges could get in trouble for flagrant acts of injustice. I suspect that by "city judges" Kekaumenos meant those in Constantinople who could rehear provincial cases if settlements were not satisfactory. That their wrath is named along with that of God and the emperor suggests that they could cause considerable damage to one's career. Their authority and the attendant danger in getting caught notwithstanding, the main objection raised to accepting bribes is that such behavior is morally wrong. Kekaumenos' exhortations to justice seem grounded in an understanding that corruption and injustice were bad, but not rare.

Despite these drawbacks, people frequently wanted the imperial judicial administration to make legal judgments settling provincial disputes, and took considerable steps to contact and awaken the interest of the imperial government. When Luke's family settled on the north coast of the Gulf of Corinth after fleeing from attacks on Aigina, the native inhabitants tried to drive them away because the newcomers were encroaching on their land. Luke's grandfather went to Constantinople to get the imperial administration to establish a legal border between the villages.[18] Settling refugees productively would have been in the best fiscal interests of the imperial administration. Yet even here provincial people had to undertake considerable effort to excite the attention of the government.

The apathy of provincial administrators could cause difficulties. One extended boundary dispute between the inhabitants of Hierissos and the monks on Mount Athos had its origin in the negligent behavior of the high-ranking fiscal official, the *epoptes* or inspector, of Thessalonike. In 943 the *epoptes* explained that the border of the Holy Mountain was in dispute because he had previously sold land to the inhabitants of Hierissos without documenting how far the territory extended. The only explanation the *epoptes* offered for his failure to record the boundary was that the land had not been disputed at the time he had made the sale. The dispute was protracted by the lack of firm evidence to back the testimony of either party.[19]

While most of our evidence shows provincial parties seeking out official help, contending parties could easily have agreed to avoid the imperial judiciary. Religious prohibitions against taking oaths may have discouraged people from using the official judicial system. When in 1033 John the Metropolitan of Philippi and the *strategos* Nicholas discovered that a monk

---

[18] *Life of Luke*, 160–1.
[19] Morris, "Dispute settlement in the Byzantine provinces in the tenth century," 134–5.

had sold them both the same vineyard, they took the case to the provincial judge. Because the judge was going to demand that both parties take oaths, John decided to come to an agreement with Nicholas outside of court.[20] Kekaumenos advised his readers to avoid taking oaths, even if they were in the right, presumably because of the Christian injunction against the practice.[21]

It seems fairly clear that the less the fisc knew about a party's holdings the better. Constantine and Maria Phasoules had a long-running dispute over territory with the Panteleemon monastery.[22] Constantine said that he had inherited the land from his parents and that he had paid a special military land-tax on it. The monks of Panteleemon said they had bought it from a third party, the *spatharokandidatos* Leo Phouskoulos. Constantine and Maria made a complaint to "Leo the famous consul, judge of the Velon of the hippodrome of Voleron, Strymon, and Thessalonike." Both parties went to court, but Leo did not hear the case. Instead, in 1058, "some God-loving men" mediated for them and arbitrated a settlement whereby Panteleemon admitted that the land belonged to the Phasoules and paid them 10 *nomismata* for half of it, 8 *modioi*. The land was not sold, but ceded to Panteleemon, and Constantine would continue to pay the taxes on it. The amount of money paid for the land would be extremely high unless one considered that Constantine would continue to pay the military tax on the land after it had been ceded to Panteleemon.[23] The parties may have come to this strange arrangement to avoid having the civil judge examine the case too closely. The military land-tax that was due on the property was a vestige of the ninth- and tenth-century system of having soldiers supply themselves from their property. In the tenth century, laws were issued restricting the sale of military land because the military estates had to be large enough to fund a soldier.[24] By the eleventh century the burden of military supply had been commuted to cash taxation payments that funded a more professional army. While there was no question of Constantine himself getting called up for military service, it may have been legally complex for him to sell the land because of its association with the military obligation. It may be that the parties came to this agreement without waiting for a decision from the judge because it was legally dubious, and it may have been advantageous to keep the imperial judges out of it. On the other hand, the administration had little incentive to enforce the laws regarding military land once the burden had been commuted to a tax

---

[20] *Vatopedi*, pp. 87–90, no. 6. [21] Kekaumenos, Litavrin, §37; Wassiliewsky, 40. Matthew 5:33–7.
[22] Nicolas Oikonomides, ed., *Actes de Dionysiou* (Paris, 1968), p. 35–42, no. 1. [23] *Ibid.*, p. 39, no. 1.
[24] On the variety of possible purposes of this legislation see Magdalino, "Army and the land," 16–25.

payment. It is possible that Leo simply did not issue a decision in a timely fashion. The state judiciary may have been available but inconvenient, slow, or expensive.

The responsive nature of provincial administration, combined with the centralization of authority in Constantinople, meant that people frequently appealed directly to friends or relatives in the city rather than work through the local administration. Formalities of jurisdiction seem not to have been observed. Legal commentaries of the eleventh and especially the twelfth century display an interest in establishing which courts were competent for which cases.[25] Legal principle held that plaintiffs had to appear in the court, or *forum*, of the defendant's residence. Constantinople, however, could function as the *forum* for everyone in the empire.[26] Plaintiffs could choose to be tried in the place of their provincial residence or in the capital. The impression arising from provincial sources is that, if an unfavorable verdict was reached by one official, the aggrieved party appealed to a different authority.

When St. Lazaros of Mount Galesion needed support for his monastery he sent embassies to Constantinople. In his long-standing dispute with the bishop of Ephesus, Lazaros gained support by going around the bishop directly to the emperor.[27] Lazaros' biographer thought it was perfectly normal to circumvent the local ecclesiastical hierarchy and accused a monk who let the bishop know that Lazaros had sent an envoy to Constantinople of being another Judas.[28] In another example, the monastery of St. Hypatios on Mount Athos had procured from the emperor Constantine Doukas a *sigillion* that said that some territories belonging to the monastery of Vatopedi were unused. The monks of St. Hypatios took over the properties on this pretext, even though the monks of Vatopedi were the legal owners. Theodosios, the superior of Vatopedi, complained to the emperor, who ordered Patriarch Constantine Leichoudes to examine the problem. Leichoudes passed the case on to Niketas, the patriarchal *chartophylax*, who ruled that the *sigillion* of St. Hypatios was spurious and returned the land to Vatopedi. This judgment was sent to the *protos* of Athos. The superior

---

[25] The most basic principles were that defendants should be tried in the courts of their residence, and that bishops had jurisdiction over their monks and priests; the *eparch*, over guild-members; and military judges, over soldiers. Ruth Macrides, "The competent court," in *Law and Society in Byzantium, Ninth–Twelfth Centuries*, ed. Angeliki Laiou and Dieter Simon (Washington, DC, 1994), 117–30.

[26] *Ibid.*, 121.

[27] On the contention between the Metropolitan of Ephesus and Lazaros' monasteries see *Life of Lazaros*, 34–48.

[28] *Life of Lazaros*, 239.

of St. Hypatios then turned to the local civil tribunal and presented the *sigillion* again. This judge found in favor of St. Hypatios. Vatopedi appealed again to the emperor and to the patriarch, who wrote to the *protos* and told him to settle the matter.[29] The emperor was probably never particularly interested in the matter and so did not provide effective help to either party. That the situation hinged on the possible forgery of an imperial decree does not seem to have made the case any more interesting to the emperor.

A dispute between the monasteries of Vatopedi and Philadelphos similarly saw several stages of appeal. The superiors of Vatopedi and Philadelphos had jointly appealed to Basil II to intervene in their dispute. Basil ordered the *magistros* and *domestikos ton scholon* Nikephoros Ouranos to settle the matter. Ouranos in turn passed the task on to a monk, Theophylakt. Theophylakt's decision that Joseph, the superior of Philadelphos, should leave immediately was approved by the *protos* and the other superiors of Athos and written up as an act of the *protos*.[30] Joseph, however, did not accept Theophylakt's judgment and he appealed again to the emperor. This time Basil passed the decision on to the patriarch Sergios. Sergios declined to make a decision because the monks of Vatopedi were not there and he only had the testimony of the envoys from Philadelphos. Sergios wrote a letter to the *protos* asking whether Joseph had really been thrown out justly. The *protos* reminded both parties that it was unseemly for monks to appear to fight continually and negotiated a settlement whereby Joseph was paid for the property taken over by Vatopedi. The final act of sale created a settlement that was substantially different from the one issued by Ouranos' monk Theophylakt.[31] Theophylakt may have been a partisan of Vatopedi or influenced by one or simply bribed.

The emperors commonly responded to appeals for intervention and judgment by asking someone to look into the matter without taking much interest in the outcome. John, the superior of Iviron monastery, took a complaint about a land dispute to Basil II. John thought it necessary to appeal to the emperor rather than to either his bishop or the locally responsible judge. Basil was insufficiently interested to do more than delegate the matter to the provincial judge and the inspector of the imperial estates.[32] The dispute involved an imperial estate that was to have been granted to a military commander, Basil the *tourmarch* of Bulgaria. The *episkeptites* Photios, who had been appointed to give Basil the *tourmarch* his estate, had given him both the property specified in the imperial order and another property

---

[29] *Vatopedi*, pp. 94–102, no. 8.   [30] *Ibid.*, pp. 67–70, no. 2.   [31] *Ibid.*, pp. 71–6, no. 3.
[32] *Iviron I*, pp. 163–72, no. 10.

belonging to Iviron. Photios had helped Basil to more territory, apparently with little concern about disobeying the emperor. Had they not taken the land from a powerful monastery whose superior had ready access to the palace, they almost certainly would have got away with it. As it was, the illegality of the matter was glossed over in the judgment restoring Iviron's rights.

The impression arising from the Athonite documents is that people appealed for judgments to the highest authority they could reach rather than to the local provincial judge. The letters of Theophylakt of Ochrid indicate that in his conflicts with fiscal officials Theophylakt did not appeal directly to the imperial officials who had formal jurisdiction over the problems at hand. In the course of one long and complex dispute, the only time Theophylakt mentioned an official was when he appealed to the official's father for a favorable word.[33] Rather, Theophylakt used his network of friends and appealed directly to the emperor's kin for intervention.[34]

The letters of Theophylakt asking for intervention with fiscal officials use the language of entreaty and petition that may have been characteristic of these various requests. In addressing Adrian, the Grand Domestic and brother of emperor Alexios Komnenos, Theophylakt wrote, "'Who am I, Lord, my Lord, that you loved me as much as this!' So to you I cry now what David then cried to God."[35] While not building quite so explicit an analogy between the powerful person and God, other letters also emphasize the disparity in power between Theophylakt and the person whose help he needs.[36] Theophylakt reminded one person of his place in an even greater hierarchy by ending the letter with the prayer: "May the Mother of God, to whom belongs land and property now suffering vexations, protect you from all vexations above."[37]

Travel to Constantinople played an extremely important role in provincial conflicts. By going to the center of power one had a better chance of being heard, and, equally important, of nullifying the slander of one's competitors. After the Mavroi lost to the *protospatharios* Michael in violent encounters, they made a formal complaint against him in Constantinople,

---

[33] Margaret Mullett, "Patronage in action: the problems of an eleventh-century archbishop," in *Church and People in Byzantium*, ed. Rosemary Morris (Birmingham, 1990), 127.
[34] Harvey, "Land and taxation," 152–4. Mullett, *Theophylact of Ochrid: Reading the Letters of a Byzantine Archbishop*, 212–13.
[35] Letter 85.3-4, citing 2 Samuel 7:18; Paul Gautier, ed., *Théophylacte d'Achrida, II, Lettres* (Thessalonike, 1986), 445.
[36] Mullett, *Theophylact of Ochrid: Reading the Letters of a Byzantine Archbishop*, 188, 196–222; Gautier, ed., *Théophylacte d'Achrida, II, Lettres*, 143, 163, 171, 465, 493, 499.
[37] Letter 26.30-1; Gautier, ed., *Théophylacte d'Achrida, II, Lettres*, 217.

which led to his condemnation.³⁸ According to Paul's biographer, they slandered Michael as the instigator of the conflicts. Had Michael thought to go to Constantinople first, he may have been able to have the head of their household condemned. When Glykeria and John found themselves in the midst of a vigorous struggle with their local bishop about the control of the monastery they founded, John went to Constantinople to get support.³⁹ When St. Luke's grandfather went to Constantinople he was able to present his petition for official adjudication of the dispute between his immigrant community and the established residents. The appropriate government official was sent out to assess and to divide the land, creating a peaceful border between the two communities.⁴⁰ On the northwest shore of the Gulf of Corinth, the established residents exerted enough authority and physical pressure to cause the immigrants to consider another move. Yet they were nothing in the face of the imperial authorities Luke's grandfather was able to marshal because he went to the imperial city.

Provincial parties could presume upon the emperor's inattention and ignore imperial judgments. Several monks took advantage of being in Constantinople for the occasion of the new emperor's coronation to make appeals for help in disputes with other monasteries on Mount Athos. In 1057 the emperor yielded judgment over all matters of dispute among monasteries of Mount Athos to the *protos*, except for one case regarding the monastery of Panteleemon, in which he made a personal judgment.⁴¹ The *protos* and the other superiors, however, did not accept the emperor's decision in the case. They called for their own investigation and judgment. Our surviving document describes their process of investigation and solution, which in the end differed from the imperial judgment. This was not a matter of quietly ignoring an imperial decision. The superiors decided to ignore the imperial ruling, described doing so in an official document, signed it, and had a copy made. In another case the *protos* was ordered by the emperor to help a particular monastery regain land that, in the emperor's judgment, had been usurped by another monastery.⁴² Again the *protos* and council of superiors did not execute the emperor's orders but made an investigation and created a settlement between the monasteries that was not as one-sided as that promulgated by the emperor.

When the emperors were interested they could settle an issue. In some cases the emperors did respond forcefully to appeals for intercession. For example, in 1089 Alexios Komnenos sent his companion Theodore Senachereim to Mount Athos with a letter and instructions to reinstate

---

³⁸ *Life of Paul*, 123.   ³⁹ *Lavra*, pp. 155–61, no. 20.   ⁴⁰ *Life of Luke*, 161.
⁴¹ *Saint-Pantéléèmôn*, pp. 51–60, no. 5.   ⁴² *Ibid.*, pp. 39–50, no. 4.

Symeon as the superior of Xenophon. Symeon was a eunuch who had been expelled for bringing three beardless boys with him when he moved to Athos.[43] The superiors on Athos had been quite decisive in their rejection of Symeon. In this case, unlike others, Alexios made certain that his wishes would be carried out by sending a personal representative to watch Symeon get reinstated in his monastery. Theodore Senachereim had no formal government office, but as a "familiar" of the emperor, people paid attention to him. There is no question that if the emperor took an active interest in a situation, his view prevailed. Yet in the vast majority of provincial disputes, people could trust that unless they took significant, usually expensive, steps to excite the interest of the government, the imperial administration would not get involved.

The imperial agents who came knocking were the tax assessors and collectors. While they could not ignore the taxation officials, provincial households had substantial opportunities for trying to elicit favorable treatment by influencing and befriending them. They could spend infinitely more time positioning themselves with regard to fiscal policy than the civil administrators could on assessing their property. A study of monastic property has revealed that monasteries engaged in:

> the use of false claims or trickery either to increase a monastery's share in the holding of the *koinosis*, or, conversely, to escape from its fiscal responsibilities. A number of cases in the *Peira*, some of which may well date from the tenth century, demonstrate the remarkable ingenuity shown by the monastic *dynatoi* and they also illustrate one of their most telling characteristics: their grasp of the intricacies of Byzantine fiscal practice, the complexities of the cadasters and systems of land measurement and inspection which only a degree of literacy could bring.[44]

While we have far less documentation for lay households, it is unlikely that they were more scrupulous than the monastic households in their efforts to avoid taxation.

The *Marcian Treatise* indicates that tax assessors had considerable latitude over the execution of fiscal principles, giving them power over the tax bills of the people in their districts. It follows that people would do whatever they could to convince the officials to favor them. An inspector could choose whether to include "previously withdrawn exemptions" when calculating a district's *epibole*, or rate of taxation.[45] This decision would directly affect how much revenue the fisc demanded from a district. Different households

---

[43] *Xenophon*, pp. 61–75, no. 1.   [44] Morris, *Monks and Laymen*, 252.
[45] *Marcian Treatise*, 117.17–18. Oikonomides, *Fiscalité*, 56–61. Kaplan, *Les Hommes et la terre*, 207–10. Neville, "Marcian Treatise," 48.

could have radically different experiences with the fiscal administration, depending on the proclivities of their particular assessor and how open he was to their persuasion. The system of assessment described in the *Marcian Treatise* included opportunities for interacting with and persuading tax officials in different levels of the administration. People with property in different locations could ask to have their tax entries brought together so that they would only pay tax once.[46] Various surcharges were added on to the land-tax at the time of collection. These apparently grew out of mandatory gratuities paid for the provisioning of the tax collectors.[47] Because these surcharges were assessed in inverse proportion to the amount of land one had, the surcharges on many small pieces of land would be much higher than those on the same land taken as a whole. It therefore could be a great advantage if one could convince the assessor to do the extra work of consolidating one's fiscal information. In the *Cadaster of Thebes* there are both those who had the records of their holdings in different villages gathered into one place in the record book and others with holdings recorded separately under the rubric for each village. Those who had their holdings brought together into one entry had a lower total tax bill than if they had paid on each parcel separately.[48] The amount of tax assessed indicates that these were not particularly wealthy households. Presumably people were able to figure out the most advantageous way for their taxes to be registered and requested that change.

The *Marcian Treatise* also assumes that the leaders of monasteries would have a hand in crafting their tax assessments. They could ask to have a regular imperial donation, or *solemnion*, changed into a tax exemption, or *logisimon*:

> A tax exemption is then a stipend whenever – having been asked by the superiors, or the officers, or the monks in the pious house – the emperor, instead of giving a stipend to this or that pious house, orders and exempts the same amount from the standard tax of some villages not subject to the pious house, so that the exempted *nomismata* are provided by the villagers to the pious house instead of by the administrator for the sake of the former stipend.[49]

This significant change in accounting and collection of taxes was done at the request of the monastery. Imperial *chrysobulls* granting exemption to monasteries from duties and taxes were seen by monastic leaders as

---

[46] *Marcian Treatise*, 122.2–9.   [47] Morrisson, "La Logarikè," 419–64.
[48] Although the sample is too small and ambiguous to support firm conclusions, in every instance where we have a basis for judgment in the *Cadaster of Thebes* the taxpayers are registered in the manner most advantageous for themselves. Neville, "Marcian Treatise," 55–7.
[49] *Marcian Treatise*, 117.38–118.3.

transferable property. Athanasios of Lavra and John the Iberian traded *chrysobulls* that they had received from Basil II. Athanasios gave John a *chrysobull* exempting him from duties on boats of 6000 *modioi* tonnage. John gave Athanasios a *chrysobull* for property on the island of Neoi.[50] The monastic leaders swapped gifts to their best advantage.

Some time after Nikon's death, the superior of his monastery in Sparta went to Constantinople to elicit imperial privileges granting the monastery tax exemptions.[51] It is unlikely that Nikon had developed a significant following in Constantinople when this mission was undertaken. The embassy presumably called on people with ties to Sparta residing in the imperial city to help them make a case that Nikon's monastery deserved the tax exemptions granted to favored monasteries.

The form of tax relief called *sympatheia* was given "because of the great poverty of the payers or of the land for which the payments were given and because of the earnest request of the payers themselves and imperial philanthropy and the thorough investigation and just alleviation of the inspector."[52] Villagers needed to elicit imperial philanthropy and justice from the inspectors, as well as look as though they were on the brink of ruin and flight. Part of the reason the Byzantine fiscal administration has at times enjoyed a reputation for ruthless efficiency is that Byzantine people were fairly consistent in trying to look too poor to pay taxes. When the tax collector arrived at Nikon's monastery the monks explained that they had not saved any money and sought through earnest entreaties and supplications to obtain mercy and forgiveness of their taxes. After a miraculous intervention from Nikon, the official donated all the taxes he had collected in Sparta to the monastery.[53] Theophylakt described imperial tax inspectors as avaricious hunting dogs.[54]

Tax assessors were supposed to vary the rate of taxation according to the fertility of the land. Three different tax rates were made for the eastern Balkans, southwestern Anatolia, and the Anatolian plateau. These basic tax rates were further modified by the prevailing local usage, regarding either land fertility or fiscal privileges.[55] This would of course open up debate and negotiation between the landowners and the tax assessors about the fertility of the land. Assessors could not possibly inspect every field in a vast estate. We can assume they consistently were shown the least productive parts of every region. The license to vary the tax rate for a particular region at their

---

[50] *Iviron I*, pp. 135–9, no. 6.   [51] *Life of Nikon*, 184.   [52] *Marcian Treatise*, 119.9–13.
[53] *Life of Nikon*, 184.   [54] Gautier, ed., *Théophylacte d'Achrida, II, Lettres*, 485–7.
[55] Lefort, "Rural economy," 300. Jacques Lefort, *Géométries du fisc byzantin* (Paris, 1991), p. 62, §54.

discretion meant that the tax assessors in effect had great freedom to tax their friends lightly and others heavily.

The possibility of obtaining a more favorable tax rate meant that different people could have significantly different experiences with the fiscal administration. The monasteries of Lavra and Esphigmenou were in fact taxed at considerably different rates in the early twelfth century.[56] The monastic archives attest to vigorous efforts on the part of monks to maintain imperial favor manifested in fiscal privileges and intervention. Lay people presumably made similar efforts to cultivate people who could help them to a more favorable assessment. Both lay and monastic households that received special fiscal privileges were proactive in having those privileges confirmed when regimes changed.[57]

Provincial households used every available means to influence officials. The author of the *Marcian Treatise* explained how work should be done by "accurate notaries" and inspectors who cared about the truth.[58] Aside from simple bribery, provincial households could pressure individual assessors and collectors through friendship and threat of denunciation. Despite the theoretical backing of the imperial administration, the boldness of fiscal officials had to be tempered by the ability of provincial households to denounce them as unjust, corrupt, or treasonous. Kekaumenos warned against taking on procurement work for the imperial administration because one would not be able to collect anything from friends or peers:

For an imperial man will come to seek you to impress beasts of burden. You will be ashamed before one as a friend, before another as a relative, another as a dynast. Then you will send your man to take either *nomismata* or *obols* to the imperial man saying, "I did not find any." And he seizing you perhaps he will flog and do you damage in your country, and you who should have been honored will be dishonored and you will have blame for generations on end. Yet if you do not spare someone but press him into service, when the imperial man leaves, you have made enemies of your friends. Even if they do not all do wrong to you, at any rate one of them will harm you, taking the others as companions. Even ten or fifteen years afterward, those from whom you have taken either the *aerikon* [tax] or something else, not only unjustly but even justly, will lead you to the provincial court. And even if you speak good words, the judge is not a prophet, but he will make demands and send you to take oaths.[59]

Bonds of respect and local dynamics of power made the requisition of goods from neighbors and supporters socially impossible. Competing government and local responsibilities made such work inherently dangerous. For some

---

[56] Harvey, *Economic Expansion*, 95.   [57] *Iviron II*, pp. 240–4, no. 52.   [58] *Marcian Treatise*, 114.31.
[59] Kekaumenos, Litavrin, §37; Wassiliewsky, 40.

extraordinary impositions it is clear that the imperial administration needed to enlist the help of locally respected people in deciding who would have to pay what. Kekaumenos advised that if an imperial imposition was being made in a community and one was pressured by "everyone" to take charge of the collection, one should observe the process but insist that others take charge:

> For thus you will be able to excuse your friend and your man, and the demanding will be light for you and no one will say anything; and if some criticism arises from the community, it will fall on those who made the assignments and you will remain blameless. But if you make the assignments, you will be able to alleviate neither your friend nor your man and they will grumble against you that you are taking more than necessary. Yet if you do excuse your man there will be a great cry against you and they will call you a bribe-taker and tax-canceller.[60]

This advice attempts to find accommodation between the pressures to help friends and the dangers of denunciation. The imperial officials appear here to have demanded that a loosely defined community come up with something, leaving the difficult task of executing the imperial order to the contention of local households. The matter of collection may have been largely one of conflict between local households, some of which had obligations to the central administration.

The tax collectors came armed, and no doubt they did not hesitate to use force to collect the tax due. The official who was trying to get the monks of Nikon's monastery to pay their taxes had some of the monks arrested until he received a threatening vision of St. Nikon.[61] The amount of physical coercion that would have been sufficient to force tax money out of humble and modest households would not have been sufficient in other cases. Many large households could bring out an armed force of their own. This is not to suggest that well-armed households fought pitched battles with the soldiers accompanying the tax collectors, but that physical presence was one of several means employed to convince the collectors that they would do better elsewhere. Yet, the taxes needed to be collected from someone. For every time an official let a friend off the hook someone else had to pay twice.

The tenth-century legislation intended to protect the empire's tax base of independent cultivators from encroachment by powerful people needs to be seen in light of the ability of some households to resist taxation. These laws have received great attention and do not need thorough treatment

---

[60] Kekaumenos, Litavrin, §38; Wassiliewsky, 42.   [61] *Life of Nikon*, 186.

here.⁶² They involve the ancient legal principle of *protimesis*, by which certain categories of persons, primarily the relatives and neighbors of the seller, have the right to buy land put up for sale before it is put on the open market. The purpose of the laws was to restrict the ability of the powerful to buy land in fiscal districts of smallholders.⁶³ The imperial administration was trying to maintain the coherence of the fiscal districts that the land-tax registration system allowed them to track and tax most effectively. While couched in a language of imperial concern for the poor, the laws were issued to protect small independent farmers in the village-based fiscal districts because they formed the tax base of the empire. Land that came under the control of the powerful seems not to have been counted upon for continued revenue. The simplest explanation for the series of laws is that powerful households did not pay their taxes. This is not directly addressed in the laws because the imperial administration stayed in power largely by convincing people that it was all-powerful. To admit that sometimes the imperial tax collectors went away empty handed would suggest to far too many citizens that they could attempt to do the same. The legislation does not seem to have been effective. The definitions of both the powerful and the poor could be construed to fit the desires and intentions of the judges. Wealthy and powerful provincial landholders apparently were able to find sympathetic judges who allowed them to buy whatever land they wanted much of the time.⁶⁴ Frequently, judges were bound through ties of friendship and household association to the people who were trying to buy as much land as possible, if they were not in fact the same people.

Besides low-level local resistance, the tax collectors had to contend with the possibility of open revolt. The revolt near Larissa, in which Kekaumenos' uncle Nikoulitzas participated, was instigated by complaints about taxation. When Nikoulitzas was in control of the revolt he wrote to the emperor telling him to cancel the tax increase that had been made in the province. The emperor is recorded as having sent a written copy of the vow: "As much as I made from the day of my reign until now, I forgive everything, and I will not exile men from your region or set up boundaries or seek public or private damages, but everything I forgive with the fear of God."⁶⁵ It seems that the emperor acknowledged that increases in taxation were grounds for

---

⁶² Svoronos and Gounaridis, eds., *Les Novelles des empereurs macédoniens*. Most recently see Papagianni, "*Protimesis*," 1071–82. Kaplan, *Les Hommes et la terre*, 399–444.
⁶³ There is a tradition of regarding this legislation as "a brave but failed attempt to save the state from the creeping tide of feudalism." Magdalino, "Justice and finance," 102. On this tradition see Kazhdan, "Russian pre-Revolutionary studies on eleventh-century Byzantium," 111–24. George Ostrogorski, "La commune rurale byzantine," *Byzantion* 32 (1962): 139–66. Lemerle, *Agrarian History*, 85–108.
⁶⁴ Kaplan, *Les Hommes et la terre*, 426–8.   ⁶⁵ Kekaumenos, Litavrin, §74; Wassiliewsky, 70.

revolt and that a promise to cancel taxation could undercut the strength of a revolt. Kekaumenos taught that it was the duty of officials in the frontier regions of the empire to report abuse by fiscal officials immediately because of the danger of revolt:

> It is praiseworthy that in every country in which you may be, if you find injustice either by the fisc or by those following the collectors, you stop these, at least in the frontier. If you are unable to stop these, write to the emperor unequivocally. For this reason many countries are destroyed and not a few desert to the gentiles and rebel against the Romans.[66]

The power of the fisc was limited by the ability of people to resist taxation. That ability varied with time and locality. Those communities that had nearby alternative rulers had far more leverage against the empire than the core provinces. In the frontier regions the local rulers would support the empire when it was giving them a better deal than they would have on their own. Even in the core provinces, however, people could violently resist taxation. Larissa was not a frontier town. The people pushing for a rebellion could not have been expecting that Larissa would become independent of the empire. Their goal would have been to change who was emperor or cause enough trouble to get their taxes forgiven. Their achievement of the latter shows the limits of the authority of the imperial administration even in the central regions of the empire.

The crux of the matter is that authority varied with the proximity of the central authorities. Although imperial officials from Constantinople posed the greater risk while they were there, once they were gone the power of local households became threatening. As in the case of the *protospatharios* Michael and the Mavroi, central officials could be counted on not to know what really happened in provincial settings. Even if one acted justly on behalf of the fisc, resentful neighbors could bring charges decades later. When Nikoulitzas was weighing the threats of the local conspirators against his family and the threat of imperial reprisal, he chose to placate the local threat first.[67] He certainly knew that the emperor was infinitely more powerful than the local rebels. The emperor, however, was in Constantinople.

As part of his efforts to reform the currency and fiscal systems Alexios Komnenos took vigorous steps to increase taxation of privileged households such as the Athonite monasteries. He sent inspectors to take stock of what monasteries actually possessed and what they were paying taxes on. His agents ignored fiscal exemptions that had been granted to Theophylakt as

---

[66] Kekaumenos, Litavrin, §20; Wassiliewsky, 18.
[67] Kekaumenos, Litavrin, §74; Wassiliewsky, 67–8.

bishop of Ochrid and resisted whatever pressures were brought to bear by Theophylakt's eloquent appeals to highly placed individuals.[68] Yet what is remarkable is that, even in the midst of what was clearly a vigorous effort to bring in more revenue, the Athonite documents show the emperor and his officials in a series of negotiations with monastic leaders over the true size of the monasteries' possessions, the tax rate to be applied, and the amount of imperial charity the monasteries were due.[69] At least some prominent provincial households had opportunities for resisting imperial demands, even in the face of the most determined of emperors.

The modes of interaction between provincial households and the imperial administration outlined above give the impression that some provincial communities had considerable authority to govern themselves. The role of the provincial administration in mediating local conflict was undercut by the administration's dual judicial and fiscal responsibilities. The administration was not proactive in enforcing imperial law where the empire's fiscal interests were not involved. Some prominent provincial households were able to influence their tax assessment by befriending imperial officials. Even less prominent households could request changes in the recording of their taxes that would lead to a more advantageous tax assessment. Provincial people could pressure and intimidate local officials who would remain in their community after the taxes were collected. The relative apathy and ignorance of the central authorities in Constantinople about provincial situations allowed prominent households and communities to have considerable autonomy in regulating their affairs and gave a decisive advantage to those who could gain access to imperial officials in Constantinople. Chapter 5 examines some of the matters that were left for local communities to manage for themselves.

---

[68] Harvey, "Land and taxation," 152–3. Morris, "Monastic exemptions in tenth- and eleventh-century Byzantium," 216.
[69] Morris, *Monks and Laymen*, 283–92. Harvey, *Economic Expansion*, 90–108. Harvey, "Financial crisis," 167–84.

CHAPTER 5

Regulation of provincial society

Aside from those tasks in which the emperors took a keen interest – chiefly military integrity and taxation – the imperial administration did not act strongly to keep order in provincial society. Unless the emperor wanted something, there was very little danger that the government would get involved. When the imperial administration was not interested, local people had the opportunity to try to order society to their liking. This chapter addresses some areas – thieving, building, and religious practice – for which provincial households managed matters for themselves. Byzantine provincial society may appear to be characterized by variety of practice and lack of regularity. Behind this irregularity was a society ordered into households, each of which had considerable autonomy.

One indication that imperial and local authorities did not regulate much is the relative prominence of thievery and fraudulent and otherwise disruptive behavior in provincial society. One of Lazaros' early miracles was to protect a bean harvest from passers-by without employing guards.[1] Later, two men are mentioned in passing as standing guard over cultivated fields at night.[2] A former monk from Lazaros' monastery planned to return to the monastery at night to steal the clothes and goods of the monks during a vigil service.[3] While this fellow repented upon hearing the singing in the church, another monk did steal money from a brother during a church service.[4] In a story from the *Life of Nikon*, Stephen, a prominent man, ordered his servants to go to the monastery and take some oil by force.[5] Dreams of Nikon quickly caused him to repent, but the monks had not been able to resist what appears to have been open theft. There was also a band of brigands who attacked travelers outside Sparta. When Nikon went to reproach them for their behavior they beat him up. Divine retribution came in the

[1] *Life of Lazaros*, 120.   [2] *Ibid.*, 344.   [3] *Ibid.*, 154.   [4] *Ibid.*, 200.   [5] *Life of Nikon*, 67.

form of an earthquake and flood that changed the brigands' settlement into a marsh.[6] The peasants who lived on one of the monastery's estates were raided by their neighbors. The robbers captured a young woman with the intention of selling her as a slave in order to get money to feed themselves.[7] Pirates raided a small island where Luke of Stiris was staying as a hermit and took the hand-mill he used to grind grain.[8] The monastic rule of Athanasios of Lavra lists prevention of theft as one of the duties of the gatekeeper and declares that: "Whoever commits such a theft of the goods, the products, and the services of the monastery should undergo the death of Ananias and Sapphira, who indeed underwent bodily death, whereas these will end up under a curse with the death of their souls."[9] Kekaumenos told those living privately to pay close attention to accounts, because otherwise "those working for you will eat your profit and make it their own."[10] These instances do not allow for a quantitative argument that stealing was commonplace, but show that the prevention of theft was a private matter. Individual households and communities protected themselves as they could without relying on the imperial administration for help.

Provincial people also needed to protect themselves against being defrauded by charlatan monks out for profit. A great many charitable gifts were given to monks, whether organized into monasteries or wandering in travel or itinerant preaching. There was concern that some of these men were less than holy. When St. Lazaros was a young man he ran away from his family and undertook to travel to the Holy Land. He fell in with a devious monk who claimed to be traveling to the Holy Land but:

did not want to travel straight [there] . . . He would thus turn aside from the direct route and go round on a detour to the villages where he would beg and collect bread and whatever else anyone offered him; he would put these things into a bag and give them to the youth [Lazaros] to carry. Then, wherever they were when evening fell, they would go in, whether it was a village or a local market, and he would sell these things and pocket the price [he got] for them.[11]

When they reached Attaleia, the monk negotiated in Armenian to sell Lazaros to one of the shipowners. Warned by a sailor who overheard and understood the conversation, Lazaros took off and joined a nearby monastery. He took the advice of the superior that it was simply too dangerous for him to travel until he got older.[12]

---

[6] *Ibid.*, 180–3.   [7] *Ibid.*, 238–43.   [8] *Life of Luke*, 194.   [9] *Typika*, 228.
[10] Kekaumenos, Litavrin, §35; Wassiliewsky, 36.   [11] *Life of Lazaros*, 85–6.   [12] *Ibid.*, 86–7.

Lazaros also encountered a fraudulent demoniac near Attaleia. This man explained his method to Lazaros:

> If you listen to me and if you want, I can make you famous and make your monastery rich... I'm not possessed by a demon, but I pretend to have this problem. If I find someone established in a church somewhere... who's compliant with my [scheme], I get him to ask around and find out who has a nice ornament or some other [such] object. After he's found this out and told me the name of these people, I take a cross and go off to some place where it's damp; I then dig [a hole] and hide it there. After several days I make myself appear to be aroused by the demon. I first go into the church and get everyone there to follow me, as though they're under orders from the saint; then I go out with them to the place where I hid the cross by burying it. I dig... pull out [the cross], pick it up, and go back to the church. I then begin to call [the people] by name and say. "Oh, so-and-so, the saint commands you to bring this [particular] object of yours here so that your whole household may not be tormented by demons." I do this every day and then, when I've gone through them all, I make myself appear to have been cured. Afterwards we split everything that's been brought, I and the person in charge of the church, and so I go off again somewhere else.[13]

Lazaros admonished the man to at least become a straightforward beggar.

Even prominent monastic leaders had to deal with suspicions that they were fraudulent. When Luke of Stiris was living as a disciple of a stylite, Luke got into a fight with a priest who claimed the stylite was a fraud.[14] Years later, a guest at Luke's monastery was well entertained and became concerned that Luke enjoyed lush living.[15] While Lazaros' *vita* contains stories of extremely devious and greedy monks, Lazaros himself is described as having traveled extensively while living entirely on pious donations he received along the way. The times when no one in a town was willing to take him in and feed him are counted among his ascetic sufferings by his hagiographer. Lazaros could easily have been charged as idiorhythmic on account of his many wanderings and frequent changes in monasteries. Skeptics speculated that his cell was stuffed with gold from the donations of the pious. The metropolitan of Ephesus was reported to have sent spies to make an accurate assessment of Lazaros' lifestyle.[16]

Judging from concern about the problem, men sometimes claimed to be priests when they were not or when they had been barred from practice. One of the regulations drawn up for the monasteries at Mount Athos under John Tzimiskes was that: "Regarding unknown priests coming here, we must insist that they do not have authority, either privately or publicly,

---

[13] Ibid., 89–91. [14] *Life of Luke*, 184. [15] Ibid., 204–5. [16] *Life of Lazaros*, 204.

to presume to celebrate the divine liturgy, unless they have an official letter from their bishops or some solid testimony in their favor."[17] A story attributed to Paul of Monemvasia deals with problems arising from a disbarred priest continuing to perform rites for money.[18] That this was an issue at all indicates a fairly low level of regulation and hierarchical organization within the Byzantine Church.

Again, the argument is not that dishonest monks and priests were numerically more prevalent in Byzantine society than elsewhere but that provincial people were left to make their own decisions about whether to trust them. The imperial administration certainly does not appear to have taken any role in regulating the actions of itinerant monastics. The ecclesiastical hierarchy also does not appear to have been particularly active in provincial society. The metropolitan of Ephesus did investigate Lazaros, but this took place in the midst of an increasingly bitter fight for control over the lands of Lazaros' monastery. We are not justified in thinking the bishop's interest was routine.

While technically the imperial government monopolized the building of civil structures, there is some evidence that provincial households took on such tasks themselves. Despite the grand Roman tradition of civil building, people in the Byzantine provinces apparently did not expect the imperial government to construct or maintain bridges and roads. Kekaumenos warned his readers about the dangers of crossing bridges: "He who goes over a wooden bridge on a horse wants to be crushed and to destroy his horse. For when cheap wood overturns or is tipped over or the horse slips even a little, he will remember my words."[19] Clearly, he did not think the imperial administration would properly maintain bridges in ordinary circumstances. A bridge across the Evrotas River just beyond the city walls of Sparta was built by Nikodemos, the superior of a monastery. A foundation stone was inscribed in 1027 with a dedication and rules governing both Nikodemos' monastery and use of the bridge.[20] Out of his own funds Nikodemos built the bridge next to the monastery's Church of the Savior. After Nikodemos' death the bridge was to remain under the control of the monastery, and the judge and *strategos* of the province were to choose a

---

[17] *Typika*, 238.
[18] John Wortley, ed., *The Spiritually Beneficial Tales of Paul, Bishop of Monembasia* (Kalamazoo, 1996), 92
[19] Kekaumenos, Litavrin, §43; Wassiliewsky, 46.
[20] The inscription, on a column of the base of the bridge, was observed and copied by Michel Fourmont in 1730. It is number 8704 in the *Corpus Inscriptionum Graecarum*. Denis and Anne Philippidis-Braat Feissel, "Inventaires en vue d'un recueil des inscriptions historiques de Byzance: inscriptions du Péléponnése," *TM* 9 (1985): 300–3. It is included in *Typika*, 323–5.

superior from among the monks of the monastery to "lovingly take care for the church and the bridge and the brothers."²¹ Tolls from the bridge probably formed an important source of the monastery's income, since crossing the river was difficult without a bridge.²² The preliminary results of an archeological survey in the area indicate that settlement on the east side of the river increased after the bridge was built.²³ While Nikodemos' inscription is an isolated piece of evidence, it significantly illustrates the imperial administration being outstripped by local efforts to provide basic civic structures. The provision of the bridge undoubtedly helped the local economy as well as the monastery.

A survey of a twelfth- and thirteenth-century fortified settlement at Mastaura in the Meander region uncovered twenty-six cisterns, fifteen of which were expensive, well-built rectangular structures able to hold more than a million liters of water. The population of the settlement seems to have been fairly well off. The surveying team considers that the cisterns' "number and distribution over the site precludes the possibility that they were built by the imperial authorities as a public service."²⁴ The surveyors have left as an open question whether the fortifications around the settlement were built through imperial sponsorship or community effort.

The ruins of a medieval aqueduct survived in Thebes until the early twentieth century. The construction has been attributed to the prominent twelfth-century bishop John Kaloktenes.²⁵ If this attribution is correct, it would be another example of a local bishop taking on what in the Roman conception was a task of the state.

These examples of private individuals building public structures speak to the limits of imperial interest in maintaining provincial towns and cities. So far as we can tell, the imperial administration did not interfere with the organic growth of medieval town fabric. In contrast to their ancient predecessors, public spaces in medieval Greek towns were replaced by streets that

---

[21] *Ibid.*, 301, lines 30–1.
[22] Pamela Armstrong, W. C. Cavanagh, and Graham Shipley, "Crossing the river: observations on routes and bridges in Laconia from the Archaic to Byzantine periods," *BSA* 87 (1992): 293–310.
[23] *Ibid.*, 300.
[24] Barnes and Whittow, "The Survey of Medieval Castles of Anatolia (1992–96): the Maeander region," in *Ancient Anatolia*, 351–3.
[25] Antonios Keramopoullos, "Thevaika," *AD* 3 (1917): 123. Vasileos Delvenakiotes, *Ho Metropolites Ioannes ho Kaloktenes kai hai Thebai* (Athens, 1970), 73. Keramopoullos cites the unpublished history of Boeotia written by Epameinondas Papavasileiou in 1904, in which Papavasileiou described twenty rounded arches of an aqueduct between 3 and 6 meters long. The unpublished life of John Kaloktenos, compiled by the bishop of Thebes in the 1830s based on older sources, credits John with bringing water to the city. This is referred to as "the 'lost ancient biography' of St. John Kaloktenes" in Aspasia Louvi-Kizi, "Thebes," in *The Economic History of Byzantium*, ed. Angeliki Laiou (Washington, DC, 2002), 634.

served residential, commercial, and production purposes.[26] There appears to be no separation between residential and industrial workspace.[27] While the evidence is admittedly meager, it seems that the imperial administration did little to regulate urban space outside of Constantinople.

Materials from ancient buildings were appropriated by whoever had the power to do so. Where ancient buildings were accessible, they were sometimes built into new structures or adapted.[28] The *Life of St. Nikon* describes stone for Nikon's church as being gathered rather than quarried.[29] A miracle in the *vita* revolves around getting the columns in the church to be the same height. It seems that who got to use which piece was a matter of initiative and personal argument. The *Testament of St. Nikon* describes the leading men in town taking for their own houses columns that Nikon wanted for his church:

At Sampson there were two columns, one of which lord Malakenos took so that he might take it to his house. I implored him and he gave it to me. Lord Rhontakios also attempted [to take] the other column with the aid of a hundred men and he was unable, but I took fifteen [men] and went and brought it there where the other one was.[30]

Who got to use classical debris seems to have been determined by who was able to find and carry it away first. Excavations have confirmed that building in medieval Sparta made heavy use of classical building materials.[31]

The use of space in towns also seems to have been left for provincial people to thrash out for themselves. An example of competition for land that had been presumed common in Sparta is found in both St. Nikon Metanoeite's foundation charter and his *vita*. According to Nikon's testament, "leading men" of Sparta opposed his efforts to build a church because it would interfere with their playing a ballgame called *tzounganion*. Nikon's *vita* locates the building site as the town marketplace.[32] The church evidently was constructed in the town's center in an open place that was traditionally used for ballgames. In his testament Nikon recalled this

---

[26] Robert Ousterhout, "Secular architecture," in *The Glory of Byzantium: Art and Culture of the Middle Byzantine Era AD 843–1261*, ed. Helen C. Evans and William D. Wixom (New York, 1997), 195.

[27] Charalambos Bouras, "Katoikies kai oikismoi sten Vyzantine Hellada," in *Oikismoi sten Hellada/ Shelter in Greece*, ed. Orestis Doumanis and Paul Oliver (Athens, 1974), 46.

[28] Charalambos Bouras, "City and village: urban design and architecture," *JÖB* 31 (1981): 640. Bouras cites examples at Corinth, Athens, Argos, Sparta, Thebes, Pergamon, and Ephesus.

[29] *Typika*, 317.   [30] *Ibid.*, 318.

[31] G. B. and J. J. Wilkes Waywell, "Excavations at the ancient theatre of Sparta 1992–94: preliminary report," *BSA* 90 (1995): 445.

[32] *Life of Nikon*, 116–17.

saying, "I do not want anything else from you but merely five beams in order that I may build arches and that you may go under [the arches] without being impeded from playing *tzounganion* and that the church stand above."[33] It is difficult to imagine how the church and field were arranged topographically. Nikon's *vita* describes the situation: "Now there was an area for ball players and lovers of horse riding were flowing there, below this divine house; for the place was at that time given to an area for ball players."[34] When services of the church were disturbed by a vigorous ballgame, Nikon rushed to censure the participants, one of whom was the local general. He was "by nature somewhat bitter and at that time was essentially wrapped up in the game and grieved at being beaten by his opponents, was roused by this to obvious madness and greater anger."[35] The general tried to have Nikon thrown out of town, but was attacked by paralysis until he begged Nikon's forgiveness. Other activities that presumably took place in the marketplace would also have been disrupted or displaced. Nikon was able to gather sufficient support in Sparta to be able to appropriate part of the town's central area.[36]

The lack of interest on the part of the Byzantine imperial administrators in civil building and regulating town fabric does not necessarily indicate their weakness. Whether the use of urban space is considered a matter for government intervention or private decisions is a cultural choice. The evidence of Roman imperial legislation suggests that the decline of imperial interest in maintaining classical forms of urban space took place in the fourth through sixth centuries.[37] The change in town fabric associated with the decline of the classical city was at least partially a matter of cultural change.[38] The pertinent point for our discussion is that the regulation of urban space and civil building projects were not among the goals of the provincial administration. Byzantine emperors did uphold the Justinianic ideal of imperial building through their role in fortifying and renewing towns.[39] The evidence suggests, however, that nearly all imperial building consisted in strengthening fortifications, with little attention paid to civil amenities. Aside from fortifications, building was undertaken by

---

[33] *Typika*, 317.   [34] *Life of Nikon*, 134–40.   [35] *Ibid.*, 136–7.
[36] *Typika*, 317–18; *Life of Nikon*, 113–31.
[37] Helen Saradi, "The dissolution of the urban space in the early Byzantine centuries: the evidence of the imperial legislation," *Symmeikta* 9 (1994): 308.
[38] Mark Whittow, "Ruling the late Roman and early Byzantine city: a continuous history," *Past & Present* 129 (1990): 19. Wolfgang Liebeschuetz, "The end of the ancient city," in *The City in Late Antiquity*, ed. John Rich (London and New York, 1992), 1–49. Averil Cameron, *The Mediterranean World in Late Antiquity: A.D. 395–600* (London and New York, 1993), 152–77.
[39] Ivison, "Urban renewal," 11.

provincial households for their own benefit. While the archeological evidence is complex and ambiguous, we have no reason to think that provincial households acted in concert regarding building projects or organizing the use of space in their towns. Rather, decisions about the space and materials were made through the competition of individual households.

The salient features of Byzantine Orthodox practice were choice and privatization. The diversity of options for religious practice is indicative of a lack of ecclesiastical regulation and uniformity. Individual households, even those of modest means, enjoyed a remarkable degree of personal control and choice regarding religious practice.

Private chapels were common. The Confraternity of Thebes describes how the brotherhood's icon was set up each month in a different member's church. It seems likely that many of these churches were private churches or perhaps chapels inside houses. Leo VI's novel xiv sanctioned baptism in private chapels and he mentions their widespread existence in novel iv.[40] One of the *Spiritually Beneficial Tales of Paul of Monembasia* takes place in the household of an *archon* in the Peloponnesos who maintained a private chapel and a priest.[41] Michael Attaleiates had private chapels in his houses at Rhaidestos and Constantinople before these buildings were turned into charitable foundations.[42] Small churches were founded by a variety of people. One study of the founders of twelfth- and thirteenth-century churches concluded that founders were not all of the same social class, and saw a "broad spectrum of founders," including "aristocrats," monks, priests, "common people," and archbishops.[43] Donor inscriptions indicating that one person or family built the church are not uncommon in other parts of Greece. For example, a donor inscription in Panagia ton Chalkeon in Thessalonike names Christopher as the founder and mentions his wife and children.[44] Hagios Merkourios in Corfu was built and decorated by the *droungarios* Nicholas and his brothers in 1074/75.[45] The churches built at Kastoria in the tenth to twelfth centuries were apparently local family donations.[46]

---

[40] Anthony Cutler, "Art in Byzantine society: motive forces of Byzantine patronage," *JÖB* 31 (1981): 765; Noailles and Dain, eds., *Les Novelles de Léon VI, le sage*, 23–5, 59.
[41] Wortley, ed., *Paul of Monembasia*, 92–4.   [42] *Typika*, 336.
[43] Charalambos Bouras, "Church architecture in Greece around the year 1200," in *Studenica et l'art byzantin autour de l'année 1200*, ed. Vojislav Korac (Belgrade, 1988), 272–3.
[44] Karin Skawran, *The Development of Middle Byzantine Fresco Painting in Greece* (Pretoria, 1982), 158.
[45] *Ibid.*, 160.
[46] Ann Wharton Epstein, "Middle Byzantine churches of Kastoria: dates and implications," *The Art Bulletin* 62 (1980): 200.

When Byzantine families had some resources they generally preferred to build their own, modest, private chapels rather than to make donations to community churches. The small size and inexpensive construction of several churches at Kastoria can be taken as evidence, along with donor inscriptions, that they were built by local families of modest means.[47] There were enough private donations by locally important people for patronage at this level to have a great effect on the fabric of the city. The taste for private spaces of worship was reflected in changes in church architecture and the "'miniaturization' of medieval church design."[48] In general, Byzantine towns had many small churches and few large-scale central churches.[49] Nineteenth-century observers in Athens noted massive destruction of churches to make room for new city planning.[50] In Thebes the remains of twenty medieval churches have been found on the Kadmeia and surrounding settlements.[51] A limited excavation in the Roman stoa in Sparta turned up a medieval church, made largely of reworked Roman buildings.[52] Households that were too modest to have a separate building or room for a chapel would still have an iconostasis for private veneration.

While the great number and intimate size of remaining chapels has been interpreted as indicating that they were private chapels, without a donation inscription it is usually impossible to tell whether a chapel was part of a private secular residence or a small monastery. In both cases the small churches were not intended for a large community. There were some large churches in provincial towns that were late antique basilicas or converted ancient temples, such as the Parthenon. It seems clear, however, that provincial Byzantine people chose to invest in building small churches for themselves rather than acting together to build large churches for the entire community. Whether they were funding monastic foundations or private household churches is in some sense less significant than that they were not building corporately or under the direction of a corporate church hierarchy. Even the members of the Confraternity did not work to build a church for their community. They came together in the churches of each

---

[47] *Ibid.*, 190, 200.
[48] Thomas Mathews, "'Private' liturgy in Byzantine architecture: toward a re-appraisal," *Cahiers Archéologiques* 30 (1982): 127.
[49] Bouras, "City and village," 646.
[50] Alison Frantz, *The Church of the Holy Apostles* (Princeton, NJ, 1971), 26. On the rebuilding of Athens see Eleni Bastéa, *The Creation of Modern Athens: Planning the Myth* (Cambridge, 2000).
[51] Sarantis Symeonoglou, *The Topography of Thebes from the Bronze Age to Modern Times* (Princeton, NJ, 1985), 164–8.
[52] Waywell, "Excavations at the ancient theatre of Sparta 1992–94: preliminary report," 427–9. G. B. and J. J. Wilkes Waywell, "Excavations at Sparta: the Roman Stoa 1988–92 Part II," *BSA* 89 (1994): 398–400.

member's house or neighborhood. Brotherhood was enacted through visits among households rather than communal investment.

In addition to building private churches, people with means had the option of building their own private monasteries. The absence of formal monastic "orders" made adopting a monastic vocation a relatively open matter. In order to become a monk, one needed to receive a monastic habit from another monk. In the ninth and tenth centuries there was considerable variety in the available forms of monastic life and an appreciation of the legitimacy of small, modest foundations.[53] The variety of monastic options gave considerable choice for those contemplating monastic life. For men there were eremitic, lavriote, and coenobitic styles of monastic experience available by the end of the tenth century. Women's choices were far more uniformly restricted to the coenobitic life.[54]

Freedom to take up a monastic profession was limited by economic contingencies. Some monasteries required substantial entrance gifts before admitting a new brother or sister.[55] On the other hand, foundation documents make it clear that some people tried to join monasteries as a means of escaping material troubles. Christodoulos expected that people would want to enter his monastery to avoid difficulties. He ordained that men should not be admitted who came:

> not simply out of love of God and desire to save his soul, but constrained by earthly contingencies, creditors, perhaps, or extreme poverty and disinclination to work, or numerous children, so that he is come to the monastery as to a refuge that will furnish escape and dispense from effort.[56]

Some Byzantine women's monasteries seem at times to have been repositories for unwanted or destitute women.[57]

Monasteries could be treated as the personal property of the founders, who sometimes tried to restrict ecclesiastical control over their monasteries.

---

[53] Morris, *Monks and Laymen*, 31.
[54] *Ibid.*, 52. Alice-Mary Talbot, "A comparison of the monastic experience of Byzantine men and women," *Greek Orthodox Theological Review* 30 (1985): 1–20.
[55] Lazaros' patron in Jerusalem paid an entrance gift to the monastery of St. Sabas both times Lazaros entered that community. The first time the patron, the archdeacon of the church of the Holy Resurrection, "gave the superior twelve *nomismata*, according to the rule of the monastery, and thus arranged for him to be received and numbered among the brothers there." Lazaros was expelled from the monastery of St. Sabas for being idiorhythmic and joined the monastery of St. Euthymios. When he rejoined St. Sabas, Lazaros had the archdeacon intercede for him again and present the superior "a Gospel valued at twelve *nomismata* and arranged for him to be received as on the first occasion." Lazaros' experiences in Palestine may not reflect the custom of Byzantine provincial society. *Life of Lazaros*, 96–8.
[56] *Typika*, 592.
[57] Alice-Mary Talbot, "Late Byzantine nuns: by choice or necessity," *BF* 9 (1985): 103–17.

A couple from the island of Skyros, Glykeria and John, vigorously disputed their bishop's authority over the monastery and church they had founded, despite the long-standing principle that bishops have authority over new ecclesiastical and monastic foundations in their jurisdiction.[58] The bishop is described as motivated by Satan in his efforts to maintain the position given to him by canon law. In the foundation document for his monastery and poorhouse Michael Attaleiates listed those who should be excluded from control over the foundation: "Every emperor and noble and dynast, and all ministers of the holy sanctuary, both bishops and priests, and everyone involved in political and ecclesiastical affairs should keep their distance from this holy property."[59] In the late eleventh century, Manuel the bishop of Stroumitza went so far as to place a ban on the taking of an inventory of his monastery of the Merciful Mother of God. He stipulated:

> I wish and prescribe that this, the monastery that I hold in private ownership and which bears the name of the Mother of God, who pities me, be self-governing and administered by itself, and that it not be subject perchance to any personage, ecclesiastical or magisterial, but to the Mother of God alone, whom, in fact, I have instituted as heir... Nor do I wish and prescribe that after my departure to the Lord an inventory be made over all these things, as the laws determine, but only an examination in the presence of my relatives by the superior of the monastery at that time and the monks in it... As a matter of fact, this monastery shall not be subjected in any way whatsoever by anyone to any keeping of accounts.[60]

In the future the bishop of Stroumitza would be able to place the seal of blessing upon the superior of the monastery during his installation but this is not to be understood "as a privilege or authority over the monastery which I hold in private ownership."[61] The right of the founder to make up the rules for the monastery was regarded as sufficiently absolute that Manuel felt justified in dictating behavior that he acknowledged was contrary to law.

That individual donors were fully responsible for their foundations meant that those foundations were only as secure as the founders were wealthy and powerful. A certain degree of insecurity was attendant on the independence of the foundations. When Michael Attaleiates founded his monastery, he included a prayer in the foundation charter that his deposition of property would remain secure:

> May thy great and all-powerful right hand keep these offerings and preserve them in perpetuity. O Lord of mercy, do not permit that a malicious man ravage and disperse this [property], nor allow that powerful men who crave after property

[58] *Lavra*, pp. 155–61, no. 20.   [59] *Typika*, 337.
[60] The monastery was founded between 1085 and 1106. *Ibid.*, 186.   [61] *Ibid.*, 185.

should gaze at the beauty of these estates with greedy and covetous eyes. Do not endure that a curious busybody, who devises the flimsiest of excuses and stirs up unjust things, should join others in villainy and throw their property rights into confusion. Do not permit an evil man, a deviser of wickedness, to insinuate himself from inside into their services, or be imposed from outside to stir up numerous petty disturbances by his cunning ways. Rather, O Lord, protect these [offerings], and defend them with thy mighty hand, and may they be a blessing on thy holy name.[62]

This prayer is a catalogue of the potential threats to rights of deposition. The prayer counts financial takeover, legal wrangling, and bad leadership as chief causes of concern.

A law of Nikephoros Phokas banning the foundation of new monasteries was issued because he thought people wanted to appease their vanity through new foundations while letting older monasteries fall apart from neglect.[63] Apparently donors far preferred to found their own monasteries than to support someone else's. Commonly the original founder's money ran out without new funds coming in to support the monks. It is unclear how, if ever, the law was enforced. Nikephoros himself was certainly one of the chief offenders in breaking it with his lavish patronage of St. Athanasios' lavra at Mount Athos. In the tenth century the practice developed of allowing a lay manager to take control of the resources of bankrupt monasteries. This practice, called *charistitki*, has been interpreted as abusive of monasteries and sparking calls for reform in the eleventh century.[64]

The privatization of religious practice meant that those with means had many options and a great deal of control over their religious experience. On the other hand, since nearly all the churches of the period belonged to either monasteries or individual households, poor people in rural areas may not have had access to priests and churches.[65] Some monasteries appear to have served communities beyond their own brothers and sisters. The monasteries of Lazaros and Luke are described as receiving local male visitors regularly. Each of these visitors probably regarded one of the monks as his spiritual father and hence had some sort of informal association with the

---

[62] *Ibid.*, 337.
[63] Svoronos and Gounaridis, eds., *Les Novelles des empereurs macédoniens*, 151–61. Morris, *Monks and Laymen*, 167–8. Peter Charanis, "The monastic properties and the state in the Byzantine Empire," *DOP* 4 (1948): 53–118.
[64] John Philip Thomas, *Private Religious Foundations in the Byzantine Empire* (Washington, DC, 1987), 186–213.
[65] Morris, *Monks and Laymen*, 91.

monastic household.⁶⁶ This relationship may have given the laymen access to Eucharist in the monastery. The problem of access to churches also may have been mitigated, at least in part, by the nature of icon veneration which fostered a form of personal devotional practice possible within private homes.

The lack of imperial regulation of religious practice extended to the choice of religion. While by the tenth century the bond between the empire and Christianity was a fundamental part of the Byzantine worldview, the imperial administration did little to dictate what religion people practiced. Formally, imperial legislation prevented pagans and Jews from holding office. Roman civil law was brought into increasing conformity with Christian law under Leo VI (886–912). Orthodoxy was a formal requirement for military service and armies were expected to invoke God before battle:

> As the enemy draws near, the entire contingent of the host, every last one of them, must say the invincible prayer proper to Christians, "Lord Jesus Christ, our God, have mercy on us, Amen," and in this way let them begin their advance against the enemy, calmly proceeding in formation at the prescribed pace without making the slightest commotion or sound. Have the signal given to them either by trumpet or another instrument for them to repeat the same prayer at the signal's end, "Lord Jesus Christ, our God, have mercy on us," and, "Come to the aid of us Christians, making us worthy to rise up and fight to the death for our faith and our brethren by fortifying and strengthening our souls, our hearts, and our whole body, the mighty Lord of battles, incomparable in power, through the intercession of the Mother of God Who bore Thee, and of all the saints, Amen."⁶⁷

The army of the Byzantine Empire was a thoroughly Orthodox army for an Orthodox empire. The emperors of Byzantium presented themselves as the champions of Orthodoxy and their courts as the mirror image of God's heavenly court. Right religion was the foundation of the emperors' power and its care was one of their primary responsibilities.

It appears that in practice, however, the universality of Orthodoxy was presumed and for the most part instances of heterodoxy were ignored by the imperial administration. Other medieval states acted on their desires for religious conformity: Jews were expelled from England in 1290 and from France first in 1306 and finally in 1394/95. Yet while Byzantine emperors supported Orthodoxy fully, the quiet existence of religious minorities

---

⁶⁶ On spiritual fatherhood in Byzantium see Rosemary Morris, "Spiritual fathers and temporal patrons: logic and contradiction in Byzantine monasticism in the tenth century," *Revue Bénédictine* 103, no. 1–2 (1993): 273–88.
⁶⁷ *Taktika* of Nikephoros Ouranos in McGeer, *Sowing the Dragon's Teeth*, 126–7.

throughout the empire speaks to the limits of imperial efforts to regulate religion.

The Armenian Church remained in formal schism with the Orthodox Church throughout the medieval period. Armenians made up a significant and increasing element in the empire's population in the tenth and eleventh centuries. If one were to judge from surviving polemical literature, the hostility between the Greek and Armenian churches was great. However, one should not overstate the degree to which the emperors tried to effect the conversion of the Armenians within the empire:

> The most that can be gathered from this disparate and fragile, or even contradictory, aggregation of testimonies appears to be that the imperial policy, generally less uniform than that of the church, oscillated between the tolerance required to accommodate the multicultural nature of the empire and attempts to impose dogmatic homogeneity.[68]

While many Armenian families who joined the empire's military aristocracy in the tenth through twelfth centuries adopted Chalcedonian Christianity, others who did not also received high imperial titles, despite legislation barring heretics.[69]

Jewish communities in the empire are not described in Byzantine literature in any way that lets us know more than that their existence was taken for granted.[70] The eleventh century may have been a period of expansion for the Jewish communities in the empire. There was a migration of Egyptian Jews to Byzantium in the wake of the persecution by the Fatimid caliph al-Hakim (1016–19).[71] In the mid-eleventh century the Nestorian patriarch of Nisibus reproached the empire for allowing Jews to build synagogues and practice their faith publicly.[72] Benjamin of Tudela famously recorded sizable Jewish communities in the empire during his tour of 1168, specifically in Patras, Corinth, and Thessalonike. Modern estimates put the size of the Jewish population of the empire at between 12,000 and 100,000, depending on whether Benjamin's figures are interpreted as counting families or individuals.[73] Late Roman legislation forbidding Jews to hold government positions, to serve in the army, or to own Christian slaves was repeated

---

[68] Nina Garsoïan, "The problem of Armenian integration into the Byzantine Empire," in *Studies on the Internal Diaspora of the Byzantine Empire*, ed. Hélène Ahrweiler and Angeliki Laiou (Washington, DC, 1998), 84–5.
[69] *Ibid.*, 100.
[70] Nicholas de Lange, "Hebrews, Greeks or Romans? Jewish culture and identity in Byzantium," in *Strangers to Themselves: The Byzantine Outsider*, ed. Dion Smythe (Aldershot, 2000), 108.
[71] Andrew Sharf, *Byzantine Jewry: From Justinian to the Fourth Crusade* (London, 1971), 112, 107–26.
[72] Jacoby, "Juifs," 119–20.
[73] Steven Bowman in Kazhdan, ed., *The Oxford Dictionary of Byzantium*, s.v. "Jews."

Regulation of provincial society 133

in Byzantine legal collections.[74] There is no evidence regarding the enforcement of the laws against Jews serving in the military and government offices. Similar laws concerning Armenian monophysites were disregarded.

There were also Slavic tribes living in the Peloponnesos that apparently had not converted to Orthodoxy by the end of the tenth century. The author of the *Life of Nikon* included an episode involving a group he called both "Milengoi" and gentiles, implying that they were not Christian. The author described them as knowing "nothing other than only constant robbery and greedily carried off of the men's property."[75] The Milengoi are described in *De administrando imperio* as Slavs settled near Lacedaemonia and Helos, who were "practically independent and self-governing" in the first half of the tenth century.[76] Nikon made no attempt to convert them.[77]

The Paulicians, originally an Armenian heterodox group, flourished in Asia Minor in the ninth century and could still be found in the Balkans in the late eleventh century. While Greek writers identified the Paulicians with Manicheans, in Armenian sources they are presented as Armenian adherents of Syrian adoptionist traditions that predated the Hellenization of the Armenian Church.[78] The *Ecloga*, a law code issued by Leo III (717–741), ordained that Manicheans and Montanists should suffer death by the sword.[79] According to the *Alexiad*, however, Manicheans were enrolled in Alexios' army for the first battle of Dyrrachion.[80] They abandoned imperial service after that disastrous defeat and Alexios confiscated the lands of their leaders. Alexios Komnenos attempted to convert them at the end of the eleventh century.

While living as a stylite, St. Lazaros of Mount Galesion was credited with converting and impressing a variety of non-Orthodox people. On two occasions he impressed Jews, one of whom said that Lazaros had outdone Elijah because he only had one old leather tunic whereas Elijah had two.[81] An Arab who had been baptized by the metropolitan of Ephesus was greatly impressed by Lazaros. A Paulician visitor to his monastery anathematized his own heresy and was baptized.[82] Much earlier in his career Lazaros was said to have converted a group of unspecified heretics living near Attaleia.

---

[74] Sharf, *Byzantine Jewry*, 91.   [75] *Life of Nikon*, 206–12.
[76] Moravcsik and Jenkins, eds., *De administrando imperio. Constantine VII Porphyrogenitus*, 232–5.
[77] Cordula Scholz, *Graecia Sacra: Studien zur Kulture des mittelalterlichen Griechenland im Spiegel hagiographischer Quellen*, vol. III (Frankfurt, 1997), 122–3.
[78] Nina Garsoïan, *The Paulician Heresy* (The Hague, 1967), 231–3.
[79] Ludwig Burgmann, ed., *Ecloga: Das Gesetzbuch Leons III und Konstantinos V* (Frankfurt, 1983), 242, §17.52.
[80] Reinsch and Kambylis, eds., *Annae Comnenae Alexias*, pp. 126–7, Book 5.3; pp. 146–7, Book 4.4.
[81] *Life of Lazaros*, 203.   [82] Ibid., 205.

Lazaros called on the bishop of Philetos to receive them into the Orthodox Church.[83] At the request of the emperor, Paul of Latros debated theology with "Manicheans" in Melitos.[84] These anecdotes are evidence that converting non-Christians was one of the things that a proper saint should do. They may also attest to the variety of religious beliefs current in the empire.

Despite the strong and consistent ideology stressing the importance of religious homogeneity, it was never achieved, and, with the exception of Alexios Komnenos, the emperors expressed little interest in combating heresy and religious pluralism. It would not push the point too far to say that religious minorities are visible in Byzantine sources only when someone of the dominant ideology wishes to reinforce his or her status through the marginalization of others. Alexios did not face an increased number of heretics, but took an unusual interest in presenting himself as the defender of Orthodoxy.[85]

Individual communities policed each other's behavior. Both the *Life* and testament of St. Nikon record that Nikon came to Sparta on the condition that the Jewish community there be expelled.[86] The town was suffering from a sickness and some people appealed to Nikon for help. Enough people in Sparta were prepared to accept Nikon's suggestion that the Jewish community was "contaminating them by its abominable customs and the pollution of its worship" that the Jews were driven out of the town.[87] This Jewish community is not attested further in written sources, but they may have returned to Sparta shortly after Nikon's purge. The formal illegality of Nikon's actions does not seem to have played any role in the affair. The choice about whether Sparta would be religiously pluralistic was left to the competition and contention among local people.

Theft, civil building, and religious practice are examples of matters that are tightly controlled by the government in some societies and not at all in others, both ancient and modern. In Byzantine provincial society these matters appear to have been regulated at the level of individual households and alliances of households. Households protected themselves against theft by standing guard over their property. Nikodemos was able to charge his neighbors tolls to cross his bridge because it was built by his monastic household. The Byzantine Church, at least in the sources reviewed here, appears to have been remarkably open to being incorporated within private

---

[83] *Ibid.*, 88.   [84] *Life of Paul*, 128.
[85] Dion Smythe, "Alexios I and the heretics: the account of Anna Komnene's *Alexiad*," in *Alexios I Komnenos*, ed. Margaret Mullett and Dion Smyth (Belfast, 1996), 232–59.
[86] *Typika*, 317; *Life of Nikon*, 110–13.   [87] *Life of Nikon*, 112–13.

households. Provincial households were largely able to do what they liked within their economic means. The main limit placed on the freedom of individual households was not the imperial government, but the opposition of neighboring households. The relative absence of formal government meant that provincial households were free, yet at each other's mercy. The following chapter looks at how provincial communities dealt with differences of opinion and conflict between households.

CHAPTER 6

Contention and authority

So long as provincial people were taxpaying and quiescent, the emperors were not proactive in regulating provincial society. The monastic superiors on Athos could blithely ignore imperial judgments in internal disputes because they knew the emperor really did not care whose vineyard it was. They knew that an imperial judgment in favor of one monastery meant only that friends or representatives of that monastery had been able to bend the proper ear and gain access to the proper official. With appropriate monastic disregard for favor-peddling, they would ignore imperial decisions with no fear that the awesome forces of empire would come to enforce the imperial will. For all the power of the imperial administration, people in the provinces were free to do whatever they liked so long as government interests were not affected.

While the emperors generally declined to exercise their own authority for regulating provincial society, they simultaneously were effective in preventing provincial figures from becoming rulers themselves. The heads of locally prominent households would benefit from exercising a degree of leadership and authority in their communities, but would not want anyone to mistake their leadership for a challenge to imperial sovereignty. In the core provinces of the empire, local aristocrats or bishops did not become the rulers of their towns as long as the imperial government was functioning effectively.[1]

Because the imperial administration ensured that no rival group would act as a government, the regulation of provincial society was informal and variable. Anyone could try to influence the course of local matters and no one was guaranteed authority. The authority to regulate behavior in Byzantine provincial society was therefore particularly fluid and subject to community consensus. Keeping order and settling disputes devolved into a

---

[1] When imperial authority broke down at the end of the twelfth century, local leaders quickly became independent rulers. Lilie, "Des Kaisers Macht und Ohnmacht," 85–112.

matter of local competition. Households were able to have their way when they had access to wealth, the capacity for physical intimidation or violence, the intervention of more powerful figures, or the support of a community. Authority seems not to have been vested in an aristocratic social status. The people who were described as *archontes* and *dynatoi* were such because they had the support of an effective household, wealth, and the community standing necessary to act authoritatively.

Provincial people put their freedom and coercive abilities to the test when they seriously disagreed about a course of action. Disputes let us see the methods provincial people employed in controlling each other and how authority was created and deployed.[2] The course of a provincial dispute would normally include episodes of actual or threatened violence against property, person, or social standing; appeals to written documents, to community opinion, and to members of more powerful households. Not every conflict involved all of the appeals and threats mentioned above, but strikingly similar patterns of struggle emerge from a disparate body of evidence. Intimidation, supplication, and intervention were actions that communicated disparities in authority between households. Authority in Byzantine provincial society lay with those who were able successfully to intimidate others and to receive intervention in their favor.

In the absence of imperial interest in moderating local affairs, provincial people were free to act against each other violently. Our sources contain numerous stories of violence in which people with physical power did what they wanted without fear of imperial justice. In the *Life of Paul of Latros* the members of the Mavroi family continually stole from and terrorized their neighbors. The conflict with their neighbor the *protospatharios* Michael seems to have taken the form of small-scale warfare.[3] Nikon used a club to beat a Jew who entered Sparta after Nikon had expelled his community.[4] Also in the *Life of Nikon* a horse trainer named John hit a poor old woman and stole the bread she was selling. John was in turn hit by his master and later struck senseless and healed by Nikon in a posthumous miracle.[5] A rich man had his servant steal oil from the monastery. Michael Choirosphaktes attacked a *metochion* of Nikon's monastery, tearing it down, stealing the sheep and beating up the monk.[6] A group of people from a non-Orthodox settlement attacked and burned down the

---

[2] For a guide to the substantial literature on dispute settlement and process see Stephen D. White, "From peace to power: the study of disputes in medieval France," in *Medieval Transformations: Texts, Power, and Gifts in Context*, ed. Esther Cohen and Mayke de Jong (Leiden, 2001), 203–18.
[3] *Life of Paul*, 123.   [4] *Life of Nikon*, 118–20.   [5] Ibid., 242–9.   [6] Ibid., 194–201.

same *metochion*.⁷ According to the narrative of his revolt in Kekaumenos, Nikoulitzas was coerced into joining the rebellion because his children could be threatened by the rebels.⁸ Monks in the monastery of Dometios attacked and tore down the boathouse of a neighboring monastery.⁹ The church and monastery that Glykeria and John built on their property on Skyros was burned down in the night. They blamed the local bishop, who later threatened Glykeria with bodily violence.¹⁰ John, a retired *droungarios*, opposed the sale of some land and acted on his opposition by violently driving out the new owner.¹¹ Theophylakt, bishop of Ochrid, was accused of arson by one of his *paroikoi*. The accusation was credible enough to make Theophylakt worry.¹² The use of physical pressure and violence in disputes seems to have been fairly normal.

Physical intimidation or implied threats also helped households enforce their wishes. After the death of his father and mother, Paul of Latros suffered extreme poverty. He worked for hire as a swineherd of the villagers. Paul's older brother Basil, who was a monk, sent another brother to find Paul and bring him back to his monastery.¹³ The villagers refused to let Paul go and sent the monk away empty-handed. The ascription of the action to "the villagers," does not imply that every member of the village had acted in concert, but that enough people opposed Paul's departure to intimidate him. While the villagers would not have had any legal authority over Paul, together they were able to prevent Paul and the monk from acting. After the third time the monk came to get Paul they let him go. The villagers probably gave up their fight once it became clear that Basil could not be put off easily. Presumably they did not want a significant fight, but would try to keep their servant if they could.

Actual and threatened violence worked through the cohesion of members of a household or associated households. Individuals did not need to have any personal capacity for violence in order to bring the threat of violence to bear on a situation. The bishop of Skyros did not burn down John and Glykeria's church himself. Yet they could reasonably hold him responsible for the actions of subordinate members of his episcopal household. We do not know what damage the members of Glykeria and John's household were doing to the bishop. Paul could probably elude any one of the peasant

---

⁷ *Ibid.*, 206–13.   ⁸ Kekaumenos, Litavrin, §74 Wassiliewsky, 67–8.
⁹ *Saint-Pantéléèmôn*, pp. 39–50, no. 4.   ¹⁰ *Lavra*, pp. 155–61, no. 20.
¹¹ *Ibid.*, pp. 97–102, no. 4.
¹² Mullett, "Patronage in action: the problems of an eleventh-century archbishop," 126–7. Mullett, *Theophylact of Ochrid: Reading the Letters of a Byzantine Archbishop*, 213–14, 270–1. Gautier, ed., *Théophylacte d'Achrida, II, Lettres*, 485.
¹³ *Life of Paul*, 119.

families that wanted him to stay in their village, but when a number of the households were of like mind, he had to stay. The peasants on Michael Choirosphaktes' estates had little capacity for violence on their own, but as his *paroikoi*, they could threaten their neighbors with their ability to provoke his anger. The ability of individuals to be violent and threatening was augmented through their household relationships.

Physical force did not always dictate the final outcome of the disputes. In the documentation we have, violence is one step in a drama that continues to develop. In the hagiography examined, the saints bring down divine retribution on their enemies. In the cases preserved in the Athonite documents, the violence was not the end of the story but a provocation for fresh negotiations. The destruction of Glykeria's church did not end her conflict with the bishop. This is a point where the testimony of the acts is certainly misleading. Disputes that ended with one party violently asserting itself at the expense of the other would not be recorded in legal documents. A fight that ended in violence either would not have written documentation or would be represented by a narrative that omitted any physical coercion. The existence of a document attesting to a peaceful resolution does not constitute evidence that physical violence did not later nullify that agreement. We should not underestimate how frequently those able to command physical power won.

Disputes among provincial households highlight both the importance placed on documents and the limits of their authority. Clearly it was best to get an agreement in writing with many witnesses. According to his testament, when St. Nikon convinced the leading men of Sparta to expel the Jews, he got them to sign a written agreement to that effect.[14] This would make it more embarrassing for those who initially supported Nikon to change their minds later. That the agreement was made in writing is as much a sign of Nikon's concern about his ability to carry out the expulsion as it is of his authority. Our surviving legal documents make frequent references to other documents used in making decisions. A group of monks whose fiscal documentation was lost in a raid by pirates petitioned the fiscal administration for new ones to be made. The lost documents included the deed of sale and description of the party from whom they purchased the land, a boundary delimitation, and their tax assessment. They felt that their title was not secure without this documentation. The imperial officials compiled a new document given to the monks so that they would

---

[14] *Typika*, 317.

not suffer "damage or confusion by anyone on account of the loss of the *libellon*."[15] From the point of view of the official who signed the document, it was perfectly reasonable for the monks to fear the loss of their land if they did not have a copy of their deed of sale. The superior of Vatopedi similarly petitioned the *protos* of Athos for new documentation regarding his monastery's possessions. He attributed the loss of the original documents to the machinations of Satan.[16]

Yet, possessing a legal written document in one's favor would not necessarily be enough to ensure that one would prevail in a dispute. One boundary dispute on Mount Athos concerned a monastery with written documentation of its purchases and borders and another that relied on oral testimony of old men and traditions to make its case. The case was settled after an on-site inspection and was not particularly one-sided.[17] In another case one monastery had a clear deed of title to a piece of land while its opponent had no documents at all. The assembly decided to settle the dispute by dividing the land in half and drawing new boundaries for both monasteries.[18] This even-handed compromise contradicts the tenet that documentary evidence was privileged.

The need for interpretation of documents placed a considerable check on the authority of written documents and guaranteed that persuasive argument and competition between households would play a role in decision making. Controversies surrounding boundaries stem, not so much from discrepancies between competing versions, but from differences in interpretation. The process of deliberation among those making the judgment was at least as important in the final outcome of the dispute as what was written on paper.

The physical location of the debate was of prime importance. In many cases of boundary disputes, but not all, those acting as judges and all parties would go in person to the place of contention and observe the lay of the land. The *protos* of Athos and the other superiors decided to settle a dispute through an on-site inspection because "seeing is more worthy of belief than hearing."[19] Some of the documents hint at vigorous struggles over whether an on-site investigation should be made.[20] The decision to make an on-site investigation was critical because such investigations allowed arguments to prevail that ran counter to the documentary evidence produced by the parties. Judgments made without physical inspections were based

---

[15] *Lavra*, p. 129, no. 11. [16] *Vatopedi*, pp. 81–6, no. 5. [17] *Pantocrator*, pp. 71–6, no. 3.
[18] *Saint-Pantéléèmôn*, pp. 60–4, no. 6. [19] *Ibid.*, pp. 51–60, no. 5.
[20] F. Miklosich and J. Müller, eds., *Acta et diplomata graeca medii aevi sacra et profana*, 6 vols. (Vienna, 1860–90), vol. IV, pp. 315–17.

on documents and personal testimony that described the situation. Once everyone was assembled in the place of contention, cases with little or no documentary support had much better chances of prevailing.

The monastery of St. Demetrios called Kynopodos had a dispute with the monastery of the Asomatos named Phalakros. Phalakros brought the case before the assembly of the superiors and the documents describing the boundaries of both were read. The superiors agreed to an on-site inspection. The settlement document describes the *protos*, superiors, and all those involved going out to the field. When the delimitations were read there the problem became clear:

And when both of the documents were read in the place, they were found to be the same regarding the names of the markers. But the contenders disagreed because the markers were not as the prosecutor – the monk Gerasimos, the superior of the monastery of St. Demetrios called Kynopodos – indicated. For the monasteries had been divided from each other by the following delimitation: "It starts from where the oak stands by the stream and returns to the high mountain." There are two mountains in the place, the one higher, the other lower. Because the delimitation was not written with directions, the accused, the monk Kosmas and superior of the monastery of Phalakros, said that the larger and higher mountain was meant in the delimitation, which was unconvincing. For if, from the direction from which the delimitation started, it came down straight from there to the higher mountain, not only most of the place and nearly all of the vineyards of St. Demetrios, but also the monastery of St. Demetrios itself would be left outside of the delimitation. And one could ask, What was the trial about if the monastery was outside of its delimitation?[21]

If the judges had not seen that there were in fact two high mountains and understood how the delimitations had been misconstrued they would probably have come to the opposite judgment.

In a dispute in Mount Latros, one party insisted that their case would be clear and persuasive if the judgment took place after an on-site inspection.[22] All the documents produced by two other parties in the case were against them. The judge, in this case a patriarchal official from Constantinople, decided not to go out to the site. Rather, when one of the other parties claimed to have more conclusive documents in Constantinople, he agreed to move the place of judgment there. All those interested in pursuing the case would have to travel to the capital after the harvest. Clearly the ultimate decision would be based entirely on documentary evidence. In this situation, the recourse to a formal court of judgment removed the dispute

---

[21] *Pantocrator*, p. 70, no. 2, lines 9–18.
[22] Miklosich and Müller, eds., *Acta et diplomata*, vol. IV, pp. 315–17.

from a realm where personal recollection and physical realities were able to influence outcomes. The decision about who would keep the land was made when the place of judgment was moved to the capital.

Usually the person writing the document was different from the person expressing first-person sentiments in the document. The space between the person with a claim or agreement and the author of the text was considerable. There are some indications that documents could be considered invalid if a case could be made that they did not express the true sentiments of all parties.

Writers of legal documents tried to ensure that their texts did express the genuine opinions of the signatories by including standard clauses expressing free will and volition.[23] For example, in 897 Georgia donated her property and ceded her inheritance rights "voluntarily, without any force, trickery, fear, violence, deceit, difficult circumstances, robbery, baiting, extortion, joking, or womanly simplicity."[24] While some sort of clause expressing free will was standard in the acts and stock phrases were used repeatedly, the clauses do vary in length and intensity in ways that correlate with the subject of the document. A normal sale between parties on good terms would have a simple statement of agreement; more complex and contentious transactions put correspondingly more emphasis on the clauses of free will as well as the penal clauses and curses against transgressors.[25] In a simple act the seller or the guarantor will promise to uphold the action of the document or suffer the curse of the 318 Holy Fathers, and be alienated from the consubstantial and Holy Trinity, not heard in any ecclesiastical or secular court, and fined. Further maledictions would be incurred if a particularly contentious resolution was disturbed:

> If then, after time, the said monk Nikephoros or some of his students or successors is found regretting the arrangement made by us, or there is some other, may he be estranged from the holy consubstantial and inseparable Trinity, stranger to the confession and faith of Christians and heir of eternal tortures and companion and fellow of the crucifiers of our Lord Jesus Christ . . . with these and included rather with the devil and all his evil angels and vengeful demons, encountering also the curse of the 318 Holy Fathers and banished from all ecclesiastical and civil courts of justice.[26]

It is clear that the writers of the documents were trying to make the documents more binding by elaborating the rhetoric.

---

[23] For a typical example see *Iviron I*, p. 133, no. 5, lines 15–18.   [24] *Lavra*, p. 89, no. 1, lines 9–10.
[25] One example of a standard sale is found in *Iviron I*, pp. 240–3, no. 26.
[26] Nicolas Oikonomides, ed., *Actes de Kastamonitou* (Paris, 1978), p. 29, no. 1, lines 13–15.

The particularly extensive statements of volition may have developed to forestall future challenges to the sale's validity on the basis that the sale was made under duress. The connection with fear of future claims is made explicitly in a number of documents in which the sellers agree to defend the sale in court should someone dispute it:

> If then at any time or year there is a movement by any person whatsoever against the farmland sold by us to you, that we, the sellers – Maria, Kale, Niketas, and Styliane – defend it from all and any sort of proceedings against it in court, and you, the person buying and your party, may be entirely undisturbed and free from further payment.[27]

While the examples of peculiarly elaborate free will clauses occur in unusually contestable arrangements, it is fair to ask whether this elaboration had any effect on the legality of the document. If one were selling land in a state of dire distress or under coercive threat, one would not be able to say that in the deed of sale. If one were forced to sell one's land, would one not also be forced to attest to one's free will and desire to sell by placing the life-giving cross on the deed of sale?

In an act of donation of 1016 Glykeria gave land to Lavra that she had previously given to her bishop.[28] She and her husband had a prolonged fight with the local bishop over control of the monastery they had founded on their land. The fight included their exclusion from communion, trips to Constantinople to obtain support from the patriarch, and the tearing down of their church in the middle of the night. While the document is badly preserved and therefore the details cannot be certain, it seems clear that Glykeria argued her previous deed was invalid because she was forced to make it under threat of violence. She used a vocabulary of unwillingness and tyranny that recalls the list of pressures explicitly denied in the standard formulae of the donors' volition.[29] Glykeria made the second donation to Lavra "freely and uncompelled and without any necessity or tyranny, but rather with all enthusiasm and choosing with my whole heart."[30] Her husband died in the low point of their dispute with the bishop. In describing the situation, Glykeria endeavored to elicit sympathy by depicting herself as a helpless, childless widow. This brings to mind the phrase included in some statements of volition made by women that they did not act out of "womanly simplicity." Glykeria seems to have been appealing to notions of female weakness in order to overturn her previous donation.

---

[27] *Iviron I*, p. 181, no. 13, lines 17–20.   [28] *Lavra*, pp. 155–61, no. 20.   [29] *Ibid.*, p. 159, no. 20.
[30] *Ibid.*, pp. 158–9, no. 20, lines 7–8.

In another case a widow, Kalida, declares that she was freely and without constraint selling land so that she could ransom her son from the Hagarenes.[31] The author of the document used a fairly standard free will clause but had Kalida and her other children promise strongly not to attempt to overturn the sale. Reasons for selling land are not usually included in acts of sale. The fact that she needed the money to ransom her son may have been mentioned in order to prevent Kalida or her children from using it later as evidence of constraint. She is made to mention the difficulty compelling her to sell her land along with the statement that she is selling it of her own free will. In donating his property to Lavra for all eternity, Jacob Kalaphatos explained that he had previously donated the land to another monastery for eternity, but disagreements with the superior caused him to change his mind.[32] Presumably the first act of donation he wrote had all the standard attestations of eternal permanence as his second one. The regulations issued by Constantine Monomachos for the monasteries on Mount Athos addressed the issue of superiors who sign agreements before witnesses but later change their minds and annul the agreements.[33]

However elaborate the statements of free will in a written document, the sentiments expressed could be denied later on the grounds that the participants had acted under duress. That all of our extant documents were preserved in monasteries means that our sample contains only cases in which the monastery prevailed. If Glykeria's first donation document followed the standard form, she would have confessed complete desire and volition in giving the land to the bishop. If that document survived instead of this one, we would think Glykeria had freely decided to give her property to the bishop. Sales could be contested on the claim that they were coerced even if the documentation contained an elaborate statement of the seller's free choice, and therefore the power of documents was limited.

From a formal legal viewpoint, dowry was the property of the wife's family. Her husband could use it while the couple was married, but it passed to the wife's children or was returned to her relatives.[34] It was therefore illegal for a married woman to sell it, except in cases of extreme need. When in 1112 Eudokia wanted to sell part of her dowry, she needed to place tremendous emphasis on both her desire and free will in selling and the dire necessity

---

[31] *Iviron I*, pp. 190–93, no. 16.   [32] *Lavra*, p. 199–203, no. 34.   [33] *Typika*, 288.
[34] N. van der Wal and D. Holwerda, eds., *Basilicorum libri LX* (Groningen, 1953–88), vol. IV, p. 1377, §28.8.19; Joëlle Beaucamp, "Les filles et la transmission du patrimoine à Byzance: dot et part successorale," in *La Transmission du patrimoine: Byzance et l'aire méditerranéenne*, ed. Joëlle Beaucamp and Gilbert Dagron (Paris, 1998), 11–35; Laiou, "Marriage prohibitions, marriage strategies and the dowry in thirteenth-century Byzantium," 136–40.

that drove her to the act. Eudokia made a case to the *pansebastos praitor* and *doux* of Thessalonike, Andronikos Doukas, the highest authority in the region, that the law restricting the sale of dowry was cruel because she and her children were in danger of death by starvation on account of their extreme poverty. This document contains some strongly worded statements of volition and repeats them several times in the course of the document. In the opening Eudokia declared:

> Eudokia the legitimate daughter of the departed Gregorios Bourion, now the wife of Stephen *protospatharios* Rasopolos, setting forth the honored and life-giving cross with my own hands at this time to the present written and signed sale of the estate of Ison, to be made clear below, i.e., of the Bryoi, with universal defense and with familial council of all my substance, with the pledge of my spouse and all other legal assurance, the action to be annulled at no time or year in any manner whatsoever by any person whatsoever or by me, but rather bound to have eternal certainty, I establish and I make willingly by my judgment, and I choose for myself with determination and desire and not from some necessity or domination or womanly simplicity or trick or law or ignorance of facts or any other reason unfit by law whatsoever, but rather with much enthusiasm on my part and great acceptance and desire, to you, Neophytos, monk and superior of the monastery of Docheiariou in the Holy Mountain, and to the same holy monastery under you, to the monks in it now and to those who should be thereafter, with the entire portion and the rights of it exactly as will be made clear.[35]

The monks of Docheiariou, who eventually bought the land, insisted that Eudokia obtain formal permission, a *dekreton*, to sell her dowry land, because they feared that she would later overturn the sale. The potential buyers were worried that their right of ownership would be compromised if they did not have proof of the legality of the sale. It suggests that another buyer, with fewer scruples or less legal savvy, would have gone ahead with the sale despite the law against selling dowry land. The monks would not have demanded such an extensive dismissal of her rights if they did not fear her ability to overturn the decision.

Eudokia appealed successfully to the *pansebastos* Doukas, who then ordered the *logariastes* Chandrenos to make a *dekreton* allowing the sale to proceed. Chandrenos then assembled a number of people to witness his questioning of Eudokia. The witnesses were an impressive set of people: *protokouropalates* and *krites* John Melidones, *protoproedros* Romanos Lazarites, four other men bearing the title *proedros*, eight men with the title *magistros*, and one monastery superior. The titles *proedros* and *magistros* had been greatly devalued by 1112, but they were better than the title *protospatharios*,

---

[35] *Docheiariou*, p. 67, no. 3, lines 1–7.

held by Eudokia's husband. Before these witnesses, Chandrenos tried to determine whether Eudokia had actually written the letter to Andronikos herself and whether she meant it:

> And we, obeying our lordly order, thoroughly questioned the woman if she sent this written supplication to our reverend master by her own will and judgment and if the things explained in it were true and if she still had this goal of selling her real estate. It was established by the council registered above that she made the entreating letter with anxious thought and care and she had dictated the things written in it to the writer and she still had the same opinion and enthusiastically wanted to sell the dowry real estate lying in the area of Bryoi.[36]

While she probably needed cash at the time of the sale, she still had other lands that she did not sell, and no mention is made of whether her husband had land. In her letter to Doukas, Eudokia explained that her husband could not provide for her and did not mention that he was a *protospatharios:*

> I was bound by my parents to a man in a marriage that was not profitable, a man who until the present managed our property as best as he could. But at these times he has been brought to complete poverty and helplessness, on account of the coming of unfortunate matters in life and from the overpowering sparseness of the times and being in no way able to provide a living for us, not having any other source of salvation, we are in danger of dying from hunger and from lack of necessities.[37]

In this narrative Eudokia is a victim of a bad marriage and her husband is a victim of bad fortune. The council was concerned with verifying that she had asked of her own free will for the letter to be written to Doukas. There may have been worry that her husband forced or pressured her into selling the land. There was a clear acknowledgment that it would be possible for someone to write such a letter without Eudokia's consent. The council concluded that she was poor and that she ought to be able to sell her land. After elaborate versions of all the normal clauses for a sale, her husband made his own declaration of support for the sale. It is unusual for a relative to make a separate declaration of agreement within an act of sale.

The repeated emphasis on Eudokia's free will and uncoerced decision making is all the more interesting because it clearly contradicts the rhetoric of necessity, poverty, and feminine weakness she employed in order to get the variance. Eudokia wrote a tale of woe and misery to Andronikos Doukas in which she claimed that the sale was necessary to save her children from death by starvation. Eudokia was far from genuine. Her husband is

---

[36] *Ibid.*, pp. 68–9, no. 3, lines 24–6.   [37] *Ibid.*, p. 68, no. 3, lines 17–19.

portrayed as entirely absent and unhelpful, although he stands by her side to sign the final agreement. She does not mention that the land she eventually does sell is only a part of her dowry, leaving her a landowner of some consequence even after the sale. She represented herself as a poor person in need of mercy from on high. Yet the monks to whom she sold the land clearly were afraid that she would try to overturn the sale later.

The people writing this document worked hard to make it binding. Their elaborate efforts provide an insight into how difficult it was to make a written text have priority over a human witness in conflict. In the resolution of conflicts, decisions were made by people. Written documents would be a significant factor in the decision making process, but they certainly were not treated as conclusive evidence in every case. People could deny that they had ever expressed the sentiments written in legal documents and even people who acknowledged that they had made a permanent sworn decision could later have that overturned.

The authority of documents was also ambiguous because those trying to settle the dispute could decide that some other source of information was more authoritative. The sworn testimony of an old eremite could be placed ahead of what was written in a monastery's archive.[38] The surviving agreements and legal decisions should be regarded as expressing one stage in conflicts that may well have continued.

One phase seen in a number of conflicts was the appeal to someone outside of the disputing group. When the local resolution was unfavorable, the losing party could try to get someone higher up in the social hierarchy to take up their cause. Making an appeal to a different authority was a way of rejecting a particular judgment or settlement. We see the same basic pattern repeated at what were obviously different social levels. Those who were able to do so appealed directly to the imperial administration in Constantinople. The higher the authority one was able to call on, the greater the likelihood of success. Appeals had the greatest chance of success when they were made to people with whom the supplicant had some sort of household connection.

People who had little coercive ability of their own would ask others to intercede for them. Michael Choirosphaktes acted against the *metochion* of Nikon's monastery at the request of the people working his land. When Michael visited his estate, "those living there brought a mixture of slanders to him," saying that the monastery's animals were damaging his field.[39]

[38] *Pantocrator*, pp. 71–6, no. 3.   [39] *Life of Nikon*, 198.

Michael responded to their complaints by gathering his men and attacking the *metochion*. The inhabitants of the village Siderokausia brought similar complaints to the provincial judge against the animals and encroachment of the Kolobou monastery in 995.[40] Kekaumenos expected that subordinate neighbors would ask one to intercede for them against an unjust powerful neighbor.[41] In the situation where one lives privately and there is a more prominent person in the area:

> If he should start to do injustice, the community will come to you saying, "We have you as our master" and, "Why have you not curbed him? Let us all go with you and speak to him freely" and, "Do not be afraid, for we are with you," do not receive them at all.[42]

Kekaumenos warned that when the matter came to a confrontation all those who had been agitating for intervention would hide. He thought that intervening on behalf of justice was important and praiseworthy, but also dangerous if one did not have sufficient support or authority. Michael Choirosphaktes clearly felt confident of success in his contest with Nikon. Those farming his land were not confident to confront the monks on their own.

When John and Glykeria came into conflict with their bishop on Skyros, John did not submit to the authority of the bishop. Rather he traveled to Constantinople to make a complaint to the patriarch and to ask for help. He apparently obtained letters from the patriarch supporting himself and his wife. John must have had some means of introduction to get the patriarch to listen to his case. The most likely scenario is that John had a physical or spiritual kinsman or friend working in Constantinople who in turn had connections with the patriarchate. The bishop, in turn, did not obey the authority of the patriarch, but had the church built by Glykeria and John burned down.[43] After John's death, Glykeria became the advocate for her household in the dispute as she became the head of the household. She eventually found a different protector in the Athonite monastery of the Great Lavra. By changing her testament to give her land to a monk of

---

[40] *Iviron I*, pp. 154–63, no. 9.   [41] Kekaumenos, Litavrin, §38; Wassiliewsky, 40–2.
[42] Kekaumenos, Litavrin, §38; Wassiliewsky, 41. The term used for the more prominent person is *hyperechousa kephale*. The term *kephale* designated a supreme governor in the later thirteenth and fourteenth centuries. The fourteenth-century usage informally denoted people in authority before it came to stand for an official designation. Ljubomir Maksimović, *The Byzantine Provincial Administration under the Palaiologoi* (Amsterdam, 1988), 117–28. In the eleventh and twelfth centuries the term was fairly rare and seems to have been one of several terms used to describe members of the highest level of Byzantine society. Cheynet, *Pouvoir et contestations*, 250–1.
[43] *Lavra*, pp. 155–61, no. 20.

the Great Lavra, she enlisted aid of one of the empire's greatest monastic households in the attempt to keep her monastery free from episcopal control. Representatives from Lavra went to Skyros to witness her donation. In undertaking the expense and difficulty of traveling to Skyros to be there in person, the monks of Lavra acknowledged the importance of personal intervention and mediation in such situations. They were not distant patrons who left Glykeria and the bishop to their own devices.

Imperial intervention was undoubtedly the most effective, when real imperial interest could be excited. In the examples discussed in chapter 4, however, the most common response of the emperor was to pass on the task of judgment to another party without actually dictating an outcome. Supplicants sought the help of the most powerful party they could reasonably expect to take an interest in their problems.

The act of petitioning a higher authority to take one's side could take place in disputes of all kinds with higher authorities of diverse stature. When the poor old woman whose bread was stolen in the *Life of Nikon* cried out for help, monks from Nikon's monastery came out to rebuke the perpetrator. This is perhaps the lowest level of intervention in the sources under examination. Similar kinds of intervention presumably took place in the arenas of women's activity and other contexts that our sources do not allow us to see. The old woman's request of help from the monks represents the same fundamental action as John's appeal to the patriarch and Symeon of Xenophon's appeal to the emperor Alexios.

Another means of gaining the upper hand in a dispute was to behave in such a manner that one's household was granted authority through the voluntary support of others. One of the central principles of provincial power seems to have been that authority came from forging agreements between relatively independent actors. The more people stood behind a disputant, the greater that person's capacity for physical intimidation. Community support also could enhance one's authority in a number of ways beyond merely lining up people willing to join one in a brawl. Community consensus and solidarity provided significant leverage to those who otherwise would be unable to oppose the actions of others.

Those with no formal authority could act authoritatively if they had sufficient support from local people. Maintaining oneself in a position of authority therefore required constant performance before the audience of potential supporters. The potential supporters were themselves constantly judging those who were trying to gain their allegiance. While in any society authority is augmented through respect and admiration, the fluid and informal nature of authority in Byzantine provincial society made attaining respect particularly important.

An individual's authority could erode quickly when his supporters decided he was no longer worthy of their support. This principle held even for those in positions of formal authority. One of the greatest concerns Kekaumenos expressed regarding military campaigning was that the soldiers would leave. If the general would not behave properly and keep the situation agreeable, he would have no power to control his soldiers: "Do not be idle or your army will be routed without battle, falling short on necessities. For being delayed and having a dearth of necessities, they will become cowardly and leave."[44] He gave examples of generals who were defeated because their armies dissolved without a fight.[45] The same advice is true for the emperor. He must treat the soldiers well or they will either desert or revolt.[46] It was dangerous for a general in the frontier to punish unruly subordinates because they would either not obey orders or revolt altogether. According to Kekaumenos, if the general acted angrily and rudely, the problem would only get worse. When the general would not behave in an appropriately temperate manner for his position, he would be disdained and ignored.[47] One would think that if anyone could enforce his views it would be a general with an army, but the reality was that a general was only in charge so long as his officers wanted him to be. Similarly, the head of a private household should turn a blind eye to most problems because "if you want to punish with severity and harshness, as truly claiming justice, either they will behave shamelessly with insolence and arrogance, or perhaps they will rush toward murder."[48]

Just as those with formal authority would lose it if they alienated their subordinates, those with no formal authority could become authoritative when people decided to support them. When physical intimidation was used in a dispute, it was often perpetrated by people who had voluntarily decided to support one of the disputants. Before attacking the *metochion* of Nikon's monastery, Michael Choirosphaktes "gathered no small band of men, finding those who happened to conform with his own ways."[49] While they became "his men" for the attack, they may have had little association with him normally. If the band included some of the peasants whose fields were in dispute, then they could be considered part of his household, broadly construed. They may have had no formal connection

---

[44] Kekaumenos, Litavrin, §28; Wassiliewsky, 24.
[45] Kekaumenos, Litavrin, §27; Wassiliewsky, 22–3.
[46] Kekaumenos, Litavrin, §80; Wassiliewsky, 94.   [47] Kekaumenos, Litavrin, §25; Wassiliewsky, 21.
[48] Kekaumenos, Litavrin, §58; Wassiliewsky, 58.   [49] *Life of Nikon*, 196–7.

Contention and authority

to Michael, but they had been convinced that they ought to support him. Somehow the bishop of Skyros presumably persuaded people to burn down Glykeria and John's church.

Common opinion was worth worrying about. Michael Attaleiates prayed that his endowment would be saved from the threat of meddlesome busybodies.[50] Such people could stir up trouble. Concern about gossip must lie behind a document in which two parties agree that they have always been in perfect agreement. The monk George declared formally to the *oikonomos* of Lavra that he had no claim on one of the monastery's fields:

> Since often I, the said monk George, suspected by some malignant man of saying that the Lavra appropriated my field in the place of Prablakas near the all-holy Theotokos... with everybody agreeing, I verified concerning the truth that, with fear of God and truthfully, this field at no time was owned by my parents, but was possessed by the Lavra from time immemorial... And now I confess as to Lord God Ruler of all that I never remember that the Lavra appropriated a field from my familial substance.[51]

Since George and Lavra had no dispute, what were they worried about if not the real effects of community opinion? Of course, it is possible that George only signed the document under duress and continued to tell people it was really his father's field as soon as the *oikonomos* and the other witnesses left. That people were gossiping about the possibility that George had owned the land was enough of a worry to make George and the steward of Lavra write up the document. Community opinion could not be shrugged off. In an act of sale between monks from 1033/34 the sale price was adjusted at the insistence, not of the seller, but of the witnesses.[52] The witnesses' ideas of a just price affected the sale. The seller may have been bargaining from a position of weakness. The witnesses may have felt that the initially negotiated price was too low to make the agreement binding.

In Nikoulitzas' account of the course of the revolt of the Larissians, preserved in Kekaumenos, the key decisions about who was going to be in charge were made in public confrontations. When Nikoulitzas received oaths from the emperor promising to end the new taxes and forgive the conspirators, he tried to break up the revolt by displaying them to the combatants:

> Calling together the people he brought before all of them the icons and showed them to them, he read out the oaths to them and he urged peace and each to go off to their own place. They did not want to but said, "You started the war, don't

---

[50] *Typika*, 337.   [51] *Lavra*, p. 134, no. 13, lines 5–10, 15–16.   [52] *Saint-Pantéléèmôn*, pp. 31–5, no. 2.

ask for peace." While he was pressing for peace, they did not agree, rising up with a great shout such as are made by disorderly host.[53]

Once he had clearly lost in his attempt to persuade the rebels to disband, Nikoulitzas changed tactics. He had two of the other leaders of the revolt arrested and threatened them with execution. Their supporters responded to the threats of execution by promising to obey Nikoulitzas, allowing him to end the rebellion:

He then ordered chosen rulers of the Vlachs and the Larissians, Sthlavotas Karmalakes and Theodore Skrivon Petastos, to be bound. All the others, seeing those led off to death, shuddered for fear of death and falling before him they all beseeched him to have sympathy on them, saying, "We will do what you order us." Then bending to their entreaties, he had sympathy with them and taking up the chosen ones of the Vlachs and the Larissians he went off to the *katepano* of Bulgaria, Andronikos Philokales, who had been sent to him with the oath of the emperor.[54]

The events show the interplay between outright force and manipulating the opinions of potential supporters. Arresting the other leaders probably entailed some risk since they as easily could have arrested Nikoulitzas. His first choice would have been to convince the host through verbal persuasion to obey his decision to accept the emperor's offer.

Nikon's hagiographer worked hard to portray as a miracle an event that had subjected the monastery to community debate and judgment. He credited Nikon with the posthumous miracle of saving the life of a boy who fell out of an upper window of the monastery. The boy, who lived in the monastery, had sneaked into one of the brother's cells to steal some money in order to buy a treat of fruit.[55] The brother caught him and locked him inside the room. The boy became so frightened that he jumped out of the window and fell on to a stone staircase, injuring his leg. While the brothers declared his survival to be a miracle, others in town spoke out against the monastery and Nikon, presumably questioning what sort of monastic behavior would motivate the boy to jump. The biographer's belabored denunciation of the malicious gossips and praise for Nikon's wisdom in allowing the boy to be injured in order to make the miracle more believable barely cloak a lively community debate. Crowds gathered around the window to judge its height and discuss whether the child's survival was miraculous. The brothers tried to influence the debate by

[53] Kekaumenos, Litavrin, §74; Wassiliewsky, 71. [54] Kekaumenos, Litavrin, §74; Wassiliewsky, 72.
[55] *Life of Nikon*, 256–64.

dropping fruits out the window to show how they smashed:

> Some of those from the monastery, being quite curious about the matter, made a test. They threw down (not from the height of the window, as being too high and extending to a great altitude, but from the parapet which lay below and was less high) some types of fruit onto the stone steps on which the child was dashed and preserved unharmed. And each time the fruits were crushed and reduced to dust so that nearly nothing at all of the shattered fruits remained on the place.[56]

This was an important matter for the brothers because, just as Nikon's monastic *oikos* would gain in prominence through the perception that the saint performed posthumous miracles, it would lose face if the brothers were perceived as behaving badly. The monastery participated in a sufficient number of conflicts after Nikon's death for us to presume that it had both detractors and adherents debating the significance of the smashing fruits. A well-respected household could act with far greater authority than one that was disregarded. Those without the respect of their neighbors would need to rely on money, and threatened violence to maintain their position. The abbot writing the life of Nikon was trying to augment his own authority by patching up the reputation of his house.

Another dispute that involved extensive community debate was Nikon's expulsion of the Jews from Sparta. According to his *vita* and the foundation charter he wrote, Nikon came to Sparta to help with a plague. In the *vita* the "chief men and the rest of the people"[57] went to find Nikon at the town of Amykleion to ask for help. In the charter the "leading men of Lakedaimon" assembled in their local church to make their plea. Nikon promised relief from the pestilence "if they drove outside of their city the Jewish race, which lived among them, lest it might be contaminating them by its abominable customs and the pollution of its worship."[58] According to the charter Nikon also required that the slaughterhouses near the church of St. Epiphanios be torn down. Neither the *vita* nor the charter provides any details about the mechanics of the expulsion, the size of the Jewish community, how the Jews responded to Nikon, or where they went. Yet the expulsion of an entire segment of the population was a major event in the life of the town. Both Roman legal precedent and Orthodox teaching protected Jews.

Nikon's attempt to expel the Jews caused a dispute that had many of the characteristics under discussion. The narrative structured events around two persons, Nikon and Aratos, who both laid verbal claims before the

---

[56] Ibid., 264. [57] Ibid., 110. [58] Ibid., 112.

community and engaged in personal acts of violence and threat. According to the hagiographer, everyone obeyed Nikon except one person, John Aratos:

> He asserted that the removal of the Jews outside the city was not just or reasonable, and the rash man, swelling with passion, did not blush to censure the Laconians for this with every word. Then on the pretext of some task, by which garments are accustomed to be finished, this boldhearted and venturesome man brought into the city one of these Jews.

Aratos made a verbal argument before the community that Nikon's actions were wrong. He also took actions – bringing Jews into the town – that showed he ignored Nikon's authority. Aratos may have had a title or an official position in the provincial administration, but none is mentioned. The titles and offices of other people with whom Nikon had both good and bad relations were noted. Even when interactions with title-holders were negative, they raised the profile of the saint. Here it seems that Aratos had no more formal authority in Sparta than Nikon. Nikon responded to Aratos' verbal attack and actions with a personal act of violence:

> The gentle man thence became a warrior... He seized a club which was lying nearby and inflicting many blows on the Jew drove him out of the city and seemed more fearful to his enemies than Herakles with his club, as they say.[59]

This prompted a verbal response and a countering act of violence from Aratos:

> But when Aratos, who got his name from madness, heard this, he considered the act a provocation to anger... The man came forth in anger at the saint, and indulging his bold and undisciplined tongue, this bold man was not at all ashamed to violently attack, to abuse, to shove, to frighten (as if he could) with threats.

In this confrontation Nikon left the field and Aratos continued to make verbal arguments before the community:

> [Nikon] answered in only a gentle voice, for he had never learned to wrangle or shout. "Depart poor wretch" he said to him, "weep for your sins, for in a short time you will know what the fruit of presumption is and the wages of evil." And having said these things and, as they say, spoken to the ears of the dead, he went back to the hermitage. His words never penetrated to the man's soul nor did he cease from his shamelessness. Nor was the all-daring soul at all content to cease with respect to his boldness toward the holy man and his ridicule of him and his disparaging of him through the whole city. He brought forth words worthy of his madness and folly, and moreover he used threats against him.[60]

[59] Ibid., 118–22.   [60] Ibid.

Right after his fight with Nikon, Aratos died. His death was interpreted as a sign of divine judgment and a warning to obey Nikon.[61] Nikon's testament mentions no resistance to the expulsion of the Jews but describes resistance to the building of Nikon's church: "One man, however, was found at that time who wanted to hinder the church from being built at that place which I had indicated. God knows that I neither cursed that man nor held anything against him, yet he happened to die."[62] This may have been the same person as Aratos or another enemy of Nikon's. That this unusual episode was mentioned, defensively, in the testament may mean that the issue was still discussed years later. Nikon was trying to clear his name from the charge that he cursed someone.

This story is our only evidence for a Jewish community in Sparta in this period.[63] We therefore do not know if Nikon's expulsion was successful. If Jews had reentered the city, the hagiographer would not have mentioned it. The weight of community opinion ultimately was the deciding factor in the expulsion because of the physical limitations of Nikon's capacity for violent enforcement. Nikon could beat up one individual Jew, but he could not physically prevent the Jewish community from resettling in Sparta if their neighbors wanted them to return. Although the author of the *vita* claimed that Nikon was not afraid of Aratos' threats, Nikon could have been driven out of town. As a newcomer who had no strong ties in the community, Nikon would have been relatively open to criticism and attack. Discussions among the general community determined who the community as a whole was going to obey. Aratos discussed the situation with people in Sparta, openly defied Nikon's decrees, confronted the saint, and continued to disparage Nikon in conversation with other inhabitants. The struggle was portrayed as between two individuals, Nikon and Aratos, but both were fighting to win over community opinion. It is difficult to tell how much support either disputant had. If everyone was firmly resolved against Aratos, he would not have found people willing to listen to him disparage and ridicule Nikon. If he had managed to persuade enough people that Nikon was unjust, he would have been able to engineer the return of the Jews to Sparta.

Informal authority was bestowed through successful disputation before a community not only in personal disputes between individuals and households but also in significant matters of local government. The fight may have been portrayed as a match between Nikon and Aratos, but the outcome

---

[61] *Ibid.*, 122–4.   [62] *Typika*, 317.
[63] Steven Bowman, "The Jewish settlement in Sparta and Mistra," *Byzantinisch-neugriechische Jahrbücher* 22 (1977): 132.

would affect the entire community and have devastating consequences on the Jewish part of the community. There may well have been officials from the imperial administration present and involved in these debates who were minimized by the hagiographer in order to magnify or exonerate Nikon's actions. If there were imperial officials present, they may not have known that the expulsion was illegal or they may not have cared. Nikon's authority was entirely informal and based on his reputation as a holy man and the perception that he had freed the city from disease. The bishop, Theopemptos, was depicted elsewhere in the *vita* as a supporter of Nikon.[64] He may have had a greater role in the debate than we can tell from the sources. Nikon was brought to the city by some prominent old men of the community. All these players were acting on informal authority that was correlated with their standing in the community. The informal authority accorded to neighbors was, in at least some cases, the authority that regulated provincial society.

The ability to gain community support was important, but it worked in conjunction with other means of maintaining authority, the most important of which was membership in an effective household. A persuasive member of a respectable and wealthy household would have more authority than a persuasive member of a poor and negligible household. A member of a powerful household could be threatening even if she had little personal capacity for physical violence. Wealth, potential for physical force, connections with more powerful people, and the ability to win the support of others all helped create the authority for enforcing a particular vision of society.

PROPER BEHAVIOR AND MANIPULATION

When the crowd, the community, or the villagers judged whether one was doing well, they did so by deciding whether one was behaving properly according to one's role and whether it was a good role. There was an ideal way to behave as father, mother, daughter, son, sister, brother, servant, and slave. The key to good behavior in Byzantine society was to assimilate one's actions to one of the proper roles. A general should care for the army as a father cares for his children. Fellow students should treat each other as their brothers and their teacher as their father. Most of Kekaumenos' advice was based on proper execution of an ideal role that remained the same regardless of rank. Certain principles of behavior are recommended for a variety of people. Kekaumenos advised those serving a general to be eager

---

[64] *Life of Nikon*, 116.

and sleepless so that they could make a name for themselves. He continued, "I advise the same things also to the soldiers. I have never seen anyone who was eager and sleepless not achieve the height of success."[65] Being alert would help in any circumstance. Likewise, if one had the opportunity "to manage and hold power over provinces" this task should be undertaken. Otherwise: "Be concerned with managing your household and make it shine."[66] Proper behavior toward a task is the same regardless of the size of the project to be managed. Kekaumenos also had the same advice for one becoming a metropolitan, bishop, or patriarch.[67] He urged the reader not to accept these positions without a clear epiphany that God had called him to the task. The description of proper conduct for a churchman is the same regardless of rank.

Ideal models of behavior could be real means of coercing the behavior of others. People were motivated to avoid certain roles and to participate in others. Monks portrayed themselves in their sales and agreements as loving brothers. In their desire to cast themselves as brothers, the monks were pushed to act that way. The monastery that built a boathouse on the shore before asking for a right-of-way through another monastery's land could have expected a conflict with their neighbors.[68] Perhaps there was considerable tension or fighting. Yet the document recording their agreement cites the need for neighborly harmony and brotherly affection and proceeds directly to the settlement agreement.

In a land dispute on Mount Athos an eremite refused to join in the decision of the superiors to allow the monastery of Panteleemon to claim a territory by virtue of the superior's oath. Neither party was described as having documents upon which to base their claim. The decision seems to have been made in favor of Panteleemon because the disputed territory was "close to the rest of their land." The vigorous opposition of the dissenter was nullified by casting him into the role of a wild, unholy man: "He appeared wild and violent, because he was not allowed to be greedy and was striving to appropriate the property of others. When the defendants saw with us his roughness and hardness, they preferred to take the oath rather than lose that which was theirs."[69] The superior who claimed the land was then able to set the boundary where he liked through a ritual procession along the boundary:

And it was truly frightening to see what occurred: A man deep in old age and having spent nearly seventy years in the monastic life, the *kathegoumenos* and most

---

[65] Kekaumenos, Litavrin, §34; Wassiliewsky, 35–6.
[66] Kekaumenos, Litavrin, §44; Wassiliewsky, 47.   [67] Kekaumenos, Litavrin, §53; Wassiliewsky, 51.
[68] *Pantocrator*, pp. 65–7, no. 1.   [69] *Saint-Pantéléèmôn*, p. 58, no. 5, lines 21–3.

reverend monk Lord Metrophanes, carrying the saintly and holy Gospels on his chest, and two other old men laudable with grey hair and virtue, the one carrying the honored cross and the other on his shoulder an immaculate and divine icon, and separating out the place, the hair of all of us shivered and our bones crumbled as we saw it. And thus with a frightful oath, the disputed place was delimited before us.[70]

By carrying the Gospels in a solemn procession and acting in a reverend manner Metrophanes created an aura of holiness. By taking on the proper role, Metrophanes achieved the support of the community that gave him the authority to set the boundary for his monastery where he thought it should go. The rude and savage monk must have had a party supporting his position or the dispute never would have been adjudicated in the first place. All those who initially had taken his position joined the consensus when it became clear that acquiescence was the only way to continue in the community. The opposition of the eremite was completely discounted when he was cast in the wrong role. The situation brings to mind Kekaumenos' warning that those who promise to support one in a public confrontation might disappear when they are needed most. The accusation of wildness was particularly difficult for an ascetic monastic leader to defend himself against because a certain degree of detachment from civilization was part of being a proper eremite.

Much of Kekaumenos' guidance about manipulating people revolved around manipulating the roles available for them to play. In advising one in imperial service about how to deal with slanderers he wrote:

If someone prattles against you, then summoning him privately, say to him with golden ways, "Brother, what harm did I do you that you talk against me? If you have been wronged somehow by me, tell me and I will correct this." And if then you have wronged him, make the correction; but if you have not wronged him, he will be put to shame by your humility and stop.[71]

Kekaumenos advised taking control of the situation by switching the relationships at play. By calling the prattler a brother and quietly asking to make amends, one could move the encounter into a familial relationship of mutual support. The prattler would be pushed into the role of brother. In the context of brotherhood prattling is shameful. Responding to the prattler with a threat would put one into the narrative of backstairs politics: "If you want to threaten him with your power, you will harm yourself. For he will then act more impudently and will lay snares for you and will harm you when you do not expect it."[72] One would need to resist the slanderer's

[70] *Ibid.*, p. 58, no. 5, lines 23–8. [71] Kekaumenos, Litavrin, §3; Wassiliewsky, 3.
[72] Kekaumenos, Litavrin, §3; Wassiliewsky, 3.

efforts to push one into the role of an enemy. Kekaumenos pointed out that punishment, even when justified, made relationships more combative. Kekaumenos wanted to work, not with enemies who would lay snares, but with brothers. In meting out punishments to subordinates a general should try to make the miscreants like children rather than enemies: "Correct... still others with good habits and mild warnings as a father his own children."[73] In giving the advice, "honor your mistress as your true lady and mother and sister," Kekaumenos was again advocating a particular role as a means of avoiding trouble.[74] Kekaumenos assumed that any contact with women posed a threat of sexual temptation. By playing brother or son, one would put the mistress into a safe role as sister or mother. In a passage discussed above, community members push one to intervene against a powerful neighbor by invoking the memory of the one's father: "'Your father,' they will say, 'was such an avenger and therefore his praises are sung by the mouths of all even until now.'"[75] In this scenario, the agitators tempt one with a highly desirable role as a powerful champion of justice. To turn down their request, one would have to admit publicly to being either a lesser man than one's father or tolerant of injustice. This sort of manipulation would be extremely difficult to brush off. Then:

In these ways enchanting your ears and you are agreed with them to do this, straightaway running in secret they will tell the prominent man, saying, "We, having faithfulness and service for you and wishing you very well, tell you what we know and heard. So and so – meaning you – has incited the entire city against you and tomorrow he will come out to you with all his people, and perhaps even they will come for murder and kill you."[76]

Kekaumenos portrayed one and the same person as perfidiously asking for intervention from and betraying the reader. Yet he was describing the actions of a community of people. It would make sense that some people within the community would push for intervention and action while others would lose their nerve and tell the opposition about the plans. Kekaumenos imagined two possible roles for the powerful person. Either he could flee to the emperor and get the reader condemned for treason. Or, the option Kekaumenos probably preferred, he could play the just, moderate, and much abused father:

Hearing these things he will flee, supposing that they speak truthfully, and he will write to the emperor against you as against a rabble-rouser and rebel, and you will be destroyed unjustly. Yet if he is steady, he will allow you to come forward to the court with the people and subduing you with a beating and cutting your hair he

---

[73] Kekaumenos, Litavrin, §58; Wassiliewsky, 57. [74] Kekaumenos, Litavrin, §4; Wassiliewsky, 5.
[75] Kekaumenos, Litavrin, §38; Wassiliewsky, 41. See note 42 above. [76] *Ibid.*

will chasten you. Then those praising you will flee and those seeing you will say "This man suffered this now because of us." They will go away in a pained fashion. While you, casting your eyes here and there and not finding any of those praising you earlier, will speak and blame yourself, saying, "Ah, my thoughtlessness!" Then the prominent man, wanting to mollify the community, will call them and say, "I recognize that your good intentions were for me and you displayed them from the first, and I have nothing against you, but I have you as my children. This did not happen because of you, but this agitator stumbled, while you are my friends."[77]

The prominent man treated those who conspired against him as friends who were looking out for his good. His possible responses illustrate well the two major avenues of redressing a grievance: first, attempt to get imperial intervention, and second, manipulate community opinion to neutralize opposition and gain supporters. The prominent man talked to the community, including his opposition, in the role of dutiful children and supporters. Just as Aratos was alone in causing all the trouble for Nikon in Sparta, here one rabble-rouser is blamed for all opposition. The tactic allowed everyone else to take on the positive roles of brothers and friends. Similarly, the eremite who did not agree to the division of property on Mount Athos was castigated as the single source of discord.

This sort of manipulation was practiced on Kekaumenos' kinsman Nikoulitzas. According to Nikoulitzas' account of it, he was forced to take part in a treasonous conspiracy against his will. When the conspirators were trying to get Nikoulitzas to join up they greeted him like a father and leader:

Leaping up immediately at the sight of him, they met him completely as befitting servants, receiving him as he dismounted from his horse and leading him into their midst, saying to him, "we have you as our father and authority and without you we would not want to do anything."[78]

By calling Nikoulitzas their father, the rebels were trying to push him into the role of the leader of the revolt. While they acted as servants, they continued to apply pressure to Nikoulitzas, who did not accept the leadership until he was persuaded that the rebels otherwise would kill him. Effective manipulation of the roles that governed relationships allowed them to gain the esteem of the anonymous crowd of observers whose opinion decided who was in charge. Throughout the revolt, Nikoulitzas' authority was least challenged when he was acting as a general. His order to have the other leaders arrested was obeyed because he managed to get the right people to consider him to be the real father and authority.

[77] *Ibid.*   [78] Kekaumenos, Litavrin, §/4; Wassiliewsky, 68.

When Nikon wanted to build a church in Sparta, he gathered support by ostentatiously chaining himself in the marketplace and walking through town, saying that he was captive to St. Barbara until her church was built.[79] The people in the town did not want Nikon in the role of a captive and so redeemed him by building the church. Nikon himself took on the role of a captive. But he also forced the townspeople to choose between the roles of captors or redeemers. In this way Nikon motivated people to help him by playing on their sense of propriety.

Eudokia's act of sale, in which she pleaded poverty to sell her dowry land, is a fascinating study in the way personal portrayal was used to coerce behavior. On the one hand, Eudokia needed to stress her independence, free will, and desire to sell her land in order to make the sale valid. On the other hand, she needed to be in a state of extreme need in order to get an exemption from the law banning the sale of dowry land. Eudokia's appeal to the *pansevastos doux* and *praitor* Andronikos Doukas emphasizes her extreme poverty, humility, and need: "Yea, my holy master, let the present accommodation (*oikonomia*) for me your unfortunate and unworthy slave stand, lest we perish most badly and pass from this world. And may God guide you. I am beseeching as a daring unworthy slave."[80] The text of this letter to Doukas was copied into the deed of sale. The appeal was emotional and sensational. She described herself as a suffering woman whose children were about to die of starvation because by taking on the role of poor supplicant she offered him the opportunity to show God-like magnanimity. Her petition can be seen as part of a tradition established in the fourth and fifth centuries, when ideas of power and justice came to be understood and exercised, in Christian terms of supplication and compassion. In this tradition the terminology of poverty became a means of establishing a claim to help from above: "the 'poor' person was the person of any status who waited, humbly but insistently, for the answer of the great."[81] While the cities, bishops, and patterns of authority that established the use of this vocabulary no longer worked in the same way in Eudokia's era, the relational and functional nature of the vocabulary persisted. Aspects of the same mental image of Christian supplication and succor lie behind the rhetoric of the tenth-century legislation in which emperors tried to regulate the economic activities of "the powerful." The goal of the legislation was to keep land in the hands of those who could

---

[79] *Life of Nikon*, 128.   [80] *Docheiariou*, p. 68, no. 3, lines 20–1.
[81] Peter Brown, *Poverty and Leadership in the Later Roman Empire* (Hanover, NH, 2002), 69–70. See also Evelyne Patlagean, *Pauvreté économique et pauvreté sociale à Byzance, 4e–7e siècles* (Paris, 1977), 25–35.

be made to pay their taxes. The emperors couched the legislation in terms of their protections for the "poor," citing Psalm 12: "Because the poor are despoiled, because the needy groan, I will now arise, says the Lord."[82] The poor were mentioned in order to allow the emperor to play the role of God, protector of the poor and helpless.[83]

Eudokia, the owner of several estates, became poor so that she could effectively call for help. Doukas' response is terse, befitting a busy man: "Since the cause for which you are about to sell the real estate seems lawful, let the *protoproedros* and *logariastes* Chandrenos, as you asked, make a *dekreton*. January, 5th indication."[84] It is clear that the other people who talked to Eudokia did not think she was so pitiful. The juxtaposition of rhetoric working to show Eudokia as acting freely and enthusiastically, and to show her dire need and extreme helplessness creates an odd tension in the document. The local officials were more exercised about verifying that she really did want to sell the land than about verifying the extent of her poverty. Eudokia promised to defend this sale in court against challenges from her children, relatives, heirs, and any others of her party. In one document she assumes simultaneously two different characters. One was the owner of a number of properties within Thessalonike and its surrounding hinterland, a woman whose father and husband held imperial titles and who made the superior of a prominent monastery nervous. Another was a helpless victim of misfortune, completely bound by necessity. In order to sell her land, Eudokia had to be both completely in her own power and under absolute restraint. By presenting herself to Doukas as bound by necessity and poverty, Eudokia got him to grant her the exemption. By presenting herself to the monks and the assembly of judges as acting willingly and of her own accord she got them to legitimate her sale.

When people had to repudiate a role they had taken previously, they could attribute their previous actions to the machinations of Satan. Monks should play the role of loving brothers. When they burn down each other's property, they are out of character. When explaining why his monks attacked and destroyed the storehouse of a neighboring monastery, the superior blamed the devil's influence.[85] The conflict between the monks of Vatopedi and Philadelphos was caused by demonic forces.[86] In the

---

[82] The novel of Romanos I of 934. Svoronos and Gounaridis, eds., *Les Novelles des empereurs macédoniens*, 82. McGeer, *Land Legislation*, 53–60.
[83] Morris, "The powerful and poor in tenth-century Byzantium," 20.
[84] *Docheiariou*, p. 68, no. 3, line 22.   [85] *Saint-Pantéléèmôn*, pp. 39–50, no. 4.
[86] *Vatopedi*, p. 74, no. 3, line 7.

settlement issued by John Tzimiskes' representative to resolve the conflict on Mount Athos between Athanasios of Athos and other monks, the author, Euthymios of Studios, declared:

> For an entire week the dispute was aired and very thoroughly investigated. Once we succeeded in acquiring a deeply spiritual understanding of the matter, it was found that both parties were absolutely guiltless, strange as this may sound. The dispute which had arisen between them was recognized as having been caused by the activity of Satan.[87]

This exonerated all parties from personal responsibility for their actions. The victim of satanic influences thus became one of the possible roles that were used to help resolve conflicts.

There is no question that Byzantine writers described situations in terms of standardized relationships and interactions. The evidence presented here suggests additionally that Byzantine people tried to align their actual behavior, as well as the descriptions of their behavior, with positive behavioral models. They also seem to have pushed those with whom they were contending into particular roles. This appears to have been a significant means of manipulation. The clever could play upon common patterns of proper behavior to elicit particular responses from others.

Money, imperial contacts, and physical force were important in creating authority. The public perception of proper behavior was also one of the central factors in creating authority in provincial society. The ability to turn local people into one's "men" could greatly enhance one's authority. Men were largely free to choose whose they would be and thus local authority was relatively easy to acquire and lose. Part of the great extent of social mobility in Byzantine society had to do with the ease with which one could acquire authority through proper behavior and manipulation of one's neighbors' perceptions.

In matters with impact beyond local provincial regulation, the imperial administration took an interest and was generally effective. Yet with the exception of Nikoulitzas' revolt, none of the events discussed here were matters that the emperors themselves cared to resolve. While the people of Sparta may have been concerned with whether John the horse-trainer was brought to justice for stealing the old woman's bread, the imperial administration was not. The methods of settling conflicts and organizing provincial communities described here applied in the absence of imperial

---

[87] *Typika*, 235.

interest in provincial regulation. The revolt is a highly significant exception because it shows the clear limits of the authority held by provincial households. When one became too powerful, the imperial administration would take an interest. Kekaumenos had it right when he said that one should never participate in a revolt because the emperor in Constantinople would always win. In the core provinces of the empire, the emperors did not allow important men to become independent princes. Nikoulitzas was the head of one of the most important households in Larissa, but he did not rule Larissa. Bishops similarly could become extremely influential in their towns, but they did not rule them. This leveling of the peaks of provincial power was a key factor in allowing provincial authority to remain informal and malleable.

Conclusions

The analysis presented here differs from earlier conceptions of Byzantine provincial society, not simply by positing a different level of imperial governmental authority, but by taking a different attitude toward the terminology of our sources. Fundamentally, Byzantines used terms that emphasized relationships rather than fixed status. Individuals had multiple relationships with others: relationships of service, of parental care, of brotherly and sisterly regard. Such relationships could change; in different situations one could be supplicant and patron to the same person. The relational vocabulary of our sources was used by the Byzantines to fit their reality into recognizable and imitable patterns of behavior. Careful attention to ideal patterns of behavior and to how Byzantine people tried to inhabit them and use them to manipulate the behavior of others can contribute to an understanding of how Byzantine people conducted themselves and what factors enabled and constrained their actions. Rather than try to sort individuals into strict categories, I have endeavored to let the reader see overlapping relationships and ambiguous identities among imperial officials and provincial people.

In an effort to move from an acknowledgement of the relational nature of authority in Byzantine society to a model that enables historical discussion while remaining true to those characteristics, I have discussed provincial society in terms of relationships and associations between households, *oikoi*. The relationships within an *oikos* – parental, fraternal, servient – were fundamental to individual identity and were also commonly used metaphorically to describe non-familial relationships. Households could form associations in several ways, including marriage, spiritual parentage, baptismal sponsorship, and proximity. Households could compensate for lack of status by forming close associations and acting in concert. The most significant way to improve one's social status was to gain an association with a more important household. Of all the various situations and interactions examined throughout this study, very few cannot be satisfactorily explained with the constellation of relationships between and within *oikoi*.

Byzantine political culture centered power and might on the emperor and allowed reasonably prominent people to participate in that power by associating themselves with the imperial majesty through acquiring imperial titles. Those who gained imperial titles greatly enhanced the prestige of their own households by becoming minor servants of the imperial household. Within the fundamentally relational Byzantine epistemology, service was a relationship, not a status. The distinctions in status that have underpinned efforts to separate the "state" from the "public" and analyze the effects of the former on the latter do not fit well with Byzantine society.

Byzantine court ceremonial played a great role in establishing and manipulating the relationship of service that tied the leading citizens of the empire into the imperial household. The ceremonial exchange of titles, offices, salaries, seals, gifts, and robes for taxes, services, prayers, and acclamations made the imperial majesty, in the words of Constantine Porphyrogenitos, "more imperial and more fearsome."[1] This ritual exaltation of imperial glory helped enforce the authority of the emperors by maintaining their majesty and ennobling service to emperors. Yet however much the political culture of title and office augmented the grandeur of imperial power and helped in sustaining imperial sovereignty in the tenth and much of the eleventh centuries, it had little to do with administration.

From the provincial standpoint, the imperial government was simultaneously sovereign and apathetic. The emperors exercised just enough authority at the right times to prevent the leaders of important households in the core provinces from becoming rulers themselves. While the efforts of the imperial administration to sustain imperial sovereignty placed some limits on local powers, the emperors were not interested in regulating the details of provincial life. The imperial administration dealt rigorously and effectively with a narrow set of objectives, chiefly collecting revenue and maintaining imperial sovereignty. Outside of these spheres, action needed to be solicited from imperial officials, leaving vast opportunities for local people to act independently of any legal strictures or fear of imperial involvement. Everyone in the provinces knew the emperor could have his way if he cared. Yet most people could act with the confidence that the emperor did not care about their business. Actions of the imperial administration in the provinces were more often matters of favors and personal appeals than regular administrative processes. The evidence for physical

---

[1] Reiske, ed., *De ceremoniis aulae Byzantinae, Constantine VII Porphyrogenitus*, 517.

Conclusions 167

travel to Constantinople in efforts to awaken imperial interest and intervention in provincial affairs speaks to the need and desire for more effective government. Far from being oppressed by an all-pervasive imperial government, people sometimes desired more imperial intervention and took steps to excite government interest in their problems.

In the relative absence of government, provincial households enjoyed great freedom to do whatever did not affect the limited interests of the imperial administration. Authority in provincial society was obtained through membership in a successful household and the acquisition of wealth and the support of others. People in provincial society attempted to control each other through physical intimidation, economic manipulation, and appeals for external intervention, and by gathering the support of community opinion. Intimidation, supplication, and intervention were central means of coercing behavior, carrying on disagreements, and forging alliances. Wealth, capacity for effective violence, and access to the imperial court were also key factors that allowed one to act with authority. The relatively fluid nature of authority allowed great scope for competition among provincial households. The significance of community consensus in creating authority made the struggle to increase the prestige of one's household a constant factor in the dynamics of provincial society.

Order, *taxis*, was created in provincial society in part by mapping human behavior to set patterns of relationships. Those who could control which roles within a paradigmatic relationship were to be assumed by whom had considerable ability to manipulate others. The correspondences between individuals in a situation and the characters in a model interaction were contested, probably more often than we can see. The attempt to cast oneself and others into particular roles within a relationship emerges as one of the main mechanisms for manipulation of others and gathering of community support.

The main factor constraining the freedom of provincial people was precisely the freedom of their neighbors. That people with physical power and the backing of some neighbors could do what they wanted did not mean that everyone in their community was pleased with that course of action. The leaders of prominent local households were able to coerce the behavior of their less powerful neighbors and posed a more immediate threat than did the distant imperial government. The considerable freedom of provincial society was thus matched by considerable insecurity.

Appendix: guide to sources

Byzantine civilization has left a rich and varied material and literary legacy. The following describes the sources used throughout this book and, where appropriate, my interpretive stance toward them. In using sources that originated outside of Constantinople whenever possible, I have perhaps presented an uncharacteristic sample of Byzantine source material. This guide is therefore not a general introduction to the sources for Byzantine history. Its purpose rather is to allow readers of all levels of training to follow and assess my arguments easily.[1]

ARCHIVES

Remarkably little Byzantine archival material survives from the tenth and eleventh centuries, but a high proportion of what has survived has been published. The largest collections of middle Byzantine legal documents are preserved in the monasteries of Mount Athos, the leading center of Byzantine monasticism since the tenth century. The oldest documents date to the late ninth century. The documents include imperial grants, agreements made between monasteries, donations, deeds of sale, deeds of exchange, and inventories of the monasteries' possessions. Although all of the documents eventually found their way into monastic archives, there are a few that record transactions made between non-monastic parties. The archives of the Monastery of St. John the Theologian on Patmos have also

---

[1] An excellent brief introduction to the major narrative sources for the eleventh century is in Michael Angold, *The Byzantine Empire, 1025–1204: A Political History*, 2nd edn (London, 1997), 1–11. The best guide to Byzantine historical writing remains Herbert Hunger's *Die hochsprachliche profane Literatur der Byzantiner*, vol. I, (Munich, 1978), 331–441; also available in Modern Greek translation by L. Benake, I. Anastasiou, and G. Makre, *Vyzantine Logotechnia: E logra kosmike grammateia ton vyzantinon* (Athens, 1991).

Appendix: guide to sources 169

survived. Some texts from the archives from monasteries in Asia Minor and southern Italy have also been published.²

Enough of these legal documents deal with standard situations for us to get a reasonable sense of what was required by convention and what was peculiar to the case at hand. Some formularies have been published.³ In their vocabulary and clausal structure, the legal documents are comparable to fifth- and sixth-century Egyptian material, showing the influence of the late Roman law schools at Beirut and Constantinople.⁴ Byzantine documents generally used more rhetorically elaborate versions of the same basic clauses in the late Roman documents. For example, the following clauses attest to the volition of the principal party. The first example was made in late sixth-century Egypt, the second in 1001 near Mount Athos, and the third in 1181 near Smyrna:

I declare voluntarily and of my own free choice, under the sacred oath by the genius of the emperor, that I give surety and pledge to Your Excellency...⁵

I, the *koubouklesios* Stephen, son of the departed *protopapas* Nikephoros, making the honored and life-giving cross with my own hand, establish and make the present sale with a defense by my voluntary decision, and I choose by will and not from some necessity, or trick, or fear, or violence, not by deceit, not by robbery, not by entrapment, nor ignorance of deeds, or some other manner forbidden by law, but rather with all eagerness and wholehearted good will...⁶

I establish and I make voluntarily and without second thoughts, not from some necessity or force, or fear or trick or fraud, or robbery, or lack of skill, or rusticity or ignorance of deeds or some other blameworthy and law-annulling reason, but

---

² The archives of many of the Athonite monasteries have been published in the series Archives de l'Athos, under the direction of Gabriel Millet, Paul Lemerle, and Nicolas Oikonomides. The archives from Patmos have been published by Era Vranuse, ed., *Byzantina Engrapha tes mones Patmou: I Autokratorika* (Athens, 1980) and Maria Nystaxopoulou-Pelekidou, ed., *Byzantina Engrapha tes mones Patmou: II Demosion Leiturgon* (Athens, 1980). Records from Asia Minor are collected in Franz Miklosich and Joseph Müller, eds., *Acta et diplomata graeca medii aevi sacra et profana*, 6 vols. (Vienna, 1860–90). The south Italian documents have been edited by André Guillou, *Les Archives de Saint-Jean-Prodrome sur le Mont Ménécée* (Paris, 1955); André Guillou, *Les Actes grecs de S. Maria di Messina; enquête sur les populations grecques d'Italie du sud et de Sicile (XIe–XIVes.)* (Palermo, 1963).
³ Dieter Simon, "Ein spätbyzantinisches Kaufformular," in *Flores Legum*, ed. R. Feenstra, J. H. A. Lokin, and N. Van der Wal (Groningen, 1971), 155–82; Dieter Simon and Spyros Troianos, "Dreizehn Geschäftsformulare," *Fontes Minores* 2 (1977): 262–95; Nicolas Oikonomides, "Contribution à l'étude de la Pronoia au XIII siècle: une formule d'attribution de parèques à un pronoiaire," *REB* 22 (1964): 158–75; Gianno Ferrari, *Formulari Notarili inediti dell'età Bizantina* (Rome, 1912).
⁴ Simon, "Ein spätbyzantinisches Kaufformular," 174–5.
⁵ E. John Rea Turner, L. Koenen, and José Fernandes Pomar, eds., *The Oxyrhynchus Papyri XXVII* (London, 1962), pp. 175–7, no. 2478.
⁶ *Iviron I*, p. 178, no. 12, lines 2–8. *Koubouklesios* was an imperial dignity bestowed on officials serving the patriarch.

with all enthusiasm and whole-hearted good will, still after having thought about the intention, time of reflection, and the approval of all my party...[7]

The rhetorical elaboration seen in the second and third examples is typical of Byzantine manifestations of the late Roman legal forms. The second and third examples also display a typical variety in vocabulary and word order among fundamentally quite similar clauses. While there is considerable continuity in clauses and vocabulary through to the thirteenth century, there was room for flexibility within these norms, so that legal documents were adapted to and reflected their particular situation.[8]

In using legal documents as historical sources it is important to appreciate the careful literary crafting behind some of these texts. Within the standard structures and stock clauses, there is room for dramatic narration. Individuals can be portrayed in a number of dramatic roles. In petitions of the fifth through seventh centuries one can find the roles and plot lines of biblical stories and Greek prose romances. In these texts local problems were described in terms clearly reminiscent of romances, with violent passions and sudden reversals of fortune, narrated with relish. At least one official, Dioskoros of Aphrodito, was explicit in approaching his task of writing official documents as literature, going so far as to point out to readers that they should notice his literary ploys.[9] While the case for Dioskoros' modeling of his petitions on romances is clear, it is possible to find petitions from the late fifth century that record plainly situations suitable for dramatic enhancement.[10] Byzantine charters of the tenth and eleventh centuries sometimes describe interactions between individuals in terms of set characters and stylized discourse. These characterizations were employed and manipulated to propel the arguments being made in the charters. The authors of these texts used their repertoire of characters and clauses to craft a compelling case for the signatory's viewpoint. Far from dramatic stylization obscuring the reality of the case, it makes the intentions of the signatories clearer.

---

[7] Miklosich and Müller, eds., *Acta et diplomata*, vol. IV, p. 122.
[8] Simon, "Ein spätbyzantinisches Kaufformular," 176.
[9] Arkady Kovelman, "From logos to myth: Egyptian petitions of the 5th–7th centuries," *Bulletin of the American Society of Papyrologists* 28 (1991): 135–52.
[10] One petition describes in a perfectly dull manner a woman's complaint that her son's unjust attempts to make her pay his debts have caused her to pledge her daughter to pay her taxes. This basic situation was ripe for the sort of passionate and dramatic treatment typical of Dioskoros' texts, yet the author limited himself to a plain statement of the situation. J. R. Rea, ed., *The Oxyrhynchus Papyri* LXIII (London, 1996), no. 4393.

Appendix: guide to sources 171

CADASTER OF THEBES

The text known as the *Cadaster of Thebes* has attracted interest because it seems to represent the middle Byzantine system of taxation based on complete registration of land. The text is on four sheets of eleventh-century paper that were added (out of order) to a fourteenth-century Greek codex when it was rebound in the early seventeenth century. The codex is in the Vatican Library (Vat. Gr. 215).[11] The text appears to be part of an imperial land-tax register written by fiscal officials to aid in the proper collection of the land-tax. Many of the place names refer to villages near Thebes. It cannot be dated precisely, but reflects fiscal practice of the eleventh century. In the late eleventh and twelfth centuries this system was superseded, but perhaps not replaced entirely, by a system that recorded the tax owed by great landowners on all their various possessions. Many of these documents, called *praktika*, have survived in the monastic archives. The *Cadaster of Thebes* on the other hand is a unique testimony to the efforts of the imperial bureaucracy to register the land of empire systematically with the people who happened to owe tax on that land. Since its preservation seems to have been accidental, the text may be a random sample of a tax register rather than one pertaining to a great monastery.

The *Cadaster of Thebes* lists villages and the individual heads of household holding land in each village. A tax amount is listed for each head of household and the tax due from the whole village is summarized at the end of that section. The text's editor assigned numbers and letters to the sections, subsections, and individual household entries.[12]

While it is clear enough that the *Cadaster of Thebes* was part of an effort to register land and tax systematically according to the principles of the ninth- through eleventh-century taxation system, the more closely one reads the document the less sense it makes. For all of the reasons explained in chapter 2 above, maintaining a comprehensive register of all the land in the empire was extraordinarily difficult, and the task became more complex as time passed and lands changed hands. Efforts to notate changes in ownership are clear in the *Cadaster of Thebes*. The meaning behind these notations is unclear, however, and they are themselves sufficiently inconsistent that I believe it is impossible to determine with confidence who was responsible for the tax on the lands listed. It is, of course, possible that one trained in

[11] Svoronos, "Recherches sur le cadastre byzantin et la fiscalité aux XIe et XIIe siècles," 1–3.
[12] *Cadaster of Thebes*, 57–63.

the art of Byzantine fiscal administration would be able to use the *Cadaster of Thebes* effectively to determine who should pay what. Yet fiscal registers also had a performative role in the process of taxation. By substantiating the claim that the emperor knew every field and farmer in the empire, the registers greatly augmented the awesome authority of the imperial officials. Collecting taxes was, at least in some places and times, an encounter bound by rituals designed to convince individuals to bow to imperial authority and hand over their money. The register book was a crucial prop in this ritual. The best explanation I can offer for the *Cadaster of Thebes* is that officials continued to maintain land registers after they ceased to contain much practically useful information because such registers still held power as performative objects.[13]

CEREMONY BOOK

Emperor Constantine VII (912–957) credited himself with writing a treatise on imperial ceremonial, usually known by its modern title *De ceremoniis aulae Byzantinae*.[14] The treatise is a compilation of diverse material dating from the fifth through the tenth centuries pertaining to imperial ceremonial.[15] Some chapters describe ceremonies that actually took place and others contain prescriptive accounts of how certain ceremonies ought to be performed. The treatise is divided into two books. Constantine explained that the first book was based on written texts and the second on oral testimony, although this distinction is not strictly maintained. Descriptions of ceremonies which took place during the reign of Constantine's successor Nikephoros Phokas (963–969) were added to the end of Book I. The last thirty-one chapters of Book II are a miscellaneous collection of records that may have been copied into the manuscript without an authorial intention that they be considered part of the treatise.[16]

---

[13] Neville, "Information, ceremony and power in Byzantine fiscal registers: varieties of function in the Cadaster of Thebes," *BMGS* 25 (2001): 20–43.

[14] On Constantine's literary activity see Ihor Ševčenko, "Re-reading Constantine Porphyrogenitus," in *Byzantine Diplomacy: Papers from the Twenty-Fourth Spring Symposium of Byzantine Studies*, ed. Jonathan Shepard and Simon Franklin (Aldershot, 1990), 167–95.

[15] Michael McCormick, "Analyzing imperial ceremonies," *JÖB* 35 (1985): 2–6. A guide to the probable dating of various sections of the text, compiled by McCormick, is provided in the entry on "De ceremoniis," in the *Oxford Dictionary of Byzantium*. See also Averil Cameron, "The construction of court ritual: the Byzantine *Book of Ceremonies*," in *Rituals of Royalty: Power and Ceremonial in Traditional Societies*, ed. David Cannadine and Simon Price (Cambridge, 1987), 106–36.

[16] On the complex history of the editions see Gilbert Dagron, André Binggeli, Michael Featherstone, and Bernard Flusin, "L'organisation et le déroulement des courses d'après le *Livre des cérémonies*," *TM* 13 (2000): 5–8. They have edited Book I.77–82, *ibid.*, 1–200. Book I through chapter 92 has

CONFRATERNITY OF THEBES

The text known as the Confraternity of Thebes is a foundation document for a lay devotional brotherhood founded in Thebes in 1048.[17] The document, in the archives of Regia Cappella Palatina in Palermo, has survived apparently by virtue of having been taken, along with its owners, to Palermo during a raid by Roger II of Sicily on central Greece in 1147.

The document opens with a miniature of the icon venerated by the association. The text contains a brief description and history of the organization, lays out responsibilities of the members, and ends with the signatures of the members. An original charter was made in 1048 when the organization was founded, but that document had become so decayed with time that the members wrote and signed a new one. This second charter, composed some time before 1089, is the document in Palermo. The association had forty-nine members, of whom four were women. Twenty members signed their own names and twenty-nine put crosses next to their names. There were twelve priests, three monks, one presbyter, one priest and monk, and one presbyter and monk. Four families had more than one relative represented in the association.

The members of the organization devoted themselves to reverence of the icon and care for each other. Each month the members would gather at the place where the icon was, partake of the Eucharist, and then process with the icon to the place that would house it for the next month. The responsibility and honor of hosting the icon was given to each member in turn. Hosting the icon entailed having Eucharist performed twice a week and praying for the emperors, the patriarch, certain local abbots and abbesses, and all members of the organization, living and dead.

While no other documents of this kind survive, there is a description of a similar brotherhood in eleventh-century Constantinople devoted to a

---

been edited with French translation and commentary: Albert Vogt, ed., *Le Livre des cérémonies*, 2 vols. (Paris, 1935). Chapters 44 and 45 of Book II, which contain financial and logistical information about imperial expeditions aimed at the recovery of Crete in 911, 935, and 949, have been edited by John Haldon, "Theory and practice in tenth-century military administration: Chapters II, 44 and 45 of the *Book of Ceremonies*," *TM* 13 (2000): 201–52. Philotheos' treatise on precedence was incorporated as chapters 52 and 53 of Book II; edited by Nicolas Oikonomides, *Les Listes de préséance byzantines des IXe et Xe siècles* (Paris, 1972), 64–235. The complete text is available in Johann Jacob Reiske, ed., *De ceremoniis aulae Byzantinae, Constantine VII Porphyrogenitus*, Corpus Scriptorum Historiae Byzantinae 9–11, ed. Barthold Georg Niebuhr (Bonn, 1829). For this edition Niebuhr incorporated corrections that Reiske had made to the edition by Leich which were originally published as notes in I. Henricus Leichius and I. Iacobus Reiskius, eds., *Constantini Porphyrogenneti Imperatoris Constantinopolitani Libri Duo de Cerimoniis Aulae Byzantinae*, 2 vols. (Leipzig, 1751–54).

[17] Nesbitt and Witta, "A confraternity of the Comnenian era," 363–6.

miraculous icon of the Theotokos Hodegetria. The activities ascribed to this group are similar to those of the Confraternity of Thebes. It is likely that there were other similar organizations. A fresco in Arta depicts such a procession of men with an icon of the Hodegetria and may illustrate the deaconate described in this text.[18] It has been suggested that other associations, *diakonia*, were responsible for maintaining bath houses in Constantinople.[19]

KEKAUMENOS

The text known as Kekaumenos, after the presumed author, is a book of practical career advice apparently written by a general to his children. It survives in a single fourteenth- or fifteenth-century manuscript in Moscow. Based on the author's remarks made in the work, especially about his relatives and ancestors, he seems to have been born around 1015 or 1020, to a family called Kekaumenos. The work was composed, probably over a period of time, between 1070 and 1081.[20]

The text of Kekaumenos in the manuscript represents a long and confused textual tradition. There is a table of contents, or *pinax*, listing topics and section numbers. The table of contents is followed by a brief metrical prologue that explains that the original prologue and some sections of the original text were missing. Section breaks are numbered throughout the text. The headings in the table of contents do not correspond to the numbered section breaks that are embedded in the text. The copyist apparently was dealing with a text that already had both the table of contents and numbered rubrics. The copyist did not attempt to rationalize either system. The numbered section breaks in the text do not make much sense as divisions. Sometimes they divide coherent arguments in half while sometimes they put two different arguments in the same segment.

The work has been understood as having four major parts: advice for the author's "sons," advice for independent princes, refutations of the existence of satyrs and dragons, and advice for emperors. It has long been assumed that the sections on satyrs and dragons had been written by a different author. Recently, however, a case has been made that some or all of

---

[18] Cutler, "Art in Byzantine society: motive forces of Byzantine patronage," *JÖB* 31, no. 2 (1981): 762–3.
[19] Paul Magdalino, "Church, bath and diakonia in medieval Constantinople," in *Church and People in Byzantium*, ed. Rosemary Morris (Birmingham, 1990), 165–90.
[20] Paul Lemerle, *Prolégomènes à une édition critique et commentée des "Conseils et récits" de Kékaumenos* (Brussels, 1960), 1–38. Georgina Buckler, "Authorship of the Strategikon of Cecaumenos," *BZ* 36 (1936): 7–26. A. Savvides, "The Byzantine family of Kekaumenos," *Diptycha* 4 (1986): 12–27.

Appendix: guide to sources 175

these sections may also have been written by Kekaumenos.[21] Between the part addressed to "sons" and that addressed to independent princes there is a break in the section numbering from 192 to 218. It has been suggested that the advice for emperors, which is exactly the right number of paragraphs, originally was placed between the advice for sons and the advice for independent princes.[22] Each edition has treated the content of the text differently.[23]

In discussing how to deal with revolts against the emperor, Kekaumenos included a lengthy narrative of a revolt in which his uncle Nikoulitzas participated. This account appears to have been based on one Nikoulitzas wrote while in prison. The chapter immediately following this account is an invective against the faithlessness of Vlachs that obeys some of the classical rules of invective taught in the *progymnasmata*.[24] It is possible that the anti-Vlach chapter was also written by Nikoulitzas, whose experiences with Vlachs in the revolt were not positive.

Kekaumenos' education was embarrassing for a rhetorician but quite impressive for a general. Kekaumenos knew some books of the Bible well and appears to have had some acquaintance with a variety of other texts, possibly from florilegia. Those passages of his advice which seem disjointed are responses to topics as arranged in common florilegia. He may have assumed that his readers would be familiar with similar collections.[25] An argument that Kekaumenos had completed the first level of basic rhetorical

---

[21] Charlotte Roueché, "The literary background of Kekaumenos," in *Literacy, Education and Manuscript Transmission in Byzantium and Beyond*, ed. Catherine Holmes and Judith Waring (Leiden, 2002), 129–35.
[22] Lemerle, *Prolégomènes*, 16.
[23] In their 1896 edition Wassiliewsky and Jernstedt preserved the numbered rubrics and sequence of the manuscript. They omitted the sections on dragons and satyrs, however, and thought that the section on advice to the emperor was a separate treatise written by a different author. This edition was the basis for Hans-Georg Beck's German translation, *Vademecum des byzantinischen Aristokraten: Das sogenannte Strategikon des Kekaumenos* (Graz, Vienna, and Cologne, 1964). In 1972 Gennadii Grigorevich Litavrin published a new edition with Russian translation and commentary under the title *Cecaumeni Consilia et Narrationes*. Litavrin removed the prologue and numbered rubrics to an appendix, and inserted his own section breaks based on the sense of the text. He placed the advice to the emperor between the advice to sons and the advice to independent princes. He put the chapters on satyrs and dragons in an appendix. This text, with Litavrin's section numbers, is reprinted with Modern Greek translation by Dimitri Tsougkarakes, *Kekaumenos Strategikon* (Athens, 1993). A third edition and Italian translation was made by Maria Dora Spadaro, who preserved the paragraph numbering of the manuscript and divided the text into five major sections. Maria Dora Spadaro, ed., *Raccomandazioni e consigli di un galantuomo (Strategikon)* (Alessandria, 1998), 29–31.
[24] Charlotte Roueché, "Defining the foreign in Kekaumenos," in *Strangers to Themselves: The Byzantine Outsider*, ed. Dion Smythe (Aldershot, 2000), 212.
[25] Roueché, "The literary background of Kekaumenos," 114–17.

training is forthcoming.²⁶ His advice about military campaigning reflects the teachings of the tenth-century military handbooks as well as tenth- and eleventh-century military practice.

One of Alexios Komnenos' key supporters was a general called Katakalon Kekaumenos. "Kekaumenos" appears to have been Katakalon's epithet rather than a family name, and for other reasons of content it does not seem that Katakalon Kekaumenos was the author.²⁷ Lemerle argued on the basis of an inscription in Georgian that the Kekaumenos family was Armenian. Oikonomides has proposed a convincing reading of the same inscription that is incompatible with Lemerle's interpretation.²⁸ Litavrin argued that Kekaumenos' family may have been of eastern or Armenian ancestry but was fully Hellenized and at home in a Balkan setting. Charlotte Rouché comments:

> What is perhaps most striking, however, is that the text should be capable of such varied interpretation... Kekaumenos was apparently unconcerned to present himself – or his ancestors – in terms of their "ethnicity." He seems to see himself as "a Roman," and to see Romanness as something that was not jeopardized by having foreign forebears.²⁹

The ethnic allegiances of Kekaumenos' grandparents do not appear to have had much impact on his perceptions. Kekaumenos' stories were from all parts of the empire.

MARCIAN TREATISE

A treatise endeavoring to explain the Byzantine fiscal system survives in a twelfth-century manuscript in the Marcian library.³⁰ This text is known as either the *Dölger Treatise* after its editor, the *Marcian Treatise* after its location, or the *Fiscal Treatise* after its content. The treatise is near the end of Marcianus Gr. 173, a manuscript of 285 folios containing laws of the tenth-century emperors and Alexios I, legal judgments, and other treatises on measurement, weights, geography, and chronology. The earliest possible date of composition is 912, the year of the death of Leo VI, who is

---

²⁶ *Ibid.*, 112. The evidence for this proposition will appear in Rouché's forthcoming edition and translation of the text.
²⁷ Lemerle, *Prolégomènes*, 38.
²⁸ Nicolas Oikonomides, "L'organisation de la frontière orientale de Byzance aux xe–xie siècle et le taktikon de l'Escorial," in *Actes du XIVe Congrès international des études byzantines I* (Bucharest, 1974), 285–302.
²⁹ Rouché, "Defining the foreign in Kekaumenos," 209.
³⁰ Dölger, *Beiträge zur Geschichte der byzantinischen Finanzverwaltung, besonders des 10. und 11. Jahrhunderts*, Byzantinisches Archiv 9 (Leipzig, 1927).

Appendix: guide to sources 177

mentioned in the treatise as deceased. Oikonomides interpreted references to the assessment of surcharges as indicating that the text was written after Alexios Komnenos issued the reform legislation known as the *Palaia kai Nea Logariki* between 1106 and 1110.[31] While this interpretation is entirely plausible, the statement regarding the surcharges in the *Marcian Treatise* is not sufficiently different from the policy created by Alexios to indicate an absolute sequence of the two texts.[32] I see the text as fitting an eleventh-century context.

The author was probably an official endeavoring to explain the reasoning behind fiscal practices and to provide a working knowledge of tax assessment for other officials in the imperial administration. The creators of the *Cadaster of Thebes* appear to have employed the system of registration described in the *Marcian Treatise*.[33]

HAGIOGRAPHY

Of the available hagiographic literature of the second half of the tenth and eleventh centuries, I have chosen to concentrate on four *vitae* that appear to have been written outside of Constantinople and reflect the concerns of provincial society.[34] The *vitae* given close attention are those of Luke the Younger of Stiris, Nikon "Metanoeite," Paul of Latros, and Lazaros the Galesiote. Luke, Nikon, Paul, and Lazaros are historically attested figures who founded provincial monasteries.

Paul of Latros was born in Elaia near Pergamon. He lived as a solitary in a cave on Mount Latros, around which a monastic community developed. He died on Mount Latros in 955. The anonymous author of his *vita* incorporated the testimony of several people who knew Paul and drew on some of Paul's own writings. A charter from the twelfth century attributes the *vita* to Symeon Metaphrastes, a prolific editor of hagiographic texts who died *c.* 1000.[35] Symeon oversaw a vast enterprise of editing saints' lives and creating a menologion, which does not contain a version of the life of Paul.[36] Symeon is not known to have undertaken any original

---

[31] Oikonomides, *Fiscalité*, 43–5.
[32] Alexander Kazhdan, Review of Nicolas Oikonomides, *Fiscalité et exemption fiscale à Byzance (*ixe–xies.*), BZ* 91 (1998): 175.
[33] Neville, "The Marcian Treatise on taxation and the nature of bureaucracy in Byzantium," *BF* 26 (2000): 47–62.
[34] On the use of middle Byzantine saints' lives as historical sources see Morris, *Monks and Laymen*, 64–89. On developments in hagiographical ideals see Bernard Flusin, "L'hagiographie monastique à Byzance au ixe et au xe siècle," *Revue Bénédictine* 103, no. 1–2 (1993): 31–50.
[35] Miklosich and Müller, eds., *Acta et diplomata*, vol. IV, p. 306.
[36] Francois Halkin, *Bibliotheca hagiographica graeca* (Brussels, 1957), 185–6.

composition.[37] An anonymous eulogy of Paul exists in addition to the *vita*.[38] The eulogy includes a testament, ostensibly by Paul, that follows the form of a monastic foundation document.[39] A number of documents attesting to the monastery's later history also have survived.[40]

Lazaros of Mount Galesion was born in the late tenth century in western Asia Minor and died in 1055 in the monastery he founded on Mount Galesion. Lazaros traveled to Jerusalem and spent several years as a monk in the Holy Land before returning to his homeland and founding several monasteries. The life of Lazaros was written by Gregory, a close associate of Lazaros who had the position of cellarer in Lazaros' monastery.[41] Some of the difficulties encountered by the monastery near the end of Lazaros' life and the monks' worries about the foundation's survival are described by Gregory. It appears that the *vita* was written in the context of an ongoing and threatening dispute with the local bishop.[42]

Luke was born before 900 in a village in Phokis. He spent most of his life as a hermit in various places around the Gulf of Corinth and died at Stiris in 953. The anonymous author of the *Life of Luke* had known Luke and probably wrote in the second half of the tenth century.[43] He collected stories from Luke's younger sister Kale and several older monks.[44] A small monastic community had developed around his last hermitage. After Luke's death, a monastery built at his tomb became the site of many healing miracles. The monastery, known as Hosios Loukas, continues to function as such. The two churches at the monastery are important monuments of tenth- and eleventh-century architecture and decoration.[45] The superior of Hosios Loukas, Theodore Leobachos, was commemorated by the members of the Confraternity of Thebes.

[37] Christian Høgel, "The redaction of Symeon Metaphrastes: literary aspects of the Metaphrastic martyria," in *Metaphrasis Redactions and Audiences in Middle Byzantine Hagiography*, ed. Christian Høgel (Bergen, 1996), 7–21.
[38] Hippolyte Delehaye, "Laudatio S. Pauli junioris," in *Der Latmos*, ed. Delehaye, in *Milet* 3.1, ed. Theodore Wiegand (Berlin, 1913), 136–53.
[39] *Typika*, 135–42.   [40] Miklosich and Müller, eds., *Acta et diplomata*, vol. IV, pp. 290–329.
[41] The most detailed study of Lazaros is the introduction by Richard Greenfield to his translation *The Life of Lazaros of Mt. Galesion: An Eleventh-Century Pillar Saint*, Byzantine Saints' Lives in Translation 3 (Washington, DC, 2000), 1–70.
[42] *Life of Lazaros*, 34–41.
[43] Demetrios Sophianos, ed., *Hosios Loukas, ho vios tou*, 2nd, edn (Athens, 1993). Sophianos' edition is available in the Dumbarton Oaks Hagiography Database: http://www.doaks.org/saints2/TEXTS/64.html. English translation by Carolyn Connor and W. Robert Connor, *Life and Miracles of Saint Luke of Steiris* (Brookline, MA, 1994). J. Da Costa-Louillet, "Saints de Grèce aux VIIIe, IXe, et Xe siècles," *Byzantion* 32 (1961): 331–2.
[44] *Life of Luke*, 162.
[45] Nicolas Oikonomides, "The first century of the monastery of Hosios Loukas," *DOP* 46 (1992): 245–55.

Nikon was born in Pontus and traveled to the Peloponnesus in the second half of the tenth century. He founded a monastery in Sparta and died there in 998. Nikon's epithet *metanoeite* is the imperative cry, "repent!" which he shouted regularly. The author of the *Life of Nikon* was the superior of Nikon's monastery, active in the eleventh century, possibly coming into office in 1042.[46] He recorded the memories of elderly people who still could remember talking with the holy man. He may himself have known Nikon, or at least been witness to events shortly after Nikon's death. The author of the *Life of Nikon* imitated the word choice and phrasing used by the author of the *Life of Luke*, especially where he was narrating an episode that was similar to one in the *Life of Luke*.[47] Significant numbers of episodes, however, occur in the *Life of Luke* and not the *Life of Nikon*, and vice versa. I regard the *Life of Nikon* as only reflecting actual events of Nikon's life once Nikon had arrived in the Peloponnesus. The stories of his early life and travels are extremely idealized. They are excellent sources of information about how a tenth-century saint was supposed to behave. Once Nikon arrives in Sparta the narrative shifts to situations that one would not expect to be included in a saint's life. A number of the episodes after Nikon's arrival in Sparta are unusual and do not put Nikon or the monastery in a particularly good light. The struggles that beset his monastery accord with the information we have from the monastic archives about the kinds of things monasteries got into fights about. Nikon's testament also survives.[48] In it Nikon begins describing his ministry with his arrival in Sparta. The testament mentions some of the events that occur in the *vita* but the accounts do not match completely.

PHILOTHEOS' TREATISE

In the late ninth century the *protospatharios* Philotheos held the post of *atriklines*, which meant he was responsible for maintaining order at imperial banquets. In 899 he completed a treatise on imperial titles and honors which is among our best sources for the theory and practice of ninth- and tenth-century Byzantine political culture. One of Philotheos' main

---

[46] *Life of Nikon*, 2–7. Sullivan's edition is available in the Dumbarton Oaks Hagiography Database: http://www.doaks.org/saints2/TEXTS/87.html. Denis Sullivan, "The versions of the *Vita Niconis*," *DOP* 32 (1978). Jan Olof Rosenqvist, "The text of the Life of St. Nikon 'Metanoeite' reconsidered," in *Leimon: Studies Presented to Lennart Rydén on His Sixty-Fifth Birthday*, ed. Jan Olof Rosenqvist (Uppsala, 1996), 93–111.
[47] *Life of Nikon*, 7–18.
[48] Odysseus Lampsidis, "Ho ek Pontou hosios Nikon ho Metanoeite," *Archeion Pontou Supplement* 13 (1982): 252–6. *Typika*, 313–22.

concerns was the order of precedence in which various officials sat during imperial banquets. He based some of his exposition on imperial invitation lists, *kletorologia*. His treatise is hence sometimes known as the "Kletorologion of Philotheos." It is one of several texts, known as *taktika*, which list imperial officials in order of their rank.[49] Philotheos' treatise was encorportated into the *Ceremony Book* in the 950s or 960s. A shortened version also survives in a separate manuscript tradition.[50]

[49] Philotheos' treatise, along with all of the known *taktika* of the ninth and tenth centuries, have been edited with French translation and invaluable commentary by Nicolas Oikonomides, *Les Listes de préséance byzantines des IXe et Xe siècles* (Paris, 1972). The treatise is also available in an edition by John Bagnell Bury, *The Imperial Administrative System in the Ninth Century, with a Revised Text of the Kletorologion of Philotheos* (London, 1911), 131–79.
[50] Oikonomides, *Listes*, 72–81.

Bibliography

This list does not include works listed in the Abbreviations, pp. viii–x.

SOURCES

Actes de Dionysiou, edited by Nicolas Oikonomides. Archives de l'Athos 4. Paris, 1968.

Actes de Kastamonitou, edited by Nicolas Oikonomides. Archives de l'Athos 9. Paris, 1978.

Actes de Kutlumus, edited by Paul Lemerle. Archives de l'Athos 2. Paris, 1988.

Acts of Patmos, edited by Era Vranouse, *Byzantina Engrapha tes mones Patmou: I Autokratorika*. Athens, 1980.
  Edited by Maria Nystaxopoulou-Pelekidou, *Byzantina Engrapha tes mones Patmou: II Demosion Leiturgon*. Athens, 1980.

Actes de Prôtaton, edited by Denise Papachryssanthou. Archives de l'Athos 7. Paris, 1975.

Actes de Xéropotamou, edited by Jacques Bompaire. Archives de l'Athos 3. Paris, 1964.

Alexiad, edited by Diether R. Reinsch and Athanasios Kambylis, *Annae Comnenae Alexias*. Corpus Fontium Historiae Byzantinae 40. New York, 2001.
  Edited by Bernard Leib, *Anne Comnène, Alexiade*, 3 vols. Paris, 1937–45.

Attaleiates, Michael, edited by W. Brunet de Presle, *Michaelis Attaliotae Historia*. Corpus Scriptorum Historiae Byzantinae 50, edited by Immanuel Bekker. Bonn, 1853.

Burgmann, Ludwig, ed. *Ecloga: Das Gesetzbuch Leons III und Konstantinos V*. Forschungen zur Byzantinischen Rechtsgeschichte 10. Frankfurt, 1983.

Ceremony Book, edited by Johann Jacob Reiske, *De ceremoniis aulae Byzantinae, Constantine VII Porphyrogenitus*. Corpus Scriptorum Historiae Byzantinae 9–11, edited by Barthold Georg Niebuhr. Bonn, 1829.
  Edited by Albert Vogt, *Le Livre des cérémonies*, 2 vols. Collection Byzantine. Paris, 1935.

Confraternity of Thebes, John W. Nesbitt and J. Witta, "A confraternity of the Comnenian era." *BZ* 68 (1975): 360–84.

Dagron, Gilbert, and Haralambie Milaescu, eds. *Le Traité sur la guérilla (De velitatione) de l'empereur Nicéphore Phocas (963–969)*. Paris, 1986.

Darrouzes, Jean. *Epistoliers byzantins du Xe siècle*. Archives de l'Orient Chrétien 6. Paris, 1960.

De administrando imperio, edited by Gyula Moravcsik and translated by Romilly Jenkins, *De administrando imperio. Constantine VII Porphyrogenitus*, new revised edition. Washington, DC, 1967.

Delehaye, Hippolyte. "Laudatio S. Pauli junioris." In *Life of Paul of Latros*, edited by Theodore Wiegand, 136–53. Berlin, 1913.

Dennis, George T. *Three Byzantine Military Treatises*. Dumbarton Oaks Texts 9. Washington, DC, 1985.

Dobschütz, E. von. "Maria Romaia: Zwei unbekannte Texte." *BZ* 12 (1903): 173–214.

Gautier, Paul, ed. "La diataxis de Michel Attaliate." *REB* 39 (1981): 5–143.

Théophylacte d'Achrida, II, Lettres. Corpus Fontium Historiae Byzantinae 16.2. Thessaloniki, 1986.

"Le typikon de la Théotokos Evergétis." *REB* 40 (1982): 5–101.

"Le typikon du sébaste Grégoire Pakourianos." *REB* 42 (1984): 5–145.

Granstrem, E., I. Medvedev, and D. Papachryssanthou. "Fragment d'un praktikon de la région d'Athènes (avant 1204)." *REB* 34 (1976): 5–44.

Guillou, André. *Les Actes grecs de S. Maria di Messina: enquête sur les populations grecques d'Italie du sud et de Sicile (XIe–XIIVe s.)*. Palermo, 1963.

Les Archives de Saint-Jean-Prodrome sur le Mont Ménécée. Bibliothèque Byzantine, Documents 3. Paris, 1955.

John Lydus, edited and translated by Anastasius Bandy, *On Powers, or, The Magistracies of the Roman State*. Philadelphia, 1983.

Karayannopulos, J. "Fragamente aus dem Vadamecum eines byzantinischen Finnanzbeamtem." In *Polychronion*, edited by Peter Wirth, 318–34. Heidelberg, 1966.

Koder, Johannes, ed. *Das Eparchenbuch Leons des Weisen*. Corpus Fontium Historiae Byzantinae 33. Vienna, 1991.

Lampsidis, Odysseus. "Ho ek Pontou hosios Nikon ho Metanoeite." *Archeion Pontou Supplement* 13 (1982): 252–6.

Liudprand of Cremona, edited by Paolo Chiesa, *Liudprandi Cremonensis: Antapodosis; Homelia paschalis; Historia Ottonis; Relatio de Legatione Constantinopolitana*. Corpus Christianorum 156. Brépols, 1998.

Translated by F. A. Wright, *Liudprand of Cremona: The Embassy to Constantinople and Other Writings*. London, 1993.

Miklosich, Franz, and Joseph Müller, eds. *Acta et diplomata graeca medii aevi sacra et profana*, 6 vols. Vienna, 1860–90.

Nesbitt, John, and Nicolas Oikonomides. *Catalogue of Byzantine Seals at Dumbarton Oaks and in the Fogg Museum of Art*. Dumbarton Oaks Catalogues. Washington, DC, 1991.

Noailles, Pierre, and Alphonse Dain, eds. *Les Novelles de Léon VI, le sage*. Paris, 1944.

Oikonomides, Nicolas, ed. *Les Listes de préséance byzantines des IXe et Xe siècles*. Paris, 1972.

Rea, J. R., ed. *The Oxyrhynchus Papyri* LXIII, Graeco-Roman Memoirs 83. London, 1996.
Svoronos, Nicolas, and Paris Gounaridis, eds. *Les Novelles des empereurs macédoniens*. Athens, 1994.
Talbot, Alice-Mary, ed. *Byzantine Defenders of Images: Eight Saints' Lives in English Translation*. Byzantine Saints' Lives in Translation 2. Washington, DC, 1998.
   Holy Women of Byzantium: Ten Saints' Lives in English Translation. Byzantine Saints' Lives in Translation 1. Washington, DC, 1996.
Theophanes Continuatus, edited by Immanuel Bekker, *Theophanes continuatus, Ioannes Caminiata, Symeon Magister, Georgius Monachus continuatus*. Corpus Scriptorum Historiae Byzantinae 33. Bonn, 1838.
Thomas, John, and Angela Constantinides Hero. *Byzantine Monastic Foundation Documents: A Complete Translation of the Surviving Founders' Typika and Testaments*, 5 vols. Dumbarton Oaks Studies 35. Washington, DC, 2000.
Turner, E., John Rea, L. Koenen, and José Fernandes Pomar, eds. *The Oxyrhynchus Papyri XXVII*. Graeco-Roman Memoirs 39. London, 1962.
van der Wal, N., and D. Holwerda, eds. *Basilicorum libri LX*. Groningen, 1953–88.
Wortley, John, ed. *The Spiritually Beneficial Tales of Paul, Bishop of Monembasia*. Kalamazoo, 1996.
Yahya of Antioch, edited by Ignace Kratchkovsky, *Histoire de Yahya ibn Sa'id d'Antioch*. Patrologia Orientalis 47.4. Brépols, 1997.
Zepos, Ioannes, and Panagiotes Zepos, eds. *Jus graecoromanum*, 8 vols. Athens, 1931. Reprint, Aalen 1962.

SECONDARY LITERATURE

Ahrweiler, Hélène. *Byzance et la mer: la marine de guerre, la politique et les institutions maritimes de Byzance aux VIIe–XVe siècles*. Bibliothèque Byzantine, Etudes 5. Paris, 1966.
   "La concession des droits incorporels. Donations conditionnelles." In *Actes du XIIe Congrès international des études byzantines II*, 103–14. Belgrade, 1964.
   Etudes sur les structures administratives et sociales de Byzance. London, 1971.
   "Recherches sur la société byzantine au XIe siècle: nouvelles hiérarchies et nouvelles solidarités." *TM* 6 (1976): 99–124.
   "Recherches sur l'administration de l'empire byzantin aux IXe–XIe siècles." *BCH* 84 (1960): 1–111. [Under the name Glykatzi-Ahrweiler.]
Angelide, Christine. "Douloi sten Konstantinoupole tou I' ai." *Symmeikta* 6 (1985): 33–51.
Angold, Michael. "Alexios I Komnenos: an afterword." In *Alexios I Komnenos*, edited by Margaret Mullett and Dion Smythe, 398–417. Belfast, 1996.
   "Archons and dynasts: local aristocracies and the cities of the later Byzantine Empire." In *The Byzantine Aristocracy, IX–XIII Centuries*, edited by Michael Angold, 236–53. Oxford, 1984.
   The Byzantine Empire, 1025–1201: A Political History. 2nd edn. London and New York, 1997.

Church and Society in Byzantium under the Comneni, 1081–1261. Cambridge, 1995.

"The shaping of the medieval Byzantine 'city'." *BF* 10 (1985): 1–37.

ed. *The Byzantine Aristocracy, IX–XIII Centuries*. British Archaeological Reports International Series 221. Oxford, 1984.

Armstrong, Pamela. "Two lives of Meletios the Younger." MA thesis, Queen's University Belfast, 1981.

Armstrong, Pamela, W. C. Cavanagh, and Graham Shipley. "Crossing the river: observations on routes and bridges in Laconia from the Archaic to Byzantine periods." *BSA* 87 (1992): 293–310.

Barnes, Hugh, and Mark Whittow. "The Oxford University/British Institute of Archaeology at Ankara Survey of Medieval Castles of Anatolia (1993)." *Anatolian Studies* 44 (1994): 187–206.

"The Survey of Medieval Castles of Anatolia (1992–96): the Meander region." In *Ancient Anatolia: Fifty Years' Work by the British Institute of Archaeology at Ankara*, edited by Roger Matthews, 347–58. London, 1998.

Barthélemy, Dominique. "Encore le débat sur l'an mil!" *Revue Historique de Droit Français et Etranger* 73 (1995): 349–60.

Bartlett, Robert, and Angus MacKay, eds. *Medieval Frontier Societies*. Oxford, 1989.

Bastéa, Eleni. *The Creation of Modern Athens: Planning the Myth*. Cambridge, 2000.

Beaucamp, Joëlle. "Difficile et dissimulée: la rébellion contre la famille à Byzance (4e–7e siècle)." In *Ordnung und Aufruhr im Mittelalter: historische und juristische Studien zur Rebellion*, edited by Marie Theres Fögen, 265–86. Frankfurt, 1995.

"Les filles et la transmission du patrimoine à Byzance: dot et part successorale." In *La Transmission du patrimoine: Byzance et l'aire méditerranéenne*, edited by Joëlle Beaucamp and Gilbert Dagron, 11–34. Paris, 1998.

"La situation juridique de la femme à Byzance." *Cahiers de Civilisation Médiévale* 20, no. 2–3 (1977): 145–76.

Beaucamp, Joëlle, and Gilbert Dagron, eds. *La Transmission du patrimoine: Byzance et l'aire méditerranéenne*. TM Monographies 11. Paris, 1998.

Beck, Hans-Georg. *Byzantinisches Erotikon: Orthodoxie, Literatur, Gesellschaft*. Munich, 1984.

Byzantinisches Gefolgschaftswesen. Munich, 1965.

Das byzantinische Jahrtausend. Munich, 1978.

Theoria: ein byzantinischer Traum? Munich, 1983.

"Theorie und Praxis im Aufbau der byzantinischen Zentralverwaltung." *Bayerische Akademie der Wissenschaften. Philosophisch-Historische Klasse Sitzungsberichte* 8 (1974): 3–33.

Vademecum des byzantinischen Aristokraten: das sogenannte Strategikon des Kekaumenos. Byzantinische Geschichtsschreiber 5. Graz, Vienna, and Cologne, 1964.

Bell, Catherine. "Performance." In *Critical Terms for Religious Studies*, edited by Mark Taylor, 205–24. Chicago, 1998.

Ritual Theory, Ritual Practice. New York, 1992.

Berger, Albrecht. "Imperial and ecclesiastical processions in Constantinople." In *Byzantine Constantinople: Monuments, Topography and Everyday Life*, edited by Nerva Necipoglu, 73–88. Leiden, 2001.
Birkenmeier, John. *The Development of the Komnenian Army 1081–1180*. History of Warfare 5. Leiden, 2002.
Bisson, Thomas, ed. *Cultures of Power: Lordship, Status, and Process in Twelfth-Century Europe*. Philadelphia, 1995.
——— "The 'Feudal Revolution'." *Past & Present* 142 (1994): 6–42.
Bon, Antoine. *Le Péloponnèse byzantine jusqu'en 1204*. Paris, 1951.
Bouras, Charalambos. "Church architecture in Greece around the year 1200." In *Studenica et l'art byzantin autour de l'année 1200*, edited by Vojislav Korac, 271–8. Belgrade, 1988.
——— "City and village: urban design and architecture." *JÖB* 31, no. 1 (1981): 612–53.
——— "Katoikies kai oikismoi sten Vyzantine Hellada." In *Oikismoi sten Hellada/Shelter in Greece*, edited by Orestis Doumanis and Paul Oliver, 30–52. Athens, 1974.
Bourdieu, Pierre. "Authorized language: the social conditions for the effectiveness of ritual discourse." In *Language and Symbolic Power*, 107–16. Cambridge, 1991.
Bowman, Steven. "The jewish settlement in Sparta and Mistra." *Byzantinisch-neugriechische Jahrbücher* 22 (1977): 131–46.
——— *The Jews of Byzantium 1204–1453*. Judaic Studies Series. Tuscaloosa, AL, 1985.
Brand, Charles, "Did Byzantium have a free market?" *BF* 26 (2000): 63–72.
——— ed. *Icon and Minaret: Sources of Byzantine and Islamic Civilization*. Englewood Cliffs, NJ, 1969.
Brandes, Wolfram. *Finanzverwaltung in Krisenzeiten: Untersuchungen zur byzantinischen Administration im 6.–9. Jahrhundert*. Forschung zur Byzantinischen Rechtsgeschichte 25, edited by Dieter Simon. Frankfurt, 2002.
Brown, Elizabeth A. R. "Introduction: ritual brotherhood in ancient and medieval Europe, a symposium." *Traditio* 52 (1997): 261–84.
——— "The tyranny of a construct: feudalism and historians of medieval Europe." *The American Historical Review* 79, no. 4 (1974): 1063–88.
Brown, Peter. *Authority and the Sacred: Aspects of the Christianisation of the Roman World*. Cambridge, 1995.
——— *Poverty and Leadership in the Later Roman Empire*. Hanover, NH, 2002.
——— *Power and Persuasion in Late Antiquity: Towards a Christian Empire*. The Curti Lectures 1988. Madison, WI, 1992.
——— *Society and the Holy in Late Antiquity*. Berkeley, CA, 1982.
Brubaker, Leslie, ed. *Byzantium in the Ninth Century: Dead or Alive*. Society for the Promotion of Byzantine Studies Publications 5. Aldershot, 1998.
Bryer, Anthony, and Mary Cunningham. *Mount Athos and Byzantine Monasticism*. Society for the Promotion of Byzantine Studies Publications 4. Aldershot, 1996.
Buckler, Georgina. "Authorship of the Strategikon of Cecaumenos." *BZ* 36 (1936): 7–26.
——— "Writings familiar to Cecaumenus." *Byzantion* 15 (1940/41): 133–43.

Burgmann, Ludwig. "A law for emperors: observations on a chrysobull of Nikephoros III Botaneiates." In *New Constantines: The Rhythm of Imperial Renewal in Byzantium, 4th–13th Centuries*, edited by Paul Magdalino, 247–57. Aldershot, 1994.

——— "Lawyers and legislators: aspects of law-making in the time of Alexios I." In *Alexios I Komnenos*, edited by Margaret Mullett and Dion Smyth, 185–98. Belfast, 1996.

——— "Reformation oder Restauration? Zum Ehegüterrecht der Ecloga." In *Eherecht und Familiengut in Antike und Mittelalter*, edited by Dieter Simon, 29–42. Munich, 1992.

——— "Sklaven in der Peira." *Fontes Minores* 9 (1993): 1–33.

Bury, J. B. *The Imperial Administrative System in the Ninth Century*. British Academy Supplemental Papers 1. London, 1911.

Cameron, Averil. *Christianity and the Rhetoric of Empire: The Development of Christian Discourse*. Berkeley, CA, 1991.

——— "The construction of court ritual: the Byzantine *Book of Ceremonies*." In *Rituals of Royalty: Power and Ceremonial in Traditional Societies*, edited by David Cannadine and Simon Price, 106–36. Cambridge, 1987.

——— *The Mediterranean World in Late Antiquity: A.D. 395–600*. London and New York, 1993.

Carney, Thomas F. *Bureaucracy in Traditional Society: Romano-Byzantine Bureaucracies Viewed from Within*. Lawrence, KS, 1971.

Charanis, Peter. *The Armenians in the Byzantine Empire*. Lisbon, 1963.

——— "The monastic properties and the state in the Byzantine Empire." *DOP* 4 (1948): 53–118.

——— *Social, Economic and Political Life in the Byzantine Empire: Collected Studies*. London, 1973.

——— *Studies on the Demography of the Byzantine Empire: Collected Studies*. London, 1972.

——— "The transfer of population as policy in the Byzantine Empire." *Comparative Studies in Society and History* 3 (1961): 140–54.

Cheyette, Fredric L., ed. *Lordship and Community in Medieval Europe: Selected Readings*. Huntington, NY, 1975.

Cheynet, Jean-Claude. "Aristocratie et héritage (xie–xiiie siècle)." In *La Transmission du patrimoine: Byzance et l'aire méditerranéenne*, edited by Jöelle Beaucamp and Gilbert Dagron, 53–80. Paris, 1998.

——— "Basil II and Asia Minor." In *Byzantium in the Year 1000*, edited by Paul Magdalino, 71–108. Leiden, 2003.

——— "Dévaluation des dignités et dévaluation monétaire dans la seconde moitié du xie siècle." *Byzantion* 53 (1983): 453–77.

——— "Du prénom au patronyme: les étrangers à Byzance (xe–xiie siècles)." In *Studies in Byzantine Sigillography 1*, edited by Nicolas Oikonomides, 57–66. Washington, DC, 1987.

——— "Les effectifs de l'armée byzantine aux xe–xiie s." *Cahiers de Civilisation Médiévale* 38 (1995): 319–35.

"Fortune et puissance de l'aristocratie (x–xii siécle)." In *Hommes et richesses dans l'empire byzantin*, edited by Vassiliki Kravari, Jacques Lefort, and Cécile Morrisson, 199–213. Paris, 1991.

"La politique militaire byzantine de Basile II à Alexis Comnene." *Zbornik Radova Vizantolosko Instituta* 30 (1991): 61–73.

"Le rôle de l'aristocratie locale dans l'état." *BF* 19 (1993): 105–12.

"Point de vue sur l'efficacité administrative entre les xe et xie siècles." BF 19 (1993): 7–16.

Pouvoir et contestations à Byzance (963–1210). Paris, 1990.

Cheynet, Jean-Claude, and Cécile Morrisson. "Lieux de trouvaille et circulation des sceaux." In *Studies in Byzantine Sigillography 2*, edited by Nicolas Oikonomides, 105–36. Washington, DC, 1990.

Cheynet, Jean-Claude, and Jean-François Vannier. *Etudes prosopographiques*. Publications de la Sorbonne, Série Byzantina Sorbonensia 5. Paris, 1986.

Chrysos, Evangelos. "Byzantine diplomacy, A.D. 300–800: means and ends." In *Byzantine Diplomacy*, edited by Jonathan Shepard and Simon Franklin, 25–39. Aldershot, 1992.

Connor, Carolyn, and W. Robert Connor, eds. *Life and Miracles of Saint Luke of Steiris*. Brookline, MA, 1994.

Cupane, Carolina. "Appunti per uno studio dell'oikonomia ecclesiastica a Bisanzio." *JÖB* 38 (1998): 53–73.

Cutler, Anthony. "Art in Byzantine society: motive forces of Byzantine patronage." *JÖB* 31, no. 2 (1981): 760–87.

"Originality as a cultural phenomenon." In *Originality in Byzantine Literature, Art and Music: A Collection of Essays*, edited by A. R. Littlewood, 203–16. Oxford, 1995.

"The pathos of distance: Byzantium in the gaze of Renaissance Europe and modern scholarship." In *Reframing the Renaissance: Visual Culture in Europe and Latin America, 1450–1650*, edited by Claire Farago, 22–45. New Haven, 1995.

Cutler, Anthony, and Alexander Kazhdan. "Continuity and discontinuity in Byzantine history." *Byzantion* 52 (1982): 429–79.

Da Costa-Louillet, J. "Saints de Grèce aux viiie, ixe, et xe siècles." *Byzantion* 32 (1961): 331–2.

Dagron, Gilbert. "Le christianisme dans la ville byzantine." *DOP* 31 (1977): 1–25.

"Le combattant byzantin à la frontière du Taurus: guérilla et société frontalière." In *Le Combattant au moyen âge*, 37–43. Paris, 1995.

Empereur et prêtre: étude sur le "césaropapisme" byzantin. Bibliothèque des Histoires. Paris, 1996.

"Guérilla, places fortes et villages ouverts à la frontière orientale de Byzance vers 950." In *Castrum 3: guerre, fortification et habitat dans le monde méditerranéen au moyen âge*, edited by André Bazzana, 43–48. Rome/Madrid, 1988.

"Lawful society and legitimate power: Ennomos politeia, ennomos arche." In *Law and Society in Byzantium, Ninth–Twelfth Centuries*, edited by Angeliki Laiou and Dieter Simon, 27–51. Washington, DC, 1994.

"Minorités ethniques et religieuses dans l'orient byzantin à la fin du xe et au xie siècle: l'immigration syrienne." *TM* 6 (1976): 177–216.

"L'ombre d'un doute: l'hagiographie en question, vie–xie siècle." *DOP* 46 (1992): 59–68.

"L'organisation et le déroulement des courses d'après le *Livre des cérémonies.*" *TM* 13 (2000): 1–200.

"La règle et l'exception. Analyse de la notion d'économie." In *Religiöse Devianz: Untersuchungen zu sozialen, rechtlichen und theologischen Reaktionen auf religiöse Abweichung im westlichen und östlichen Mittelalter*, edited by Dieter Simon, 1–18. Frankfurt, 1990.

"The urban economy, seventh–twelfth centuries." In *The Economic History of Byzantium from the Seventh through the Fifteenth Century*, edited by Angeliki Laiou, 393–462. Washington, DC, 2002.

Darrouzes, Jean. *Recherches sur les "offikia" de l'église byzantine*. Archives de l'Orient Chrétien 11. Paris, 1970.

Davies, Wendy, and Paul Fouracre, eds. *Property and Power in the Early Middle Ages*. Cambridge, 1995.

de Lange, Nicholas. "Hebrews, Greeks or Romans? Jewish culture and identity in Byzantium." In *Strangers to Themselves: The Byzantine Outsider*, edited by Dion Smythe, 105–18. Aldershot, 2000.

"Jews and Christians in the Byzantine Empire." In *Christianity and Judaism*, edited by Diana Wood, 15–32. London, 1992.

Delvenakiotes, Vasileos. *Ho Metropolites Ioannes ho Kaloktenes kai hai Thebai*. Athens, 1970.

Ditten, Hans. "Zu den Mauroi der Vita s. Pauli Junioris in Monte Latro (10 Jh.), dem Personennamen Mauros (um 700), der Maurousias der vita S. Petri Atroensis und den Athiopiern der Vita SS 42 Martyrum Amoriensium (9 Jh.)." *Klio* 72 (1990): 254–69.

Dölger, Franz. *Beiträge zur Geschichte der byzantinischen Finanzverwaltung, besonders des 10. und 11. Jahrhunderts*. Byzantinisches Archiv 9. Leipzig, 1927.

Dölger, Franz, and Johannes Karayannopulos. *Byzantinische Urkundenlehre: Die Kaiserurkunden*. Handbuch der Altertumswissenschaft 12; Byzantinisches Handbuch 3.1. Munich, 1968.

Durliat, Jean. *Les Finances publiques de Dioclétien aux Carolingiens (284–889)*. Sigmaringen, 1990.

Eastmond, Anthony, ed. *Eastern Approaches to Byzantium*. Society for the Promotion of Byzantine Studies Publications 9. Aldershot, 2001.

Epstein, Ann Wharton. "Middle Byzantine churches of Kastoria: dates and implications." *The Art Bulletin* 62, no. 2 (1980): 190–206.

Erickson, John H. "Oikonomia in Byzantine canon law." In *Law, Church and Society: Essays in Honor of Stephan Kuttner*, edited by Kenneth Pennington and Robert Somerville, 225–36. Philadelphia, 1977.

Feissel, Denis, and Anne Philippidis-Braat. "Inventaires en vue d'un recueil des inscriptions historiques de Byzance: inscriptions du Péloponnèse." *TM* 9 (1985): 300–3.

Ferrari, Gianno. *I documenti Greci medioevali di diritto privato dell'Italia meridionale*. Byzantinische Archiv 4. Leipzig, 1910.
Formulari Notarili inediti dell'età Bizantina. Bullettino dell'Istituto Storico Italiano 33. Rome, 1912.
Flusin, Bernard. "L'hagiographie monastique à Byzance au ixe et au xe siècle." *Revue Bénédictine* 103, no. 1–2 (1993): 31–50.
Fögen, Marie Theres. "Legislation in Byzantium: a political and bureaucratic technique." In *Law and Society in Byzantium, Ninth–Twelfth Centuries*, edited by Angeliki Laiou and Deiter Simon, 71–92. Washington, DC, 1994.
"Muttergut und Kindesvermögen bei Konstantin d. Gr., Justinian und Eustathios Rhomaios." In *Eherecht und Familiengut in Antike und Mittelalter*, edited by Dieter Simon, 15–27. Munich, 1992.
"Reanimation of Roman law in the ninth century: remarks on reasons and results." In *Byzantium in the Ninth Century: Dead or Alive?*, edited by Leslie Brubaker, 11–22. Aldershot, 1998.
Foss, Clive. "Archeology and the 'twenty cities' of Byzantine Asia." *American Journal of Archaeology* 81 (1977): 469–86.
Ephesus after Antiquity: A Late Antique, Byzantine, and Turkish City. Cambridge, 1979.
History and Archaeology of Byzantine Asia Minor. Aldershot, 1990.
Foss, Clive, and Robin Fursdon. *Survey of Medieval Castles of Anatolia*. BAR International Series 261. Oxford, 1985.
Foss, Clive, and David Winfield. *Byzantine Fortifications: An Introduction*. Pretoria, 1986.
Frantz, Alison. *The Athenian Agora*, vol. 20: *The Church of the Holy Apostles*. Princeton, NJ, 1971.
Galatariotou, Catia. "Byzantine ktetorika typika: a comparative study." *REB* 45 (1987): 77–138.
The Making of a Saint: The Life, Times and Sanctification of Neophytos the Recluse. Cambridge and New York, 1991.
"Open space/closed space: the perceived worlds of Kekaumenos and Digenes Akrites." In *Alexios I Komnenos*, edited by Margaret Mullett and Dion Smyth, 302–28. Belfast, 1996.
Garsoïan, Nina. *The Paulician Heresy*. The Hague, 1967.
"The problem of Armenian integration into the Byzantine Empire." In *Studies on the Internal Diaspora of the Byzantine Empire*, edited by Hélène Ahrweiler and Angeliki Laiou, 53–124. Washington, DC, 1998.
Gascou, Jean "Les grands domaines, la cité et l'état en Egypte byzantine." *TM* 9 (1985): 1–89.
Geary, Patrick. *The Myth of Nations: The Medieval Origins of Europe*. Princeton, NJ, 2002.
Glykatzi-Ahrweiler, H. "Recherches sur l'administration de l'empire byzantin aux ixe–xie siècles." *BCH* 84 (1960): 1–111.
Greenfield, Richard P. H. *Traditions of Belief in Late Byzantine Demonology*. Amsterdam, 1988.

Guilland, Rodolphe. *Recherches sur les institutions byzantines*. Berlin, 1967.
    Titres et fonctions de l'empire byzantin. London, 1976.
Haldon, John. *The Byzantine Wars*. Stroud, 2001.
    Byzantium: A History. Stroud, 2000.
    Byzantium in the Seventh Century: The Transformation of a Culture. Cambridge, 1990.
    The State and the Tributary Mode of Production. London, 1993.
    "Theory and practice in tenth-century military administration: Chapters II, 44 and 45 of the *Book of Ceremonies*." *TM* 13 (2000): 201–52.
    Warfare, State and Society in the Byzantine World. London, 1999.
Harries, Jill D. *Law and Empire in Late Antiquity*. Cambridge, 1999.
Harvey, Alan. *Economic Expansion in the Byzantine Empire, 900–1200*. Cambridge, 1989.
    "Economic expansion in central Greece in the eleventh century." *BMGS* 8 (1982): 21–8.
    "Financial crisis and the rural economy." In *Alexios I Komnenos*, edited by Margaret Mullett and Dion Smythe, 167–84. Belfast, 1996.
    "The land and taxation in the reign of Alexios I Komnenos: the evidence of Theophylakt of Ochrid." *REB* 51 (1993): 139–53.
    "Land, taxation and trade in the eleventh century monastic economy: the case of Evergetis." In *The Theotokos Evergetis and Eleventh Century Monasticism*, edited by Margaret Mullett and Anthony Kirby, 124–36. Belfast, 1994.
    "The middle Byzantine economy: growth or stagnation?" *BMGS* 19 (1995): 243–61.
    "Peasant categories in the tenth and eleventh centuries." *BMGS* 14 (1990): 250–6.
Heather, Peter. "New men for new Constantines? Creating an imperial elite in the eastern Mediterranean." In *New Constantines: The Rhythm of Imperial Renewal in Byzantium, 4th–13th Centuries*, edited by Paul Magdalino. London, 1991.
Hendy, Michael F. "Byzantium, 1081–1204: the economy revisited, twenty years on." In *The Economy, Fiscal Administration and Coinage of Byzantium*, 1–48. London, 1989.
    Coinage and Money in the Byzantine Empire, 1081–1261. Washington, DC, 1969.
    "The economy: a brief survey." In *Byzantine Studies: Essays on the Slavic World and the Eleventh Century*, edited by Speros Vryonis, 141–52. New Rochelle, NY, 1992.
    The Economy, Fiscal Administration and Coinage of Byzantium. Northampton, 1989.
    Studies in the Byzantine Monetary Economy, c. 300–1450. Cambridge, 1985.
Høgel, Christian. "The redaction of Symeon Metaphrastes: literary aspects of the Metaphrastic martyria." In *Metaphrasis Redactions and Audiences in Middle Byzantine Hagiography*, edited by Christian Høgel, 7–21. Bergen, 1996.

Hohlweg, Armin. *Beiträge zur Verwaltungsgeschichte des ostromischen Reiches unter den Komnenen*. Miscellanea Byzantina Monacensia 1, edited by Hans Georg Beck. Munich, 1965.

Holmes, Catherine. "Basil II and the government of empire: 976–1025." DPhil thesis, Oxford, 1999.

——— "Byzantium's eastern frontier in the tenth and eleventh centuries." In *Medieval Frontiers: Concepts and Practices*, edited by David Abulafia and Nora Berend, 83–104. Aldershot, 2002.

——— "'How the east was won' in the reign of Basil II." In *Eastern Approaches to Byzantium*, edited by Anthony Eastmond, 41–56. Aldershot, 2001.

——— "Political elites in the reign of Basil II." In *Byzantium in the Year 1000*, edited by Paul Magdalino, 35–69. Leiden, 2003.

Howard-Johnston, James. "Crown lands and the defense of imperial authority in the tenth and eleventh centuries." *BF* 21 (1995): 75–100.

Hunger, Herbert. *Die hochsprachliche profane Literatur der Byzantiner*. Handbuch der Altertumswissenschaft 12; Byzantinisches Handbuch 5. Munich, 1978.

——— *Prooimion: Elemente der byzantinischen Kaiseridee in den Arengen der Urkunden*. Wiener Byzantinische Studien 1. Vienna, 1964.

Hussey, J. M. *Church and Learning in the Byzantine Empire, 867–1185*. London, 1937.

Ivison, Eric. "Urban renewal and imperial revival 730–1025." *BF* 26 (2000): 1–46.

Jacoby, David. "The encounter of two societies: western conquerors and Byzantines in the Peloponnesus after the Fourth Crusade." *The American Historical Review* 78, no. 4 (1973): 873–906.

——— "From Byzantium to Latin Romania: continuity and change." *Mediterranean Historical Review* 4 (1989): 1–44.

——— "Les Juifs de Byzance: une communauté marginalisée." In *Oi perithoriakoi sto Byzantio (Marginality in Byzantium)*, edited by Chryssa A. Maltezou, 117–25. Athens, 1993.

——— "Silk in western Byzantium before the Fourth Crusade." *BZ* 85 (1992): 455–500.

James, Liz. *Women, Men, and Eunuchs: Gender in Byzantium*. London, 1997.

Janin, Raymond. *Constantinople byzantine: dévelopement urbain et répertoire topographique*. Paris, 1950.

Jeffreys, Elizabeth. "Akritis and outsiders." In *Strangers to Themselves: The Byzantine Outsider*, edited by Dion Smythe, 189–202. Aldershot, 2000.

Jenkins, Romilly. *Byzantium: The Imperial Centuries, AD 610–1071*. London, 1966.

Kamer, Stephen Arnold. "Emperors and aristocrats in Byzantium 976–1081." PhD thesis, Harvard University, 1983.

Kaplan, Michel. "L'église byzantine des vie–xie siècles: terres et paysans." In *Church and People in Byzantium*, edited by Rosemary Morris, 109–23. Birmingham, 1990.

——— *Les Hommes et la terre à Byzance du vie au xie siècle: propriété et exploitation du sol*. Paris, 1992.

"Maisons impériales et fondations pieuses: réorganisation de la fortune impériale et assistance publique de la fin du VIIIe siècle à la fin du xe siècle." *Byzantion* 61, no. 2 (1991): 340–65.

"Les moines et leurs biens fonciers à Byzance du VIIIe au xe siècle: acquisition, conservation et mise en valeur." *Revue Bénédictine* 103, no. 1–2 (1993): 209–223.

"Le saint, le village et la cité." In *Les Saints et leur sanctuaire à Byzance: textes, images et monuments*, edited by Catherine Jolivet-Lévy, Michel Kaplan, and Jean-Pierre Sodini, 81–94. Paris, 1993.

Kazhdan, Alexander. "Aristocracy and the imperial ideal." In *The Byzantine Aristocracy, IX–XIII Centuries*, edited by Michael Angold, 43–57. Oxford, 1984.

"The Armenians in the Byzantine ruling class, predominantly in the ninth through twelfth centuries." In *Mediaeval Armenian Culture*, edited by T. Samuelian and M. Stone, 439–51. Philadelphia, 1984.

L'aristocrazia bizantina: dal principio dell'XI alla fine del XII secolo. (New edition of *Sotsial'nyi sostav gospodstvuiushchego klassa Vizantii XI–XII vv.*, translated by Silvia Ronchey, Moscow, 1974.) Palermo, 1997.

Authors and Texts in Byzantium. Aldershot, 1993.

"Do we need a new history of Byzantine law?" *JÖB* 39 (1989): 1–28.

"Heremitic, ceonobitic and secular ideals in Byzantine hagiography of the ninth through the twelfth centuries." *Greek Orthodox Theological Review* 30 (1985): 472–85.

"The notion of Byzantine diplomacy." In *Byzantine Diplomacy*, edited by Jonathan Shepard and Simon Franklin, 3–24. Aldershot, 1992.

"Pronoia: the history of a scholarly discussion." *Mediterranean Historical Review* 10 (1995): 133–63.

"Russian pre-Revolutionary studies on eleventh-century Byzantium." In *Byzantine Studies: Essays on the Slavic World and the Eleventh Century*, edited by Spyros Vryonis Jr., 111–24. New Rochelle, 1992.

"Small social groupings (microstructures) in Byzantine society." In *Congrès international des études byzantines: Actes 16*, 3–11. Vienna, 1982.

"Some observations on the Byzantine concept of law." In *Law and Society in Byzantium, Ninth–Twelfth Centuries*, edited by Angeliki Laiou and Dieter Simon, 199–216. Washington, DC, 1994.

"State, feudal and private economy in Byzantium." *DOP* 47 (1993): 83–100.

ed. *The Oxford Dictionary of Byzantium*. New York, 1991.

Kazhdan, Alexander, and Giles Constable. *People and Power in Byzantium: An Introduction to Modern Byzantine Studies*. Washington, DC, 1982.

Kazhdan, Alexander, and Simon Franklin. *Studies on Byzantine Literature of the Eleventh and Twelfth Centuries*. Cambridge, 1984.

Kazhdan, Alexander, and Michael McCormick. "Social composition of the Byzantine court." In *Byzantine Court Culture from 829–1204*, edited by Henry McGuire, 169–72. Washington, DC, 1997.

Kazhdan, Alexander, and Annabel Jane Wharton. *Change in Byzantine Culture in the Eleventh and Twelfth Centuries*. Berkeley, CA, 1985.

Keramopoullos, Antonios. "Thevaika." *AD* 3 (1917): 1–484.
Kolias, Georgios Taxiarchou. *Amter- und Wurdenkauf im fruh- und mittelbyzantinischen Reich*. Texte und Forschungen zur Byzantinisch-neugriechischen Philologie 35. Athens, 1939.
Köpstein, Helga. *Zur Sklaverei im ausgehenden Byzanz*, Berliner Byzantinistische Arbeiten 34. Berlin, 1966.
Kovelman, Arkady. "From logos to myth: Egyptian petitions of the 5th–7th centuries." *Bulletin of the American Society of Papyrologists* 28 (1991): 135–52.
Laiou, Angeliki. "The Byzantine economy: an overview." In *The Economic History of Byzantium from the Seventh through the Fifteenth Century*, edited by Angeliki Laiou, 1145–64. Washington, DC, 2002.
— "Exchange and trade, seventh–twelfth centuries." In *The Economic History of Byzantium from the Seventh through the Fifteenth Century*, edited by Angeliki Laiou, 697–770. Washington, DC, 2002.
— "The festival of 'Agathe'; comments on the life of Constantinopolitan women." In *Byzantium: Tribute to Andreas N. Stratos*, 111–22. Athens, 1986.
— *Gender, Society and Economic Life in Byzantium*. Aldershot, 1992.
— "God and Mammon: credit, trade, profit and the Canonists." In *Byzantium in the 12th Century: Canon Law, State and Society*, edited by Nicolas Oikonomides, 266–85. Athens, 1991.
— *Mariage, amour et parenté à Byzance aux XIe–XIIIe siècles*. Paris, 1992.
— "Marriage prohibitions, marriage strategies and the dowry in thirteenth-century Byzantium." In *La Transmission du patrimoine: Byzance et l'aire méditerranéenne*, edited by Joëlle Beaucamp and Gilbert Dagron, 129–60. Paris, 1998.
— *Peasant Society in the Late Byzantine Empire: A Social and Demographic Study*. Princeton, NJ, 1977.
— ed. *Consent and Coercion to Sex and Marriage in Ancient and Medieval Societies*. Washington, DC, 1993.
— ed. *The Economic History of Byzantium from the Seventh through the Fifteenth Century*. Washington, DC, 2002.
Laiou, Angeliki, and Dieter Simon, eds. *Law and Society in Byzantium, Ninth–Twelfth Centuries*. Washington, DC, 1994.
Lampsidis, Odysseus. "Ho ek Pontou hosios Nikon ho Metanoeite." *Archeion Pontou Supplement* 13 (1982): 252–6.
Lefort, Jacques. "Anthroponymie et société villageoise xe–xive siècles." In *Hommes et richesses dans l'empire byzantine*, edited by Vassiliki Kravari, Jacques Lefort, and Cécile Morrisson, 63–82. Paris, 1991.
— "Le Cadastre de Radolibos (1103), les géomètres et leurs mathématiques." *TM* 8 (1981): 269–313.
— *Géométries du fisc byzantin*. Réalités Byzantines 4. Paris, 1991.
— "Radolibos: population et paysage." *TM* 9 (1985): 195–234.
— "Rural economy and social relations in the countryside." *DOP* 47 (1993): 101–13.

"The rural economy, seventh–twelfth centuries." In *The Economic History of Byzantium from the Seventh through the Fifteenth Century*, edited by Angeliki Laiou, 231–310. Washington, DC, 2002.

Villages de Macédoine: notices historiques et topographiques sur la Macédoine orientale au moyen âge. Paris, 1982.

Lemerle, Paul. *The Agrarian History of Byzantium: From the Origins to the Twelfth Century*. Galway, 1979.

Cinq études sur le XIe siècle byzantin. Paris, 1977.

"Présence de Byzance." *Journal des Savants* (1990): 247–68.

Prolégomènes à une édition critique et commentée des "Conseils et récits" de Kékauménos. Brussels, 1960.

"'Roga' et rente d'état aux xe–xie siècles." *REB* 25 (1967): 77–100.

Leyser, Karl. "Concepts of Europe in the early and high Middle Ages." *Past & Present* 137 (1992): 25–47.

Rule and Conflict in an Early Medieval Society: Ottonian Saxony. Bloomington, IN, 1979.

Liebeschuetz, Wolfgang. "The end of the ancient city." In *The City in Late Antiquity*, edited by John Rich, 1–49. London and New York, 1992.

Lightfoot, Christopher. "Amorium 2001." *Anatolian Archaeology: British Institute of Archaeology at Ankara* 7 (2001): 9–10.

"The survival of cities in Byzantine Anatolia: the case of Amorium." *Byzantion* 68, no. 1 (1998): 56–71.

Lilie, Ralph-Johannes. "Des Kaisers Macht und Ohnmacht." *Poikila Byzantina* 4 (1984): 9–120.

"Die Zentralbürokratie und die Provinzen zwischen dem 10. und dem 12. Jahrhundert. Anspruch und Realität." *BF* 19 (1993): 65–75.

Lim, Richard. *Public Disputation, Power, and Social Order in Late Antiquity*. Berkeley, CA, 1995.

Litavrin, Gennady G. "Family relations and family law in the Byzantine countryside of the eleventh-century: an analysis of the Praktikon of 1073." *DOP* 44 (1990): 187–94.

Lock, Peter. "The Frankish towers of central Greece." *BSA* 81 (1986): 100–23.

"The medieval towers of Greece: a problem in chronology and function." In *Latins and Greeks in the Eastern Mediterranean after 1204*, edited by Benjamin Arbel, Bernard Hamilton, and David Jacoby, 129–45. London, 1989.

Lock, Peter, and Guy Sanders, eds. *The Archaeology of Medieval Greece*. Oxbow Monographs 59. Oxford, 1996.

Louvi-Kizi, Aspasia. "Thebes." In *The Economic History of Byzantium*, edited by Angeliki Laiou, 631–8. Washington, DC, 2002.

McCormick, Michael. "Analyzing imperial ceremonies." *JÖB* 35 (1985): 1–20.

Eternal Victory: Triumphal Rulership in Late Antiquity, Byzantium, and the Early Medieval West. Cambridge, 1986.

McGeer, Eric. *The Land Legislation of the Macedonian Emperors*. Toronto, 2000.

Sowing the Dragon's Teeth: Byzantine Warfare in the Tenth Century. Washington, DC, 1995.

MacKay, Camilla Martha. "The road networks and postal service of the eastern Roman and Byzantine empires (first–fifteenth centuries AD): social effects on the provincial population." PhD thesis, University of Michigan, 1999.
Macrides, Ruth. "The Byzantine godfather." *BMGS* 11 (1987): 139–62.
    "The competent court." In *Law and Society in Byzantium, Ninth–Twelfth Centuries*, edited by Angeliki Laiou and Dieter Simon, 117–30. Washington, DC, 1994.
    "Dynastic marriages and political kinship." In *Byzantine Diplomacy*, edited by Jonathan Shepard and Simon Franklin, 263–80. Aldershot, 1992.
    "Killing, asylum and the law." *Speculum* 63 (1988): 509–38.
    Kinship and Justice in Byzantium, 11th–15th Centuries. Aldershot, 1999.
    "Kinship by arrangement: the case of adoption." *DOP* 44 (1990): 109–18.
    "Nomos and kanon, in paper and in court." In *Church and People in Byzantium*, edited by Rosemary Morris, 61–85. Birmingham, 1990.
McKitterick, Rosamond, ed. *The Early Middle Ages*. Short Oxford History of Europe, edited by T. C. W. Blanning. Oxford, 2001.
Magdalino, Paul. "The Byzantine aristocratic oikos." In *The Byzantine Aristocracy, IX to XIII Centuries*, edited by Michael Angold, 92–111. Oxford, 1984.
    "The Byzantine army and the land: from stratiotikon ktema to military pronoia." In *Byzantium at War 9th–12th C.* Athens, 1997.
    "The Byzantine holy man in the twelfth century." In *The Byzantine Saint*, edited by Sergei Hackel, 51–66. London, 1981.
    "Byzantine snobbery." In *The Byzantine Aristocracy, IX to XIII Centuries*, edited by Michael Angold, 58–78. Oxford, 1984.
    "Church, bath and diakonia in medieval Constantinople." In *Church and People in Byzantium*, edited by Rosemary Morris, 165–90. Birmingham, 1990.
    "Constantinople and the 'exochorai' in the time of Balsamon." In *To Vyzantio kata ton 120 aiona*, edited by Nicolas Oikonomides, 179–98. Athens, 1991.
    "Constantinople and the outside world." In *Strangers to Themselves: The Byzantine Outsider*, edited by Dion Smythe, 149–62. Aldershot, 2000.
    Constantinople médiévale: études sur l'évolution des structures urbaines. Paris, 1996.
    The Empire of Manuel I Komnenos, 1143–1180. Cambridge, 1993.
    "Honour among Romaioi: the framework of social values in the world of Digenes Akrites and Kekaumenos." *BMGS* 13 (1989): 183–218.
    "Innovations in government." In *Alexios I Komnenos*, edited by Margaret Mullett and Dion Smythe, 146–66. Belfast, 1996.
    "Justice and finance in the Byzantine state, ninth to twelfth centuries." In *Law and Society in Byzantium, Ninth–Twelfth Centuries*, edited by Angeliki Laiou and Dieter Simon, 93–116. Washington, DC, 1994.
    "Medieval Constantinople: built environment and urban development." In *The Economic History of Byzantium from the Seventh through the Fifteenth Century*, edited by Angeliki Laiou, 529–38. Washington, DC, 2002.
    The Perception of the Past in Twelfth-Century Europe. London, 1992.
    "The reform edict of 1107." In *Alexios I Komnenos*, edited by Margaret Mullett and Dion Smythe, 199–218. Belfast, 1996.

"'What we heard in the Lives of the saints we have seen with our own eyes': the holy man as literary text in tenth-century Constantinople." In *The Cult of the Saints in Late Antiquity and the Middle Ages: Essays on the Contributions of Peter Brown*, edited by James Howard-Johnston and Paul Anthony Hayward, 84–112. Oxford, 1999.

ed., *New Constantines: The Rhythm of Imperial Renewal in Byzantium, 4th–13th centuries*. Aldershot, 1994.

Maguire, Henry. "The heavenly court." In *Byzantine Court Culture from 829 to 1204*, edited by Henry Maguire, 247–58. Washington, DC, 1997.

ed. *Byzantine Court Culture from 829 to 1204*. Washington, DC, 1997.

Maksimović, Ljubomir. *The Byzantine Provincial Administration under the Palaiologoi*. Amsterdam, 1988.

Malamut, Elisabeth. *Les Iles de l'empire byzantin: VIIIe–XIIe siècles*. Série Byzantina Sorbonensia 8 Paris, 1988.

Mango, Cyril. "Discontinuity with the classical past in Byzantium." In *Byzantium and the Classical Tradition*, edited by Margaret Mullett and Roger Scott, 48–57. Birmingham, 1981.

Mango, Cyril, and Gilbert Dagron, eds. *Constantinople and Its Hinterland*. Society for the Promotion of Byzantine Studies Publications 3. Aldershot, 1995.

Mango, Cyril, and Ihor Ševčenko. "A new manuscript of the *De ceremoniis*." *DOP* 14 (1960): 247–9.

Martin-Hisard, Bernadette. "Constantinople et les archontes caucasiens dans le *Livre des cérémonies*, II, 48." *TM* 13 (2000): 359–530.

Mathews, Thomas. "'Private' liturgy in Byzantine architecture: toward a reappraisal." *Cahiers Archéologiques* 30 (1982): 125–38.

Metcalf, D. M. "Monetary recession in the middle Byzantine period: the numismatic evidence." *The Numismatic Chronicle* 161 (2001): 110–53.

Miller, Timothy S., and John W. Nesbitt, eds. *Peace and War in Byzantium: Essays in Honor of George T. Dennis, S.J.* Washington, DC, 1995.

Morris, Rosemary. "Dispute settlement in the Byzantine provinces in the tenth century." In *The Settlement of Disputes in Early Medieval Europe*, edited by Wendy Davies and Paul Fouracre, 125–47. Cambridge, 1986.

"Divine diplomacy in the late eleventh century." *Byzantine and Modern Greek Studies* 16 (1992): 147–56.

"Emancipation in Byzantium: Roman law in a medieval society." In *Serfdom and Slavery: Studies in Legal Bondage*, edited by Michael Bush, 130–43. London, 1996.

"Monastic exemptions in tenth- and eleventh-century Byzantium." In *Property and Power in the Early Middle Ages*, edited by Wendy Davies and Paul Fouracre, 200–20. Cambridge, 1995.

Monks and Laymen in Byzantium, 843–1118. Cambridge, 1995.

"The political saint of the eleventh century." In *The Byzantine Saint*, edited by Sergei Hackel, 43–50. London, 1981.

"The powerful and poor in tenth-century Byzantium: law and reality." *Past & Present* 73 (1976): 3–27.

Spiritual fathers and temporal patrons: logic and contradiction in Byzantine monasticism in the tenth century." *Revue Bénédictine* 103, no. 1–2 (1993): 273–88.
ed. *Church and People in Byzantium*. Birmingham, 1990.
Morrisson, Cécile. "Byzantine money: its production and circulation." In *The Economic History of Byzantium from the Seventh through the Fifteenth Century*, edited by Angeliki Laiou, 909–66. Washington, DC, 2002.
"La Logarikè: réforme monétaire et réforme fiscale sous Alexis 1er Comnène." *TM* 7 (1979): 419–64.
"Monnaie et finances dans l'empire byzantin xe–xive siècle." In *Hommes et richesses dans l'empire byzantin*, edited by Jacques Lefort and Cécile Morrisson V. Kravari, 291–315. Paris, 1989.
"Numismatique et sigillographie: parentes et méthode." In *Studies in Byzantine Sigillography 1*, edited by Nicolas Oikonomides, 12–26. Washington, DC, 1987.
Morrisson, Cécile, and Jean-Claude Cheynet. "Prices and wages in the Byzantine world." In *The Economic History of Byzantium from the Seventh through the Fifteenth Century*, edited by Angeliki Laiou, 815–78. Washington, DC, 2002.
Mullett, Margaret. "Byzantium: a friendly society?" *Past and Present* 118 (1988): 2–24.
"The madness of genre." *DOP* 46 (1992): 233–43.
"The 'other' in Byzantium." In *Strangers to Themselves: The Byzantine Outsider*, edited by Dion Smythe, 1–22. Aldershot, 2000.
"Patronage in action: the problems of an eleventh-century archbishop." In *Church and People in Byzantium*, edited by Rosemary Morris, 125–47. Birmingham, 1990.
Theophylact of Ochrid: Reading the Letters of a Byzantine Archbishop. Aldershot, 1997.
"Theophylact of Ochrid's In Defense of Eunuchs." In *Eunuchs in Antiquity and Beyond*, edited by Shaun Tougher, 177–98. London, 2002.
"Writings in early medieval Byzantium." In *The Uses of Literacy in Early Medieval Europe*, edited by Rosamond McKitterick. Cambridge, 1990.
Mullett, Margaret, and Anthony Kirby, eds. *The Theotokos Evergetis and Eleventh-Century Monasticism*. Belfast, 1994.
eds. *Work and Worship at the Theotokos Evergetis, 1050–1200*. Belfast, 1997.
Mullett, Margaret, and Roger Scott, eds. *Byzantium and the Classical Tradition*. Birmingham, 1981.
Mullett, Margaret, and Dion Smythe, eds. *Alexios I Komnenos*. Belfast, 1996.
Neville, Leonora. "Information, ceremony and power in Byzantine fiscal registers: varieties of function in the Cadaster of Thebes." *BMGS* 25 (2001): 20–43.
"Local provincial elites in eleventh-century Hellas and Peloponnese." PhD thesis, Princeton University, 1998.
"The Marcian Treatise on taxation and the nature of bureaucracy in Byzantium." *BF* 26 (2000): 47–62.

Oikonomides, Nicolas. "La chancellerie impérial de Byzance." *REB* 43 (1985): 167–96.
———. *A Collection of Dated Byzantine Lead Seals*. Washington, DC, 1986.
———. "The contents of the Byzantine house from the eleventh to the fifteenth century." *DOP* 44 (1990): 205–14.
———. "Contribution a l'étude de la Pronoia au XIII siècle: une formule d'attribution de parèques à un pronoiaire." *REB* 22 (1964): 158–75.
———. "The donation of castles in the last quarter of the 11th century." In *Polychronion: Festschrift Franz Dölger zum 75. Geburtstag*, edited by Peter Wirth, 413–17. Heidelberg, 1966.
———. "L'évolution de l'organisation administrative de l'empire byzantin au XIe siècle." *TM* 6 (1976): 125–52.
———. "The first century of the monastery of Hosios Loukas." *DOP* 46 (1992): 245–55.
———. *Fiscalité et exemption fiscale à Byzance (IXe–XIe s.)*. Institut de Recherches Byzantines Monographies 2. Athens, 1996.
———. "The holy icon as an asset." *DOP* 45 (1991): 35–44.
———. "The Jews of Chios (1049): a group of excusati." *Mediterranean Historical Review* 10, no. 1–2 (1995): 218–25.
———. *Les Listes de préséance byzantines des IXe et Xe siècles*. Paris, 1972.
———. "Middle Byzantine provincial recruits: salary and armament." In *Gonimos: Neoplatonic and Byzantine Studies Presented to Leendert G. Westerink at 75*, edited by John Duffy and J. Peradoto, 121–36. Buffalo, 1988.
———. "Mount Athos: levels of literacy." *DOP* 42 (1988): 167–78.
———. "L'organisation de la frontière orientale de Byzance aux Xe–XIe siècle et le taktikon de l'Escorial." In *Actes du XIVe Congrès international des études byzantines I*, 285–302. Bucharest, 1974.
———. "On sigillographic epigraphy." In *Studies in Byzantine Sigillography 6*, edited by Nicolas Oikonomides, 37–42. Washington, DC, 1999.
———. "The 'Peira' of Eustathios Romaios: an abortive attempt to innovate in Byzantine law." *Fontes Minores* 7 (1986): 169–92.
———. "The role of the Byzantine state in the economy." In *The Economic History of Byzantium from the Seventh through the Fifteenth Century*, edited by Angeliki Laiou, 973–1058. Washington, DC, 2002.
———. "Some Byzantine state annuitants: *Epi Tes (Megales) Hetaireias* and *Epi Ton Barbaron*." *Symmeikta* 14 (2001): 9–19.
———. "St. George of Mangana, Maria Skleraina, and the 'Malyj Sion' of Novgorod." *DOP* 34–5 (1980–81): 239–46.
———. "Tax exemptions for the secular clergy under Basil II." In *Kathegetria: Essays Presented to Joan Hussey for Her 80th Birthday*, edited by Julian Chrysostomides, 317–26. Camberley, Surrey, 1988.
———. "Terres du fisc et revenu de la terre." In *Hommes et richesses dans l'empire byzantine II: VIIIe–XVe siècle*, edited by Vassiliki Kravari, Jacques Lefort, and Cécile Morrisson, 321–37. Paris, 1989.
———. "Title and income at the Byzantine court." In *Byzantine Court Culture from 829 to 1204*, edited by Henry Maguire, 199–215. Washington, DC, 1997.

"The usual lead seal." *DOP* 37 (1983): 147–58.

"Das Verfalland im 10.–11. Jahrhundert: Verkauf und Besteuerung." *Fontes Minores* 7 (1986): 161–8.

Ostrogorski, George. "Agrarian conditions in the Byzantine Empire in the Middle Ages." In *Cambridge Economic History of Europe*, vol. 1: *The Agrarian Life of the Middle Ages*, edited by M. Postan, 205–34. Cambridge, 1966.

"La commune rurale byzantine." *Byzantion* 32 (1962): 139–66.

History of the Byzantine State. Revised ed. New Brunswick, NJ, 1969.

"Die ländliche Steuergemeinde des byzantinischen Reiches im x. Jahrhundert." *Vierteljahrschrift für Sozial-und Wirschaftsgeschichte* 20 (1927): 32–5.

"The peasant's pre-emption right: an abortive reform of the Macedonian emperors." *Journal of Roman Studies* 37 (1947): 118–26.

Ousterhout, Robert. "Secular architecture." In *The Glory of Byzantium: Art and Culture of the Middle Byzantine Era AD 843–1261*, edited by Helen C. Evans and William D. Wixom, 192–9. New York, 1997.

Papadatou, Daphne. "Divorce by mutual consent and its customary application in Byzantium." *BS* 58 (1997): 269–73.

Papagianni, Eleutheria. "Byzantine legislation on economic activity relative to social class." In *The Economic History of Byzantium from the Seventh through the Fifteenth Century*, edited by Angeliki Laiou, 1083–93. Washington, DC, 2002.

"Legal institutions and practice in matters of ecclesiastical property." In *The Economic History of Byzantium from the Seventh through the Fifteenth Century*, edited by Angeliki Laiou, 1059–69. Washington, DC, 2002.

"*Protimesis* (preemption) in Byzantium." In *The Economic History of Byzantium from the Seventh through the Fifteenth Century*, edited by Angeliki Laiou, 1071–82. Washington, DC, 2002.

Patlagean, Evelyne. "Christianisation et parentes rituelles: le domaine de Byzance." *Annales Economies, Sociétés, Civilisations* 3 (1978): 625–36.

"Les débuts d'une aristocratie byzantine et le témoignage de l'historiographie: système des noms et liens de parenté aux IX–X siècle." In *The Byzantine Aristocracy*, edited by Michael Angold. Oxford, 1984.

"Familles et parentèles à Byzance." In *Histoire de la famille*, vol. 1, edited by André Burgière, 421–41. Paris, 1986.

Pauvreté économique et pauvreté sociale à Byzance, 4e–7e siècles. Paris, 1977.

"Sainteté et pouvoir." In *The Byzantine Saint*, edited by Sergei Hackel, 88–105. London, 1981.

Structure sociale, famille, chrétienté à Byzance :IVe–XIe siècle. London, 1981.

Poly, Jean-Pierre, and Eric Bournazel. "Que faut-il préférer au 'mutationnisme'? Ou le problème du changement social." *Revue Historique de Droit Français et Etranger* 72 (1994): 401–12.

Rapp, Claudia. "For next to God, you are my salvation: reflections on the rise of the holy man in Late Antiquity." In *The Cult of the Saints in Late Antiquity and the Middle Ages: Essays on the Contribution of Peter Brown*, edited by James Howard-Johnston and Paul Anthony Hayward, 64–81. Oxford, 1999.

"Ritual brotherhood in Byzantium." *Traditio* 52 (1997): 285–326.
Reynolds, Susan. *Fiefs and Vassals: The Medieval Evidence Reinterpreted*. Oxford, 1994.
Kingdoms and Communities in Western Europe, 900–1300. Oxford, 1984.
Ringrose, Katharine. "Living in the shadows: eunuchs and gender in Byzantium." In *Third Sex, Third Gender: Beyond Sexual Dimorphism in Culture and History*, edited by Gilbert Herdt, 85–109. New York, 1994.
Roberts, Simon. "Law and dispute process." In *Companion Encyclopedia of Anthropology*, edited by Tim Ingold, 962–82. London, 1994.
Rodley, Lyn. "Patron imagery from the fringes of the empire." In *Strangers to Themselves: The Byzantine Outsider*, edited by Dion Smythe, 163–78. Aldershot, 2000.
Rosenqvist, Jan Olof. "The text of the life of St. Nikon 'Metanoeite' reconsidered." In *Leimon: Studies Presented to Lennart Rydén on his Sixty-Fifth Birthday*, edited by Jan Olof Rosenqvist, 93–111. Uppsala, 1996.
Rosenwien, Barbara, Thomas Head, and Sharon Farmer. "Monks and their enemies: a comparative approach." *Speculum* 66 (1991): 764–96.
Roueché, Charlotte. "Defining the foreign in Kekaumenos." In *Strangers to Themselves: The Byzantine Outsider*, edited by Dion Smythe, 203–14. Aldershot, 2000.
"The Literary Background of Kekaumenos." In *Literacy, Education and Manuscript Transmission in Byzantium and Beyond*, edited by Catherine Holmes and Judith Waring, 111–38. Leiden, 2002.
Runciman, Steven. "Blachernae Palace and its decoration." In *Studies in Memory of David Talbot Rice*, edited by Giles Robertson and George Henderson, 277–83. Edinburgh, 1975.
Sanders, G. D. R. "Corinth." In *The Economic History of Byzantium from the Seventh through the Fifteenth Century*, edited by Angeliki Laiou, 647–54. Washington, DC, 2002.
"New relative and absolute chronologies for 9th to 13th century glazed wares at Corinth: methodology and conclusions." In *Byzanz als Raum: Zu Methoden und Inhalten der historischen Geographie des östlichen Mittelmeerraumes*, edited by Klaus Belke, Friedrich Hild, Johannes Koder, and Peter Soustal, 153–73. Vienna, 2000.
Saradi, Helen. "The Byzantine tribunals: problems in the application of justice and state policy (9th–12th c.)." *REB* 53 (1995): 165–204.
"A contribution to the study of the Byzantine notarial formulas: the infirmitas sexus of women and the sc. Velleianum." *BZ* 83 (1990): 72–90.
"The dissolution of the urban space in the early Byzantine centuries: the evidence of the imperial legislation." *Symmeikta* 9, no. 2 (1994): 295–308.
"On the 'archontike' and 'ekklesiastike dynastei' and 'prostasia' in Byzantium with particular attention to the legal sources: a study in social history of Byzantium." *Byzantion* 64 (1994): 69–117, 314–51.
Sargent, Thomas J., and François R. Velde. *The Big Problem of Small Change*. Princeton, NJ, 2002.

Savvides, A. "The Byzantine family of Kekaumenos." *Diptycha* 4 (1986): 12–27.
Scheltema, H. J. "Byzantine law." In *The Cambridge Medieval History*, vol. IV: *The Byzantine Empire*, Part II: *Government, Church and Civilization*, edited by J. M. Hussey. Cambridge, 1966.
Schilbach, Erich. *Byzantinische Metrologie*. Handbuch der Altertumswissenschaft 12. Munich, 1970.
Schminck, Andreas. *Studien zu mittelbyzantinischen Rechtsbüchern*. Forschungen zur Byzantinischen Rechtsgeschichte 13. Frankfurt, 1986.
Scholz, Cordula. *Graecia Sacra: Studien zur Kulture des mittelalterlichen Griechenland im Spiegel hagiographischer Quellen*. Studien und Texte zur Byzantinistik 3, edited by Peter Schreiner. Frankfurt, 1997.
Schreiner, Peter. *Byzanz*. Munich, 1986.
Seibt, Werner. "Beinamen 'Spitznamen,' Herkunftsnamen, Familiennamen bis ins 10. Jahrhundert: Der Beitrag der Sigillographie zu einem prosopographischen Problem." In *Studies in Byzantine Sigillography 7*, edited by Werner Seibt, 119–36. Washington, DC, 2002.
Ševčenko, Ihor. "Constantinople viewed from the Eastern provinces in the middle Byzantine period." In *Eucharisterion: Essays Presented to Omeljan Pritsak* = Harvard Ukrainian Studies III /IV part 2, 712–47. Cambridge, MA, 1982.
―― "Re-reading Constantine Porphyrogenitus." In *Byzantine Diplomacy*, edited by Jonathan Shepard and Simon Franklin, 167–95. Aldershot, 1990.
―― "Was there totalitarianism in Byzantium? Constantinople's control over its Asiatic hinterland in the early ninth century." In *Constantinople and Its Hinterland*, edited by Cyril A. Mango and Gilbert Dagron, 91–108. Aldershot, 1995.
Sharf, Andrew. *Byzantine Jewry: From Justinian to the Fourth Crusade*. London, 1971.
Shaw, Brent. "Ritual brotherhood in Roman and post-Roman societies." *Traditio* 52 (1997): 327–56.
Shepard, Jonathan. "Byzantium expanding, 944–1025." In *The New Cambridge Medieval History*, vol. III: *c. 900–c. 1024*, edited by Timothy Reuter, 586–604. Cambridge, 1999.
―― "Constantine VII, Caucasian openings and the road to Aleppo." In *Eastern Approaches to Byzantium*, edited by Anthony Eastmond, 19–40. Aldershot, 2001.
―― "'Father' or 'scorpion'? Style and substance in Alexios's diplomacy." In *Alexios I Komnenos*, edited by Margaret Mullett and Dion Smythe, 68–132. Belfast, 1996.
―― "The uses of the Franks in eleventh-century Byzantium." *Anglo-Norman Studies* 15 (1993): 275–305.
Shepard, Jonathan, and Simon Franklin, eds. *Byzantine Diplomacy, A.D. 300–800: Means and Ends*. Society for the Promotion of Byzantine Studies Publications 1. Aldershot, 1992.
Sideris, George. "'Eunuchs of light': power, imperial ceremonial and positive representations of eunuchs in Byzantium (4th–12th centuries)." In

Eunuchs in Antiquity and Beyond, edited by Shaun Tougher, 161–76. London, 2002.

Simeonova, Liliana. "Foreigners in tenth-century Byzantium: a contribution to the history of cultural encounter." In *Strangers to Themselves: The Byzantine Outsider*, edited by Dion Smythe, 229–44. Aldershot, 2000.

Simon, Dieter. "Byzantinische Provinzialjustiz." *BZ* 79 (1986): 310–43.

——— "Das Ehegüterrecht der Pira: Ein systematischer Versuch." *Fontes Minores* 7 (1986): 193–238.

——— "Die Epochen der byzantinischen Rechtsgeschichte." *Ius commune: Veröffentlichungen des Max-Planck-Instituts für Europäische Rechtsgeschichte* 15 (1988): 73–106.

——— "Legislation as both a world order and a legal order." In *Law and Society in Byzantium, Ninth–Twelfth Centuries*, edited by Angeliki Laiou and Dieter Simon, 1–25. Washington, DC, 1994.

——— "Ein spätbyzantinisches kaufformular." In *Flores Legum*, edited by R. Feenstra, J. H. A. Lokin, and N. Van der Wal, 155–82. Groningen, 1971.

Simon, Dieter, and Spyros Troianos. "Dreizehn Geschäftsformulare." *Fontes Minores* 2 (1977): 262–95.

Skawran, Karin. *The Development of Middle Byzantine Fresco Painting in Greece*. Pretoria, 1982.

Skinner, Patricia. *Family Power in Southern Italy: The Duchy of Gaeta and Its Neighbours, 850–1139*. Cambridge, 1995.

Smythe, Dion. "Alexios I and the heretics: the account of Anna Komnene's *Alexiad*." In *Alexios I Komnenos*, edited by Margaret Mullett and Dion Smythe, 232–59. Belfast, 1996.

——— "Outsiders by *taxis*: perceptions of non-conformity." *BF* 24 (1997): 229–50.

——— ed. *Strangers to Themselves: The Byzantine Outsider*. Society for the Promotion of Byzantine Studies Publications 8. Aldershot, 2000.

Sorlin, Irene. "Publications soviétiques sur le xie siècle." *TM* 6 (1976): 367–98.

Soteriou, Georgos. "Ta ereipia tou para ton Areion Pagon vyzantinou naou." *AD* 2 (1916): 139–42.

Stavrakas, Spyros. "The Byzantine provincial elite: a study in social relationships during the ninth and tenth centuries." PhD thesis, University of Chicago, 1978.

Stephenson, Paul. "Byzantine policy towards Paristrion in the mid-eleventh century: another interpretation." *BMGS* 23 (1999): 43–63.

——— *Byzantium's Balkan Frontier: A Political Study of the Northern Balkans, 900–1204*. Cambridge, 2000.

——— "Conceptions of otherness after 1018." In *Strangers to Themselves: The Byzantine Outsider*, edited by Dion Smythe, 245–57. Aldershot, 2000.

——— "A development in nomenclature on the seals of the Byzantine provincial aristocracy in the late 10th century." *REB* 52 (1994): 187–211.

Stolte, Bernard. "Not new but novel. Notes on the historiography of Byzantine law." *BMGS* 22 (1998): 264–79.

Sullivan, Denis. "The versions of the *Vita Niconis*." *DOP* 32 (1978): 157–73.
Svoronos, Nicolas. "L'épibolè à l'époque des Comnènes." *TM* 3 (1968): 375–95.
— *Etudes sur l'organisation intérieure, la société et l'économie de l'empire byzantin.* London, 1973.
— "Recherches sur le cadastre byzantin et la fiscalité aux xie et xiie siècles." *BCH* 83 (1959): 1–166.
Symeonoglou, Sarantis. *The Topography of Thebes from the Bronze Age to Modern Times.* Princeton, NJ, 1985.
Talbot, Alice-Mary. "The Byzantine family and the monastery." *DOP* 44 (1990): 119–29.
— "A comparison of the monastic experience of Byzantine men and women." *Greek Orthodox Theological Review* 30 (1985): 1–20.
— "An introduction to Byzantine monasticism." *Illinois Classical Studies* 12 (1987): 229–41.
— "Late Byzantine nuns: by choice or necessity." *BF* 9 (1985): 103–17.
Thomas, John Philip. *Private Religious Foundations in the Byzantine Empire.* Washington, DC, 1987.
Tjäder, Jan-Olof. *Die nichtliterarischen lateinischen Papyri Italiens aus der zeit 445–700.* Stockholm, 1982.
Tougher, Shaun. "Byzantine eunuchs: an overview, with special reference to their creation and origin." In *Women, Men and Eunuchs: Gender in Byzantium*, edited by Liz James, 168–84. London, 1997.
Toumanoff, Cyril. *Studies in Christian Caucasian History.* Washington, DC, 1963.
Travlos, J. *Poleodomike exelixis ton poleos ton Athenon.* Athens, 1960.
Treadgold, Warren T. *A History of the Byzantine State and Society.* Stanford, CA, 1997.
Vasiliev, A. A. *A History of the Byzantine Empire.* Madison, WI, 1928.
Vryonis, Speros Jr. "The Peira as a source for the history of Byzantine aristocratic society in the first half of the eleventh century." In *Near Eastern Numismatics, Iconography, Epigraphy and History: Studies in Honor of George C. Miles*, edited by Dickran Kouymjian, 279–84. Beirut, 1974.
Waywell, G. B., and J. J. Wilkes. "Excavations at Sparta: the Roman stoa 1988–92 Part II." *BSA* 89 (1994): 337–432.
— "Excavations at the ancient theatre of Sparta 1992–94: preliminary report." *BSA* 90 (1995): 435–60.
Weber, Max. *The Theory of Social and Economic Organization*, translated by A. M. Henderson and Talcott Parsons. New York, 1947.
Weiss, Gunter. "Antike und Byzanz. Die Kontinuität der Gesellschaftstruktur." *Historische Zeitschrift* 224 (1977): 529–56.
— *Ostromische Beamte in Spiegel der Schriften des Michael Psellos.* Munich, 1973.
White, Stephen D. "Feuding and peace-making in the Touraine around the year 1100." *Traditio* 42 (1986): 195–263.
— "From peace to power: the study of disputes in medieval France." In *Medieval Transformations: Texts, Power, and Gifts in Context*, edited by Esther Cohen and Mayke de Jong, 203–18. Leiden, 2001.

"The politics of exchange: gifts, fiefs and feudalism." In *Medieval Transformations: Texts, Power, and Gifts in Context*, edited by Esther Cohen and Mayke de Jong, 169–88. Leiden, 2001.

Whittow, Mark. "How the east was lost: the background to the Komnenian reconquista." In *Alexios I Komnenos*, edited by Margaret Mullett and Dion Smythe, 55–67. Belfast, 1996.

The Making of Byzantium, 600–1025. Berkeley, CA, 1996.

"Ruling the late Roman and early Byzantine city: a continuous history." *Past & Present* 129 (1990): 3–29.

"Rural fortifications in western Europe and Byzantium, tenth to twelfth century." *BF* 21 (1995): 57–74.

Wickham, Chris. *Early Medieval Italy: Central Power and Local Society, 400–1000*, Totowa, NJ, 1981.

"The other transition: from the ancient world to feudalism." *Past & Present* 103 (1984): 3–36.

Winkelmann, F. *Byzantinische Rang- und Ämterstruktur im 8. und 9. Jahrhundert*. Berlin, 1985.

Wolska-Conus, Wanda. "Les écoles de Psellos et de Xiphilin sous Constantin IX Monomaque." *TM* 6 (1976): 223–43.

Zuckerman, Constantine. "A propos du *Livre des cérémonies*, II, 48." *TM* 13 (2000): 531–94.

Index

Note on names
All personal names are indexed by the given name, with a cross-reference from the more significant family names of the Empire.
Saints of the Orthodox Church are listed under their personal names where there is a reference to the historical personage, under "St." where the name appears only as the title of a religious institution.

adelphopoiia see brotherhood
administration, imperial 3–4, 5–6, 65
    changes in 6–10, 13–14, 31–4, 36–7, 38, 58
    distinguished from political system 6
    operational methods 102–3
    see also bureaucracy; emperors; officials; taxation; *names of emperors especially* Alexios I
Adrian Komnenos 109
Alexios I Komnenos, emperor 31, 75, 110–11, 149, 176–7
    appointments of family members 31–4, 38
    fiscal policy 12, 48, 52, 55, 63–5
    military organization 12–13, 176
    relations with foreign rulers 89
    religious views/policy 133, 134
    social/political reforms 12, 26, 31–4, 37, 38, 74, 100–1, 117–18
Anatolia 113
    archaeological findings 42
Andronikos Doukas 33, 145–6, 161–2
Anna Dalassene 12
appeals, role in legal process 107–9, 147–9
Aratos *see* John
aristocracy
    financial assets 84–5
    types/structure 37–8
Armenian Church 132, 133
army
    construction skills 42
    payment/status of officers 24
    qualities/failings 40, 41
    role in governance 7–8, 41
    social structure 73, 150

Asomatos *see* Phalakros
Asotios of Taron 30
Athanasios of Lavra, St. 113, 120, 130, 163
Atteleiates *see* Michael
authority
    acquisition/sources 117, 118, 136–7, 163, 167
    defined 1
    limitations 164
    loss of 150
    role of community in 149–51, 155–6, 167
    surviving descriptions 36–7

Balkans 113
    conflicts over 10, 11
Balsamon *see* Theodore
baptism, role in social alliances 87, 92
Basil I, emperor 58
Basil II, emperor 8, 20, 46, 55, 108–9, 112, 113, 116–17
Basil of Anysos (villager) 93
Basil of Latros (brother of St. Paul) 138
Beck, Hans-Georg 34, 37
Benjamin of Tudela 132
Botaneiates *see* Nikephoros III
bridges, building of 122, 123
brotherhood, ritual 87–8
Bulgaria 8, 9–10
bureaucracy, role in Empire 5–6, 35–6, 38
    compared with modern systems 34, 39
    modern perceptions of 5, 31, 34–5

Cadasters see taxation: registers
ceramic industry 84

206 Index

ceremonial, role in Byzantine culture 14–15, 16, 82–3, 166, 172
  in family alliances 87–8
  see also titles, granting of
Chandrenos (*logariastes*) 145–6
children
  adoption 88–9
  titles purchased for 26
Choirosphaktes *see* Michael
Christodoulos of Katzari 54–5
Christodoulos of Patmos, St. 40, 128
churches, building of 126–30
Confraternity of Thebes 72–4, 81, 82, 83, 89
  meetings 126, 127–8
  surviving documentation/membership 73, 173–4
Constantine I, emperor 31
Constantine VII, emperor 14, 26–7, 46
  Book of Ceremony 14, 166, 172–3
Constantine IX Monomachos, emperor 144
Constantine X Doukas, emperor 52, 107–8
Constantine Leichoudes, patriarch 107–8
Constantine Lips 29
Constantine Phasoules 106–7
Constantinople
  role in imperial power structure 7, 10, 31, 37, 100, 107, 109–10, 166–7
  social conditions 81, 86
construction 122
  materials, sources of 124
  regulation 123–4, 125–6
  see also fortification
corruption (in fiscal system) 27–8, 81, 104–5, 114
Court (imperial)
  composition/hierarchy 15–16, 33–5, 37–8
  officials, role/functions of 16–17, 20–1;
    see also titles
  (re)location 31
Crete 8
crime, in provincial society 119–22
currency 9–10, 22–4
  devaluation 9–10
  reform 12

Dallassene *see* Anna
Demetrios, St., monastery of *see* Kynopodos
Digenes Akritas 70
Dioskoros of Aphrodito 170
disputes, means of conducting 137
  community involvement 149–51, 155–6, 160
  see also appeals; documents; litigation; location; violence
Docheiariou, monastery of 57–8, 145–7

documents, legal
  authority 147
  challenges to 143–4
  creation 142, 147
  role in disputes 139–42
  style/vocabulary 66, 142–3, 161–2, 169–70
Dometios, monastery of 138
Doukas *see* Andronikos; Constantine X; Michael VII
dowry, legal status of 144–7
duress *see* documents, challenges to

economy, imperial 7–9, 11–12, 22, 23–4, 26, 47;
  see also taxation
Elpidios 25–6
emperor(s)
  appointments policy 20–1, 28–30, 31–4, 85
  breakdown of authority 136
  foreign relations 11, 72
  involvement in legal procedure 108–9, 110–11, 149
  policy towards provinces 2, 13, 41, 65, 119, 136, 163–4
  role in court ceremony 5–6, 17–18, 19, 21–3, 166
  role in financial administration 58, 60–1
  social pre-eminence 80, 166
  symbolic status 71–2
  theological justification 44
  see also Court; sovereignty; *names of individual rulers*
Empire *see* administrative structure; bureaucracy; Constantinople; Court; economy; emperors; provinces
Ephesus, bishop of 107, 121, 122
Esphigmenou, monastery of 54–5, 114
estates 49, 83–4
  defined 80
  imperial, role in economy 8, 9, 63
Eudokia (testatrix) 144–7, 161–2
eunuchs 19
Euthymios of Peristerai 52
Euthymios of Studios 163
Euthymios of Tryphonos 54–5

family
  imperial *see under* Alexios I
  as social unit *see* oikos
fathers, role in family structure 69–70
fines, payment of 101, 103
fortification(s), as imperial prerogative/monopoly 41–2, 44, 125–6
Fourmont, Michel 122
friendship, role in social framework 90–1
  false offers of 91–3

frontiers 2–3
  defence of 11
  enemy raids/incursions 40–1, 51

generals *see* army
George (monk) 151
George (notary) 33
George of Douchos (villager) 93
George Xeros 33–4
Georgia (testatrix) 142
Glykeria of Skyros 110, 129, 138, 139, 143, 144, 148–9
godparents *see* baptism
Gregory (Lazaros' biographer) 178
Gregory Pakourianos 23, 43–4
guilds 79
Guiscard, Robert 10, 13

hagiographies, as sources 177; *see also under names of saints*
Hagios Merkourios, monastery of (Corfu) 126
al-Hakim, caliph 132
Hierissos (village) 61–2, 95, 96, 105
household *see oikos*

icons, role in fraternities/ceremonies 173–4
Ioannikios (monk) 33
Isaac I Komnenos, emperor 32, 110
Isaac Komnenos, sebastokrator 33
Iviron, monastery of 35, 45, 55, 77, 108–9

Jacob Kalaphatos, bishop 144
Jenkins, Romilly, *Byzantium: The Imperial Centuries* 13
Jews
  expulsion from Sparta 134, 137, 139, 153–5
  expulsion from Western nations 131
  treatment under Empire 132–3
John I Tzimiskes, emperor 8, 41, 121–2, 163
John Aratos 153–5, 160
John (*doungarios*/litigant) 103–4, 138
John Kaloktenes, bishop 123
John Lydus 15–16
John Malakenos 46
John Melidones 33, 145
John of Iviron 108–9
John of Larissa, bishop 75
John of Skyros 110, 129, 138, 143, 148
John the Iberian 113
John the Metropolitan of Philippi 105–6
John Xenos 82
Joseph of Philadelphos 108

judges, role/responsibilities 100–1, 102, 103, 104–6, 116
Justinian I, emperor 37

Kale Pakourianos 45
Kalida (testatrix) 144
Kastoria 126–7
Katakalon Kekaumenos 176
Kazhdan, Alexander 68, 94
Kekaumenos
  characteristics of text 174–5
  identity/personal characteristics 175–6
  modern editions 175, 176
  on family relationships 86–7
  on finance 81–2, 120
  on friendship 91–3
  on legal process 106, 148
  on military matters 42, 43, 44, 45, 150, 164
  on officials' duties 81, 100, 104–5, 117
  on service 74–6
  on social interaction 78–9, 80, 156, 158–60
  on tax system 49, 61, 114–15
  on titles 28, 32
  on travel 122
klasmata (abandoned lands) *see under* taxation
Kolobou, monastery of 95, 96, 148
Komnenian era *see individual rulers especially* Alexios I
Komnenos *see* Adrian; Alexios I; Isaac (I); Manuel
Krikorikios of Taron 29–30
Ktenas 27
Kynopodos, monastery of St. Demetrios of 141

Lacapenos *see* Romanos I
land
  fertility/taxability 66, 113–14
  ownership 50, 51, 52–5, 56, 69, 116
  transfer/confiscation 51–2, 55, 56, 62, 85
Larissa, rebellion in 116–17, 151–2, 160, 164; *see also* Nikoulitzas
Lavra, monastery of 103–4, 114, 151
  donations to 143–4, 148–9
  see also Athanasios
law (Byzantine), principles/customs 101–2, 107; *see also* documents; judges; litigation; Roman Empire
Lazaros of Mt. Galesion, St. 177, 178
  events of life 71, 107, 120–1, 128, 133–4, 178
  miracles 119
  monastery of 107, 119, 122, 130–1
legacies 82
Leichoudes *see* Constantine
Lemerle, Paul 26, 176
Leo, bishop of Athens 43

Leo VI, emperor 15, 24, 26–7, 28–30, 73, 88, 126, 131, 133, 176–7
Leo (judge) 106–7
Litavrin, Gennadii 175, 176
literature (Byzantine) 162, 168
  influence on legal texts 170
  style/vocabulary 66–7, 80, 163, 165
litigation
  avoidance 105–7
  communal 95–6
  over titles 25–6
  see also appeals; disputes; documents; location; violence
location, significance in legal process 109–10, 140–2
Luke of Stiris, St. 177, 178
  events of life 40, 46, 51, 71, 74, 80, 105, 110, 120, 121, 178, 179
  miracles 94
  monastery of 130–1

Magdalino, Paul 13–14
Malakenos *see* John
Manichaean sect 133
Manuel I Komnenos, emperor 32
Manuel of Stroumitza, bishop 129
Manuel of Tekis 28–9
Marcian Treatise 48, 176–7
Maria of Alania, empress 89
Maria Phasoules 106–7
marriage, role in social fabric 87
Mastaura, archaeological findings at 123
Matthew, Gospel of 82
Mavroi family 45–6, 97, 103, 109–10, 137
Melessenos *see* Nikephoros
Merciful Mother of God, monastery of 129
Mesopotamia 28–9
Metrophanes of Panteleemon 157–8
Michael IV "the Paphlagonian," emperor 78–9
Michael VII Doukas, emperor 43
Michael Atteleiates 23, 49, 78
  religious foundations 126, 129–30, 151
Michael Choirosphaktes 97, 137–8, 139, 147–8, 150–1
Michael (*protospatharios*), feud with Mavroi 45–6, 97, 103, 109–10, 137
Michael Psellos 25–6, 90, 101
monasteries/monks
  archives 168–9, 170
  attitude to imperial judgments 136
  criminal activities 120–2
  entry options/requirements 128–9
  fortification 43–4
  foundation 128–30
  public image 157, 162–3

regulation(s) 121–2
  role in rural communities 130–1
  social/financial structure 23, 70–1, 89–90
  taxation 63, 111, 112–13, 117–18
  tenant peasantry 77
  territorial disputes 66, 140–2, 157–8
  see also names of specific institutions
Mount Galesion, monastery of *see* Lazaros
Mount Latros, monastery of 141–2
Mullett, Margaret 90, 92
Mu'tasim, Caliph 42

Nicholas, patriarch 40, 88
Nicholas, son of Agathon 52
Nicholas (*doungarios*) 126
Nicholas (provincial official) 105–6
Nikephoros II Phokas, emperor 8, 73, 130, 172
Nikephoros III Botaneiates, emperor 32, 33
Nikephoros Melessenos 33
Nikephoros Ouranos 20, 108
Nikephoros (religious leader) 54
Niketas (provincial official) 107–8
Nikodemos (religious leader) 122–3, 134
Nikon, St. 177, 179
  attacks on Jews 134, 137, 139, 153–6
  events of life 46, 71, 80, 81, 133, 160, 161, 179
  "miracles" ascribed to 119–20, 137, 152–3
  monastery of 40, 97, 113, 115, 120, 124–5, 137–8, 147–8, 149, 150–1, 153
Nikoulitzas, rebel 45, 116–17, 138, 151–2, 160, 164, 175
Nisibus, patriarch of 132
nobility, foreign/provincial: grants of titles to 11, 28–1, 89
Normans, conflicts with 10, 12–13

officials, administrative (imperial/provincial)
  conflicts of interest 101
  personal appeals to 99, 105, 109, 111–12, 114, 118, 166–7
  role in provincial society 100–1
  shortcomings 105–7
  titles/functions 12, 15
oikonomia (= husbandry/accommodation), as legal principle 101–2
Oikonomides, Nicolas 48, 176, 177
oikos/oi (household(s))
  associations between 68, 85–98, 165–6
  domestic structure 68, 69–70, 74–6, 91
  implications of terminology 67–8
  as metaphor for larger concepts 67, 69–72, 76, 77, 156–7, 158–60, 165
  religious practices 127–8
  role in society 68–9, 119, 134–5, 137, 156, 167
Orthodox Church *see* religion

Ouranos *see* Nikephoros
ownership *see* land

Pakourianos *see* Gregory; Kale; Symbat
Panteleemon, monastery of 106–7, 110, 157–8
Papavasileiou, Epameinondas 123
paroikoi (rent-paying peasants) 76–7
  etymology 77
  social advantages 97–8, 139
Patmos, monasteries on *see* Christodoulos;
  St. John the Theologian
Paul of Latros, St. 177–8
  events of life 134, 138–9
  life 45–6, 71, 74, 80, 103
  miracles 46
Paul of Monemvasia 122, 126
Paulician sect 133
peasantry 68
  economic conditions 83–4
  see also paroikoi; taxation; villages
Peter (monk) 54–5
Phalakros, monastery of 141
Phasoules *see* Constantine
Philadelphos, monastery of 108, 162
Philip (imperial official) 90
Philotheos 15, 16, 17–18, 19, 35, 179–80
Poletiane, daughter of Basil 93
Polygyros, monastery of 62
population
  of Empire 9, 51
  transfers of 41
Pothos, general 46
'power'
  legal definitions 79–80, 85–6
  public perceptions 80–1
property *see* land
provinces
  adminstrative structure 100–1, 103
  conquest/acquisition 7, 8, 28–9
  "core," *vs.* outlying 2–3, 11, 46
  geographical disposition 7
  relationship with Empire 2, 3, 39–40, 46–7,
    65, 99, 118, 166–7 (*see also* Emperors)
  social events/customs 81
  social organisation/hierarchy 2, 3, 39–40,
    69–70, 99–100, 119, 134–5, 136–7, 167
Psellos *see* Michael

Radochastos (village) 96
rebellion(s) 44, 116–17
  accusations of 45–7
  reprisals 44–5
  see also Larissa
relationships, role in Byzantine culture/writing
  66, 67, 165; *see also* family; *oikos*

religion
  conversions 133–4
  legislation 131, 133
  minorities, treatment under Empire 131–4
  Orthodox practices 126, 130–1
  relationship with law 102, 161–2
  see also churches
ritual *see* ceremonial
Roger II of Sicily 173
Roman Empire 1
  family law 88
  influence on Byzantine legal system 50, 100,
    169–70
  land/tax laws 50–1, 54
  town planning 125
Romanos I Lacapenos, emperor 30, 53
  social legislation 79, 85–6
Romanos III, emperor 21–2
Romanos Lazarites 145
Roudabon, monastery of 96
Roueché, Charlotte 176

St. Hypatios, monastery of 52, 107
St. John the Theologian, monastery of 168–9
St. Sabas, monastery of 128
salaries, payment of 24–5, 35; *see also under*
  army; emperor, role in court ceremony;
  titles
"sandaled senate" 15–16, 35
Satanic influence, as defence 162
seals 36
  nature of inscriptions 19–20
  as research tool 35–6, 38
Seljuk Turks, conflict with 10–11, 13, 40, 63
Senachereim *see* Theodore
Sergios, patriarch 108
service, rights/obligations of 73–6
Siderokausia (village) 95, 148
silk industry 84
Skylitzes (historian) 49
Skyros, bishop of 129, 138, 139, 143, 148–9
Skyros, monastery of *see* Glykeria; John
slavery *see* service
Slavic tribes/religion 133
social events/gatherings 81
society (Byzantine), organisation/structure 78
  appropriate behavior, importance of 156–7,
    163, 167
  mobility, role of 78–9, 163
  status, attainment/markers of 78, 82–5, 86
  status, loss of 81–2
  see also provinces
sovereignty, imperial 39–40
  architectural symbols of 41–2
  means of maintaining 46–7, 166

Sparta, archaeological findings 124, 127; *see also* Nikon, St.
Stephen Chrysodaktylos 33
Sviatoslav of Kiev 8
Symbat Pakourianos 31, 45
Symeon Metaphrastes 177–8
Symeon of Xenophon 110–11, 149
sympatheia see tax exemptions/rebates

Taron 29–30
tax(ation) 39, 47–64
    of abandoned lands 40–1, 50–1, 52, 62
    assessment methods 47–8, 55, 57, 60, 70, 111–14
    basic principles 50, 53
    changes/developments in 47–50, 58, 63–4, 115–16
    collection 114–15, 172
    delegation (*pronoia*) 48–9, 72
    evasion 116–17
    exemptions/rebates 112–13
    farming 49
    inconsistencies of system 59–61
    jurisdiction 53–4
    officers 111–12, 115
    problems of 47, 61–3, 64–5, 171–2
    registers 47, 48, 53, 55–6, 57, 58–9, 60, 62–4, 83, 93, 112, 171–2
    rural communities 62–3, 83–4, 93–4
territorial gains/losses *see* provinces: conquest/loss
Thebes
    archaeological findings 123, 127
    Cadaster of 171–2, 177
themata 7–8
Theodore Balsamon 88–9
Theodore Kladon 77
Theodore Leobachos 178
Theodore Senachereim 75, 110–11
Theodosius (monk) 90
Theodosius of Vatopedi 107–8
Theoktistos (religious leader) 54

theology *see* religion
Theopemptos, bishop of Sparta 156
Theophylakt (monk) 108
Theophylakt of Ochrid, bishop 63, 90–1, 109, 117–18, 138
Thessalonike, town/monastery 52, 105, 126, 162
Thomaïs of Lesbos 74
titles 100
    financial rewards/obligations 15, 17, 21–3, 24–8, 84, 85
    granting of 17, 18, 19, 28–31
    multiple 20
    social/political significance 28, 76, 86, 100, 166
    types/ranking structure 18–19, 32–3, 35, 169
towns
    layout 123–6, 127
    rents 84
Tzimiskes *see* John I

Vatopedi, monastery of 107–8, 140, 162
villages
    administrative definition 94
    common land 96–7
    migrations between 93
    modern studies of 68–9, 93–4
    social structure 93–7
violence, recourse to 137–9, 150–1
volition, treatment in legal documents 142–7, 169–70

wars, imperial involvement in 10–11, 12–13
wealth, relationship with social status 83–5
Western Europe (laws/culture), relationship with Byzantine system 1, 31, 78
witnesses, role in legal process 95, 145–6, 151
women, role in household/society 70, 72–3, 159

Xenophon, monastery of *see* Symeon

Zoe Karbonopsina 88

Printed in the United Kingdom by
Lightning Source UK Ltd., Milton Keynes
137117UK00001B/460-462/P